MW00678091

Preventing and Managing Workplace Violence
Legal and Strategic Guidelines
Editor Mark A. Lies, II

**Section of State and
Local Government Law**

Cover design by ABA Publishing.

The materials contained herein represent the opinions and views of the authors and/or the editors, and should not be construed to be the views or opinions of the law firms or companies with whom such persons are in partnership with, associated with, or employed by, nor of the American Bar Association or the Section of State & Local Government Law, unless adopted pursuant to the bylaws of the Association.

Nothing contained in this book is to be considered as the rendering of legal advice, either generally or in connection with any specific issue or case; nor do these materials purport to explain or interpret any specific bond or policy, or any provisions thereof, issued by any particular franchise company, or to render franchise or other professional advice. Readers are responsible for obtaining advice from their own lawyers or other professionals. This book and any forms and agreements herein are intended for educational and informational purposes only.

Printed in the United States of America.

11 10 09 08 07 5 4 3 2 1

Library of Congress Cataloging-in-Publication Data
Preventing and managing workplace violence / edited by Mark A. Lies II.
    p.   cm.
    Includes index.
    ISBN 978-1-59031-973-4
    1. Violence in the workplace—United States.   2. Violence in the workplace—Law and legislation—United States.   I. Lies, Mark A.
    HF5549.5.E43W6716   2008
    658.4'73—dc22   2008014690

Discounts are available for books ordered in bulk. Special consideration is given to state bars, CLE programs, and other bar-related organizations. Inquire at Book Publishing, ABA Publishing, American Bar Association, 321 North Clark Street, Chicago, Illinois 60610-4714.

www.ababooks.org

Contents

Foreword

FOR WORKERS IN THE PUBLIC SECTOR, the threat of violence is not an abstract concept. While statistics show that workplace violence, overall, began to decline in the early 1990s along with the general decline in violence throughout the United States, statistics continue to show that the risk of being a victim of workplace violence for public employees remains great. All employees need to be concerned about violence in the workplace because no one is immune to the threat. It is for that reason we chose to participate in this project, in the hope that by gathering the lessons learned from those who work daily to find ways to make people safer on the job, we give employers the resources they need to ensure that their workers will be less likely to fall victim to a violent attack.

According to the U.S. Bureau of Labor Statistics' (BLS) most recent survey on workplace violence (based on 2005 data), while fewer than 5 percent of private employers reported that they had experienced an incident of workplace violence in the previous twelve months, 32 percent of state government and nearly 15 percent of local government employers reported that they had experienced an incident during the same time period. In trying to explain the significant differences between the rates of violence in the private and public sectors, the BLS pointed to factors more closely associated with workers in the public sector: working directly with the public, having a mobile workplace (i.e., working in the field), working with unstable or violent persons (e.g., incarcerated, mental health, social services populations), working in high-crime areas, and working in community-based settings.

Unfortunately, the threat of violence remains a critical issue in U.S. society in the new millennium. Various societal issues, including insecurity over globalization of jobs, concerns over perceived fairness in employment opportunities among various groups based on ethnicity, religion, race, gender, and the like, and anxiety over the perceived lack of a social safety net regarding such things as the availability of affordable health care, create stressors outside the workplace which naturally find their way into the workplace. Since governmental agencies must interact with the public—and are often perceived as the place of last resort in finding a solution to these societal issues—employers in the public sector have genuine reason to be concerned that their workplaces (and their employees) will be targeted by those who feel a need to vent their frustrations in destructive ways.

Can public employers shield their employees from all acts of violence in the workplace? The short answer is no. As the BLS survey reflects, there are certain inherent characteristics among jobs performed in the public sector that do not lend themselves to a fail-safe solution to the problem of workplace violence. Moreover, as one former FBI agent observed in an op-ed piece written shortly after the shootings at Virginia Tech, "all the profiling and counseling in the world" will not put a halt to every violent act in the workplace.

Thus, starting with the premise that workplace violence cannot be eradicated, public employers need to proactively ask and answer the following question: What measures can we put into place to *reduce* the likelihood that violence will occur in the workplace? As this book goes to great lengths to outline, there are many things that employers can do to create a safer workplace for their employees. First and foremost, however, employers need to identify what risks for workplace violence exist in *their* work settings. Depending on the nature of the workplace—be it working at a vehicle licensing facility, a courthouse, or a community mental health center—the risks vary. If there is only one lesson to be learned from this study, it is the importance of drafting a workplace violence policy that is tailored to the particular work hazards of one's job site, not to some generic job site.

Surprisingly, the BLS survey found that a significant number of employers still do not have a workplace violence prevention policy or program in effect. According to the survey, among state government employers, nearly 22 percent had no policy or program; among local government employers, nearly half (49.9 percent) had none.

While the anecdotal evidence confirms that workplace violence cannot be eradicated, it is critical to consider that the failure to adequately respond to an incident in the aftermath can be just as detrimental to an employer's workforce as the incident itself. To measure the impact of such an incident solely by the number of those injured fails to recognize the fallout these events have on such intangibles as employee morale, fear levels, and productivity. According to the BLS survey, employee morale is most likely to be adversely affected by a workplace violence incident, followed by employee fear levels.

That notwithstanding, the BLS survey found that an overwhelming majority of employers did not change their workplace violence policies or programs following a violent incident. Among state government employers, only 6.2 percent made any changes to their policies or programs; among local government employers, only 4.3 percent did so. Any response to a workplace violence incident should involve all stakeholders or parties with an interest in securing the workplace from further violence. That means that employers need to join forces with employees and unions to determine what measures can be put into place to make employees feel safe and secure again.

Rather than advocating a single viewpoint, this book reflects the range of experiences and opinions of its contributors, who include mental health clinicians, security experts, workplace safety researchers and practitioners, and lawyers—many of whom have made workplace safety their life's calling. As such, no attempt was made to encourage the book's contributors to speak in one voice.

This volume is intended to serve as a practical reference guide for those charged with addressing workplace violence concerns, either on behalf of their employer or their client. To ensure accessibility, contributions, as much as possible, have been written with the understanding that many readers are not likely to have any expertise in workplace safety issues or be well-versed in the concepts that have proven useful for analyzing workplace violence.

While efforts were made to avoid significant overlap, not all redundancies could be eliminated. Each chapter has been written to stand on its own, recognizing that not everyone will read the book from cover to cover. That said, the thirteen chapters address four general areas of focus: (1) the problem of workplace violence and the different forms it takes (Chapter 1); (2) the underlying psychological factors that may prompt someone to act out violently (Chapter 2); (3) legal issues that can arise, such as employer liability or due process rights of public employees, and state legislation addressing workplace violence concerns (Chapters 3–6); and (4) tools that are available to employers to avert or reduce the likelihood of a violent incident or measures to undertake in the aftermath of an incident (Chapters 7–13).

More than two years have passed since work began on this book; it has been nothing short of a labor of love. We are greatly indebted to all the contributors for taking time out of their busy schedules to offer their resources and wisdom to the project. Since this project began, not surprisingly, numerous acts of workplace violence have occurred—most notably, the shootings at Virginia Tech and Northern Illinois University. These tragic events, where lives were lost or injured, only renewed and reinvigorated our commitment to the project and to our belief in the value and importance of the guidance and counsel this book imparts to those who believe that employees are entitled to a safe and secure workplace.

Mark A. Lies II
Ina R. Silvergleid
Seyfarth Shaw LLP

Acknowledgments

I WANT TO EXTEND MY SINCERE GRATITUDE and thanks to all those who have played a role in seeing this book through from its infancy and growing pains to a successful conclusion. A project such as this takes on a life of its own as the authors share professional and personal experiences on the subject matter and eventually coalesce into a team. We have all learned much from each other.

Besides those individuals whose names appear in the book as chapter authors, I also want to extend my sincere thanks to those individuals, namely Patricia Biles and Eugene Rugala, who offered their time and expertise to the project but were unable to contribute written materials to the final project because of other significant commitments. Finally, I would especially like to thank my colleague Ina Silvergleid, who worked tirelessly to keep the project moving forward. Without her continuing assistance, this project would not have come to fruition.

Mark A. Lies II

About the Editor

Mark A. Lies II is a partner in the Chicago office of Seyfarth Shaw LLP. His practice areas include product liability, occupational safety and health, workplace violence, construction litigation, and related employment litigation which arises in these areas. He has extensive experience in the refining and petrochemical industry, defending litigation involving the failure of process equipment and the resulting fires and explosions. He has developed related expertise in defending employers against claims of inadequate hazardous materials and fire safety response. Mr. Lies has advised numerous clients on a national basis from 1975 to the present on compliance with federal OSHA regulations for the control, removal, and handling of asbestos. Because of his work in this industry, he has defended related toxic tort litigation involving exposure to hydrogen sulfide, benzene, lead, silica, and other toxic substances.

He also has significant experience in construction law in the areas of design and construction of roofing systems on various structures and their performance and premature failure. He is an adjunct member of several national safety organizations including the American National Standards Institute (ANSI) and the National Fire Protection Agency (NFPA). Mr. Lies has also litigated numerous cases involving various products, including mobile cranes, overhead cranes, elevators, wire drawing equipment, extrusion machines, paper cutting devices, and electrical control and transmission devices. He is a frequent speaker before various employer and trade associations on these topics.

Mr. Lies represents employers in employment discrimination cases in federal and state court and before administrative agencies involving Title VII, ADA, FMLA, retaliation cases under OSHA, and retaliatory discharge cases under workers' compensation.

About the Contributors

Larry Barton, Ph.D., is a world-class expert in crisis prevention and response who has created the crisis plans for Honda, Nike, Disney, Gap Inc., ESPN, and dozens of government agencies. He is former vice president of crisis communications for Motorola, Inc. and has led the response to over 800 violent incidents at work worldwide. A former professor at Pennsylvania State University and Harvard Business School, he is the author of three books and a frequent speaker at meetings of government and corporate leaders on crisis response.

Steven M. Bierig is engaged in the practice of arbitration and mediation specializing in labor and employment and has received appointments for cases both on an *ad hoc* basis as well as being a member of numerous arbitration and mediation panels, some of which include the U.S. Postal Service, the City of Chicago, the Federal Aviation Administration and the Internal Revenue Service. He serves on the roster of arbitrators, mediators, and fact-finders for the Illinois State and Educational Labor Relations Boards and is a member of the National Academy of Arbitrators.

A graduate of IIT/Chicago Kent College of Law (with honors), Bierig is currently an instructor at the School of Continuing Education at the University of Wisconsin–Milwaukee. He has written numerous articles on various labor and employment issues.

Matt Bowyer, B.S.E.E., is an engineer currently serving as a member of the NIOSH Fire Fighter Fatality Investigation and Prevention Program. He earned his B.S. degree in electrical engineering from West Virginia University in 1983. He has worked for NIOSH in various scientific and technical positions since 1995. From 2002 through 2004, Mr. Bowyer was part of the NIOSH team implementing the

Workplace Violence Research and Prevention Initiative. He served as the chair of the planning committee for the NIOSH conference, Partnering in Workplace Violence Prevention: Translating Research to Practice, which was convened in Baltimore, Maryland, in November 2004.

Michelle Camden is a Chicago-area labor arbitrator and attorney. As a full-time neutral, she serves on various arbitration rosters and panels, including the Federal Mediation and Conciliation Service, the National Mediation Board, the Illinois Department of Labor, the Better Business Bureau, the City of Chicago, and the FOP Lodge #7. Ms. Camden is also an Ombudsperson for the Illinois Chapter of the Employer Support of Guard and Reserve, where she facilitates resolution of disputes between employers and returning service members, as well as educating employers and service members. Ms. Camden also teaches at the School for Police Staff and Command through Northwestern University's Center for Public Safety. She also teaches Arbitration for the Executive Management Program at Northwestern. She is an adjunct faculty member of Triton College.

Ms. Camden co-authored the chapter update entitled "Public Employment" for the Illinois Institute of Continuing Legal Education's *Labor Law Handbook*. Ms. Camden obtained her undergraduate degree from the University of Illinois at Urbana-Champaign and her law degree from Northern Illinois University.

Brian Clauss is an arbitrator and mediator of labor and employment disputes. As a full-time neutral, he serves on various arbitration and mediation rosters and panels, including the Federal Mediation and Conciliation Service, the American Arbitration Association, the National Mediation Board and the National Railroad Adjustment Board. Clauss is a licensed attorney and a graduate of Lake Forest College and the John Marshall Law School. He began his legal career as a felony prosecutor in Chicago, Illinois, and later defended Cook County, Illinois, in labor and employment matters before beginning a practice as an arbitrator and mediator in 2004. Clauss is a member of the Board of Directors of the Labor and Employment Relations Association (Chicago Chapter), the Executive Committee for the Illinois Committee for Employer Support of the Guard and Reserve and is the Ombudsman Coordinator for Illinois. Clauss is the author of several published articles.

Gary S. Cohen co-founded Employee Resource Systems, Inc. (ERS) with William R. Heffernan. For more than 29 years he has worked as a corporate consultant specializing in Employee Assistance Programs, managed mental health care, and chemical dependency treatment. Mr. Cohen holds a bachelor's degree and a master's in social work from the University of Wisconsin at Madison. He is a Licensed Clinical Social Worker (LCSW), a Certified Employee Assistance Professional (CEAP), a Diplomate in Clinical Social Work (DCSW), and a Qualified Clinical Social Worker (QCSW). In 2000, he was chosen as the Northern Illinois Employee Assistance Professional of the year. He was also the Co-Chairperson of the EAPA Consultants Group, as well as Treasurer, Vice-President, President, and now President *ex officio* of the Illinois Chapter of the Employee Assistance Professionals Association (EAPA). Mr. Cohen has been an active member of the Chicagoland Chamber of Commerce and its Drug-Free Workplace and Workplace Excellence Committees. He was a member of the Board of Directors for the AIDS Foundation of Chicago from November 1997 to November 2003.

Among Mr. Cohen's many responsibilities at ERS are business development, account services, consultation, and training.

Michael A. Crane is Executive Vice President & General Counsel of IPC International Corporation, a full-service security consulting, investigative, and protective services company licensed in all 50 states and Puerto Rico. After he was an attorney for the Chicago Police Department, Mr. Crane then became a trial attorney in the Cook County State Attorney's Office, after which he moved to a Chicago law firm, handling both civil and criminal cases. He has lectured extensively on workplace violence and legal liability in the security industry, has been called as an expert witness in security related litigation, and has taught at Webster University in the graduate program for Security Management.

In 2001, Mr. Crane was selected to participate in the FBI's Critical Incident Response Group's Workplace Violence Planning Meeting held at the FBI Academy in Quantico, Virginia. He also was invited to attend the FBI's Violence in the Workplace Symposium held in Leesburg, Virginia.

Mr. Crane has been designated a Certified Protection Professional (CPP) by ASIS International (ASIS) and is a Certified Fraud Examiner (CFE). He is currently an ASIS Council Vice President and a member of the ASIS Guidelines Commission. He is a member of the Board of Directors of the Chicago Chapter of the Association of Threat Assessment Professionals (ATAP) and formerly served as a member of their National Board of Directors. He is a member of the Illinois and Chicago Bar Associations, and the Association of Corporate Counsel. In June, 2005, he was appointed co-chairman of the Private Sector Committee of the Illinois Terrorism Taskforce working with the Statewide Terrorism & Intelligence Center (STIC) and its private sector Infrastructure Security Awareness (ISA) program.

Richard V. Denenberg is the Co-Director of Workplace Solutions, a not-for-profit organization founded with the support of the Hewlett Foundation. He is an author of *The Violence-Prone Workplace: A New Approach to Dealing with Hostile, Threatening and Uncivil Behavior* (Cornell University Press). He has published articles in the *Dispute Resolution Journal* and *Perspectives on Work,* and he is the co-editor with Tia Denenberg of the *Attorney's Guide to Drugs in the Workplace* (American Bar Association, 1996). His work also has been published in the *International and Comparative Law Quarterly* and in the *Dictionary of Modern Thought*. A former editor on the staff of the *New York Times*, Mr. Denenberg has been awarded fellowships and grants by the Ford Foundation, the American Political Science Association, and the Alicia Patterson Foundation. He was educated at Cornell, Stanford, and the University of Cambridge in England, and he served as Lecturer in Political Theory and Government at the University of Wales.

Tia Schneider Denenberg is an arbitrator mediator who serves on conflict resolution panels of the American Arbitration Association (AAA), the Federal Mediation and Conciliation Service, the National Mediation Board, and the New York State Public Employment Relations Board. Ms. Denenberg was a member of the U.S. Foreign Service Labor Relations Board for six terms and a Presidential appointee to an Emergency Board. The AAA has conferred on her its Distinguished Service Award (the Crystal Owl). Ms. Denenberg is a member of the National Academy of Arbitrators and a Director of the NAA Research and Education Foundation. She is the co-author with R.V. Denenberg of *Alcohol and Other Drugs: Issues in Arbitration* (BNA Books). She was elected to the Executive Board of the Labor and Employment Relations Association (2001–2004) and co-chaired the organization's Dispute Resolution Section. A graduate of the Cornell University School of Industrial and Labor Relations, Ms. Denenberg has been designated as the school's Neutral in Residence in 2008. She is a Town Justice in New York's Hudson River Valley.

Richard A. Devine was elected Cook County State's Attorney in November 1996. He was re-elected to a third term in November 2004. During his tenure as State's Attorney, Devine established the office's first Domestic Violence Unit, now nationally acclaimed.

Devine is a cum laude graduate of Loyola University and North-western University School of Law, where he was the Managing Editor of the Northwestern Law Review. He has argued cases before the Illinois Appellate Court, the Illinois Supreme Court, the 7th Circuit Court of Appeals, and twice before the U. S. Supreme Court. He has been a trial lawyer handling both civil and criminal cases for more than 35 years. Over the years he has received numerous awards and recognitions for his work as State's Attorney. Devine serves as a member of the Boards of the National District Attorneys Association and the Illinois State's Attorneys Association. He is a past president of the ISAA. He has also served as a member of the Criminal Justice Section of the American Bar Association.

Jack F. Dowling, CPP, PSP, is President of JD Security Consultants, LLC in Downingtown, Pennsylvania He has over 35 years of police and security management experience and is a court qualified security expert witness. Mr. Dowling has conducted numerous security site assessments in a variety of settings, including the development of workplace violence programs. He is on the faculty of the Criminal Justice Administration program at the University of Phoenix.

Brigitte M. Duffy is a partner in the Labor & Employment Department at Seyfarth Shaw LLP. Her practice focuses on both counseling and litigation. She has extensive experience counseling employers on compliance with state and federal laws on such issues as discrimination, leaves, layoffs, wage and hour compliance, and background checks. She routinely litigates employment matters before administrative agencies and in state and federal courts. She has trial experience defending management against claims brought under common law and federal and state anti-discrimination laws. Ms. Duffy received her bachelor of arts degree, cum laude, from Harvard University, and her law degree, cum laude, from Suffolk University.

Andrew L. Eisenberg is a partner in Seyfarth Shaw LLP's Labor and Employee Relations Department. Based in its Boston office, Mr. Eisenberg represents the firm's union and non-union clients in all aspects of labor and employment law. He regularly appears before state and federal courts and administrative agencies and conducts management training programs on a variety of subjects related to labor and employment issues.

Alan F. Friedman, Ph.D., specializes in threat assessments and management, violence prevention training, fitness for duty evaluations, and pre-employment psychological screening. He develops workplace violence prevention and crisis management plans and procedures and provides signal detection training to managers and supervisors for identifying employees at risk for problematic behaviors. Since 1983, Dr. Friedman has been an Associate Professor in the Department of Psychiatry and Behavioral Sciences at Northwestern University Medical School and is a Fellow in the Society for Personality Assessment. He is also a member of the American and Illinois Psychological Associations. He is the senior author of three highly acclaimed textbooks on psychological assessment and pre-employment screening which are frequently cited and used by practitioners and researchers around the country.

Bridget Healy Ryan is the Director of Public Affairs and Violence Against Women Policy Advisor for the Cook County State's Attorney's Office. In her role as Director, she advises the State's Attorney on a broad range of issues, especially domestic violence and sexual assault, involving the nation's second largest prosecuting office. Prior to this recent appointment she was the Deputy Supervisor of the domestic violence division for the State's Attorney's Office.

Among her other achievements, Ms. Healy Ryan has had numerous national speaking engagements on domestic violence, workplace violence and stalking. She is also on the faculty of the National

College of District Attorneys, the National District Attorney's Association, the American Prosecutor's Research Institute, and the Department of Homeland Security's Federal Law Enforcement Training Center. In August 2006 Ms. Healy Ryan was named one of the top 40 Lawyers Under 40 in the state of Illinois. She received her B.A. in English from Indiana University, and her J.D. from the John Marshall Law School.

William R. Heffernan co-founded Employee Resource Systems, Inc. (ERS) with Gary S. Cohen in 1993. Mr. Heffernan holds a master's degree in rehabilitation counseling and is a Certified Employee Assistance Professional (CEAP). He has served as the chairperson for the Chicagoland Chamber of Commerce's Drug-Free Workplace Taskforce. In 2002 he was elected Vice President of the Northern Illinois Chapter of the Employee Assistance Professionals Association (NIEAPA) and currently holds the position of President of that organization. Mr. Heffernan serves as the Chairman of the Board of Community Health Charities, the largest federation representing health agencies. In 1999, he was named Employee Assistance Professional of the Year for his many contributions to the Northern Illinois chapter.

Mr. Heffernan is skilled in organizational development and has significant expertise in developing drug-testing policies and procedures for labor unions as well as large and small companies. He is an engaging trainer and travels extensively, conducting workshops, presenting seminars, and facilitating programs.

John Howard, M.D., J.D., is the Director of the National Institute for Occupational Safety and Health in the U.S. Department of Health and Human Services in Washington, D.C. Before his appointment as Director of NIOSH, Dr. Howard served as Chief of the Division of Occupational Safety and Health in the California Department of Industrial Relations from 1991 through 2002. In 1995, he wrote the *Cal/OSHA Guidelines for Workplace Violence Prevention.*

Dr. Howard received his Doctor of Medicine from Loyola University of Chicago in 1974, his Master of Public Health from the Harvard School of Public Health in 1982, his Doctor of Law from the University of California at Los Angeles in 1986, and his Master of Law in Administrative Law from the George Washington University in Washington, D.C., in 1987. Dr. Howard is board-certified in internal medicine and occupational medicine and is admitted to the practice of medicine and law in the state of California and in the District of Columbia. He has written numerous articles on occupational health law and policy.

E. Lynn Jenkins, Ph.D., is a Senior Scientist in the National Institute for Occupational Safety and Health (NIOSH) Office of Research and Technology. She previously served for five years as the Chief of the Analysis and Field Evaluations Branch within the Division of Safety Research at NIOSH. From 1996 to 1999, she served as a Senior Scientist in the NIOSH Office of the Director. Lynn earned her Ph.D. in public policy analysis from the Department of Political Science at West Virginia University (WVU) in 2006, her bachelor's degree in psychology from WVU in 1987, and her master's degree in applied social research, also from WVU, in 1988. Dr. Jenkins has authored, co-authored, or edited more than 30 journal articles, book chapters, or NIOSH documents focused on workplace violence and other occupational safety and health topics. She has made more than 100 professional presentations to labor, business, and academic audiences, primarily on risk factors and prevention strategies for workplace violence.

Michael H. LeRoy is a Professor of Law, and Labor and Industrial Relations, at the University of Illinois at Urbana-Champaign. He has published extensively on strikes and lockouts, voluntary and mandatory arbitration, employee involvement teams, and more recently on employment and labor law implications stemming from 9/11 and domestic terrorism. Professor LeRoy has testified before the full U.S. Senate Committee on Labor and Human Resources; consulted at the request of the President's Council of Economic Advisers in connection with the Taft-Hartley labor dispute involving Pacific Maritime Association and International Longshore and Warehouse Union; and served as an advisor to the President's Commission on the United States Postal Service. This bipartisan commission adopted Professor LeRoy's recommendations to Congress for the use of final offer interest arbitration in place of conventional arbitration in contract impasses with various postal worker unions. His research has been cited as authority by two federal appeals courts and the Minnesota Supreme Court. Recent research publications appear in *Northwestern University Law Review*, *Notre Dame Law Review*, *Harvard Negotiation Law Review*, *UCLA Law Review*, *Southern California Law Review*, *Emory Law Journal*, and *Stanford Law & Policy Review*.

Jane Lipscomb, RN, PhD, FAAN, is Professor and Director of the School of Nursing's Center of Excellence, the Work and Health Research Center. She is Principal Investigator on three NIOSH-funded intervention evaluation R01s. In each of three separate grant projects, Dr. Lipscomb has successfully led a team of researchers, union, and management partners in the development, implementation, and evaluation of workplace interventions. Dr. Lipscomb is an epidemiologist with more than 25 years of experience conducting research focusing on health care and other groups of workers. She has conducted research on workplace violence for the past ten years and intervention effectiveness research over the past seven years. Dr. Lipscomb, while a senior scientist in the NIOSH Office of the Director, was a member of the U.S. Office of Personnel Management's interagency workgroup that developed the document entitled *Dealing with Workplace Violence: A Guide for Agency Planners*. Dr. Lipscomb has authored a widely cited review article on the topic of health care workers and workplace violence (Lipscomb and Love, 1992). She has presented both peer-reviewed and invited papers on the topic of violence and other workplace hazards among health care workers to national and international audiences. She has authored a chapter on health care workers for two occupational health textbooks.

Matthew London, M.S., has worked in occupational health and safety for 25 years. He earned an M.S. in industrial hygiene from the University of Cincinnati, received epidemiologic training as a member of the CDC's Epidemic Intelligence Service (EIS), and then worked from 1982 to 1987 at the National Institute for Occupational Safety and Health (NIOSH) conducting health hazard evaluations. Beginning in 1987, Matt worked at the New York State Department of Health (DOH), helping to develop New York's statewide Occupational Health Clinic Network and overseeing DOH's industrial hygiene activities. Since May 2004, Mr. London has worked as project coordinator for two NIOSH-funded workplace violence prevention projects being conducted within the New York state government.

Kathleen M. McPhaul, PhD, MPH, BSN, RN, is Assistant Professor and core faculty member of the University of Maryland Work and Health Research Center. She is a co-investigator on several ongoing and completed workplace violence research projects. She is an occupational health nurse specialist with over 20 years' experience in occupational health services, program development, policy, and research in the Maryland/Baltimore region. She served as the first occupational nurse intern at the Federal Occupational Safety and Health Administration (OSHA) and currently serves on the Maryland Commission for the Nursing Workforce representing occupational health and safety. She was the project manager of "Evaluation of OSHA Violence Prevention Guidelines in Mental Health" (PI, Jane Lipscomb) and co-investigator on "Workplace Violence Intervention Evaluation" (PI, Jane Lipscomb). Her dissertation project was an R-21 pilot project funded by the CDC titled "Workplace Violence Risk in the Home Health Workplace," which developed and tested measures of risk of workplace violence in the home and community setting. Ms. McPhaul has authored or co-authored several publications on workplace violence and has presented widely on the topic at scientific, clinical, and public meetings. She provides consultation to health care systems and facilities on workplace violence prevention. She teaches courses on leadership and safety in the healthcare work environment.

Jonathan L. Moll was appointed Vice President and General Counsel of Babson College in 2007. A former partner in Seyfarth Shaw's Boston office, Mr. Moll was a member of the Business Services Department and Co-Chair of the firm's Education Group. Mr. Moll's experience also includes business sales and acquisitions, the acquisition and development of land, project management, financing, and drafting and negotiating architectural, engineering and construction agreements. Mr. Moll is admitted in the U.S. District Court for the District of Massachusetts and the U.S. Court of Appeals for the First Circuit. He is the author of several publications and presentations. Mr. Moll is a member of the Boston Bar Association and the Massachusetts Bar Association, and is a member of Harpur College Alumni National Law Advisory Council (Board Member).

Pamela A. Paziotopoulos began her career as a prosecutor for the Cook County State's Attorney's office in 1990 and quickly focused on the area of domestic violence. In 1996 she joined the American Prosecutor's Research Institute's Criminal Prosecution Division as a Senior Attorney, conducting training and speaking on domestic violence. In 1997, she was recruited to the Cook County State's Attorney's Office to create and supervise the Domestic Violence Division. In 2002, Paziotopoulos left the Cook County State's Attorney's office to form her own consulting group, serving both the public and private sectors. Paziotopoulos has appeared on CNN, CNBC, and the *Oprah Winfrey Show* to speak on domestic violence. She has appeared on the FBI's Training Network discussing domestic violence in the workplace and was a consultant and participant in the FBI's Violence in the Workplace Symposium. She has authored numerous articles on the issues of domestic violence and stalking. Her article "Violence Against Women Act: Federal Relief for State Prosecutors" has been cited by Federal Courts of appeal as decisive in defending the landmark legislation VAWA. She is licensed to practice law in Illinois and in Federal Court.

James J. Powers is an associate at Seyfarth Shaw LLP in Chicago, where he concentrates his practice in labor and employment law, with a special emphasis in public sector labor and employment matters. Mr. Powers is active with the Illinois Public Employer Labor Relations Association, for which he co-edits its monthly newsletter and drafts *amicus curiae* briefs and opinions on matters of legal interest to public employers. Mr. Powers received his B.A. with distinction from Northwestern University in 1992 and his J.D. with highest honors from IIT/Chicago-Kent College of Law in 1998. He was the valedictorian of his law school graduating class.

Jonathan D. Rosen, MS, CIH, has served as Director of the Occupational Health & Safety Department for NYS Public Employees Federation, AFL-CIO since 1990. In this capacity he has facilitated PEF's 130 joint health and safety committees and developed programs addressing infectious disease, chemical, ergonomic, and safety hazards, including workplace violence prevention. Jonathan has conducted workshops on workplace violence for the George Meany Institute, the Albany Law Center, the SUNY School of Public Health, the American Psychiatric Association, the Oregon Industrial Relations Research Association, the 1999 Montreal International Conference on Occupational Health for Healthcare Workers, the

University of Iowa Workplace Violence Intervention Research Workshop, and the Veteran's Health Administration. He is a contributing author to Lewis Publishers Volume 4, Essentials of Modern Hospital Safety: "A Joint Labor/Management Experience in Implementing OSHA's Violence Prevention Guidelines in the NYS Office of Mental Health" and the author of "A Labor Perspective of Workplace Violence Prevention," published in the February 2001 issue of the *American Journal of Preventive Medicine*. He is currently co-investigator on a federal NIOSH intervention research grant studying workplace violence intervention in New York State social service agencies. Jonathan has completed a master's degree in industrial health at the University of Michigan and is a certified industrial hygienist.

Robin R. Runge, Esq., is the Director of the Commission on Domestic Violence at the American Bar Association. Robin has been a domestic violence victim advocate for fourteen years and practiced employment law for five years with a focus on women's rights in employment, specifically the Family and Medical Leave Act, Title VII, the Americans with Disabilities Act, and employment protections for victims of domestic violence, sexual assault, and stalking. Robin is a nationally recognized expert on the employment rights of victims and speaks and provides trainings regularly on these issues. She has co-authored several articles on employment law and domestic violence, and has worked on state and federal legislation providing job-guaranteed leave from work, unemployment insurance, and anti-discrimination in employment for domestic violence and sexual assault victims.

Previously, Robin was Deputy Director and Coordinator of the Program on Women's Employment Rights (POWER) at the D.C. Employment Justice Center and the coordinator of the Domestic Violence and Employment Project at the Employment Law Center, Legal Aid Society of San Francisco. In these capacities, she was responsible for the development and supervision of the legal, policy,

and public education components of each program, including supervising legal clinics, supervising attorneys providing legal representation to low income women, and conducting trainings on these
issues for domestic violence victims, advocates, policy-makers, attorneys, and human resource managers. In 1997, Robin was the first
George Washington University Law School graduate to receive one
of fourteen Equal Justice Fellowships from Equal Justice Works (formerly the National Association for Public Interest Law) to create the
Domestic Violence and Employment Project at the Legal Aid Society of San Francisco—one of the first programs in the country
devoted exclusively to advocating for the employment rights of domestic violence victims. In 2000, Robin was a public policy attorney
for the National Coalition Against Domestic Violence in its Washington, DC office.

Robin currently serves on the advisory board of the Corporate
Alliance to End Partner Violence (CAEPV) and the Women's Information Network. In 2006, she was also appointed to the Washington,
DC Mayor's Commission on Women. From 2001 to 2005, she was a
member of the board of directors of Women Empowered Against Violence (WEAVE), a nonprofit agency providing legal, counseling,
and economic literacy support to domestic violence victims in Washington, DC, and co-chair of the board in 2005. She has also served
on the board of the California Alliance Against Domestic Violence
(1998–2000), and as co-chair of its Public Policy and Research
Committee (1998–2000). Robin is currently an Associate Professo-
rial Lecturer in Law at the George Washington University Law
School teaching Public Interest Lawyering and an Adjunct Professor
at the American University Washington College of Law, where she
teaches Domestic Violence Law.

Robin is a member of the California Bar and the District of Columbia Bar. She received her law degree from the George Washington University Law School, where she received the West Publishing
Award for Clinical Achievement in Family Law and the Baer Award
for Individual Excellence from the George Washington University.

She received her B.A. in history and French, *cum laude*, from Wellesley College. Robin is from Collinsville, Illinois, outside of St. Louis, Missouri.

Ina R. Silvergleid is a staff attorney with Seyfarth Shaw LLP, where she provides research and writing support for the firm's Labor & Employment Practice Group. Prior to joining Seyfarth Shaw, Ms. Silvergleid practiced labor and employment law in the public and private sectors, representing both management and labor. Following her graduation from IIT Chicago-Kent College of Law, she clerked two years for the Honorable H. Dean Whipple, who is a federal district court judge in Kansas City, Missouri.

CHAPTER 1

Introduction: The Phenomenon of Workplace Violence

Richard V. Denenberg
and Tia Schneider Denenberg

▌ Prudence or Panic: Estimating a Danger

Two books with the word "fear" in the title were published nearly simultaneously at the close of the last century. One was *The Gift of Fear* by Gavin de Becker (1997), the other *The Culture of Fear* by Barry Glassner (1999). Their messages were quite dissimilar, however. De Becker, a security consultant to the glitterati, advised that we should be keenly attuned to the subtle "survival signals" sent by our instinct for self-preservation, because the threat of violence, including violence on the job, is omnipresent. Sociologist Glassner, on the other hand, argued that concern about violence was a spurious panic induced by media hype and that the chances of being victimized at work were about as slight as the likelihood of being struck by a comet.

The books' disparate views epitomize a debate that has permeated the study of workplace violence. Despite well-publicized mass murders at factories, offices, brokerages, hospitals, shopping centers, and postal facilities, a basic question has persisted: Is workplace violence a serious threat, justifying comprehensive preventive measures, or is it merely a figment of the public's overstimulated imagination? The controversy highlights how difficult it has been to determine the prevalence of workplace violence, its causes, and how best to prevent it from occurring.

The specter of violence in the workplace has become deeply embedded in our national psyche. The appearance of a computer pastime called Postal (advertised as a "brutal shooter strategy game"), an R-rated film titled *Office Killer* (1997), and rap lyrics with lines like "I'm going to kill my boss today" (Ludacris) evidently reflects a macabre fascination with headline-grabbing massacres. There is even a thriving market in boredom-busting toys like the Airzooka Fun Gun, a faux weapon whose loud noises frighten coworkers for amusement. (The manufacturer suggests that you "sneak up on your friends . . . your boss . . . and kerpow!")

The popular stereotype is that actual workplace violence is the product of deviancy. A similar belief among employment specialists has promoted personality profiling and preemployment screening. For example, industrial psychologists at the University of Tennessee have developed a 25-question reasoning test that identifies potentially hostile workers with a "high probability of getting in trouble on the job," according to the test's creators.[1] Filters like the Tennessee temper test are superficially attractive, but the possibility of predicting which persons will commit violence has never been proven scientifically. Millions of utterly peaceable workers fit the best-known profile of a violent worker: a white, male loner who is a military veteran and a gun enthusiast. A rigid catalog of supposed predictive traits is no substitute for the exercise of informed and nuanced judgment.

The focus on personality traits leads to a hunt for the few "bad apples in the barrel." But experience has shown that the barrel itself often needs to be checked, because the working environment may be highly volatile. Detailed study of previous incidents suggests that systemic risk factors increase the probability of danger, much as a high cholesterol level increases the likelihood of a cardiac incident. Here are several risk factors:

- *Failure to react to warning signals.* The conventional wisdom is that the signals are difficult to detect. In reality, many coworkers seem to be aware that something is amiss when they begin to horripilate (feel goose bumps), even though they cannot yet articulate a reason. It is the failure of the organization to *respond* to these warnings that typically leads to disaster.

- *Failure to resolve conflict early.* Chronic interpersonal conflict among employees is often ignored or regarded as trivial. Fellow workers tiptoe around the feuding coworkers without interceding. Yet such low-key quarrels may suddenly escalate and endanger everyone who works nearby.

- *Failure to deal with victimization.* Persistent harassment, teasing, psychological abuse, and other insults to the dignity of employees often leaves them seething with resentment. Few organizations have developed policies to relieve such tension and protect the victims.

The professionals who guard corporate facilities have certainly focused on the threat of violence. When the famed Pinkerton agency surveyed security directors to discover their estimation of the top ten threats to corporate well-being,[2] the results were as follows:

1. Workplace violence
2. Executive protection
3. Fraud/white collar crime
4. Employee screening
5. Hardware/software theft

6. General employee theft
7. Internet/intranet security
8. Drugs in the workplace
9. Unethical conduct
10. Property crime

Violence, at number one, outranked even drug use, theft, and Internet security, a trio of issues that has long preoccupied security executives.

Although the Pinkerton organization and the labor movement have had a contentious history, in this instance the former antagonists are in agreement. The American Federation of Labor–Congress of Industrial Organizations also has been concerned about the threat of violence to its members and has offered a course in the subject at the National Labor College in Maryland. David Alexander, who taught the course for many years, summarizes the organization's dual goal as "protecting the due process rights of an individual while meeting a larger responsibility to protect the lives of other members." In addition, union officers are sometimes the target of violence perpetrated by those who feel alienated by the workplace power structure.

For most employees, protection against workplace violence has evidently become a cornerstone of job satisfaction. A survey published by the Society for Human Resource Management (SHRM) found that in the eyes of workers "feeling safe" was among the five most significant features of a job.[3] It was preceded in importance only by compensation, benefits, security of job tenure, and work/life balance—factors that are close to the heart of every employee. Safety was regarded as more important than such factors as fully using one's skills on the job, the opportunity to communicate with management, receiving recognition for one's job performance, the meaningfulness of the job, or the nature of the work itself. Significantly, managers who responded to the survey could not always state with certainty what employees valued most, which suggests that some decision makers may be underestimating their workers' desire to be shielded from violence.

▌ Prevalence and Scope of Violence

The prevalence of workplace violence had been largely undocumented until SHRM began surveying its own members, who are human resource specialists at public and private workplaces. In the initial survey, conducted in 1996, almost half of the members reported that an incident involving violence of some kind had occurred in their own organizations. The significance of the incidents probably varied greatly, since there was no attempt to measure their magnitude. Nevertheless, the survey demonstrated that a strikingly large proportion of the profession had directly experienced a violent incident in the workplace. Three years later, in 1999, SHRM conducted a follow-up survey. The proportion of members reporting incidents grew to 57 percent, a major increase. Clearly, a large and rapidly growing trend lay behind the headlines.

The SHRM survey contributed valuable data by examining the cause of the reported incidents. Respondents were presumably well informed about events in their own workplaces and familiar with the employees involved.

The cause most commonly reported was personality conflict (55 percent of survey respondents). The result is surprising in that tension between two coworkers is typically viewed as a personality conflict in order to minimize its importance. Yet here is evidence that garden variety conflict, which tends to be disregarded, may fester and escalate into violence, endangering the participants and those near them. The finding suggests that low-level but chronic conflict deserves more attention; intervening at an early stage may be essential to risk reduction (see Phases of Policy Development, later in this chapter).

Family and marital problems were cited as a cause of violence by 36 percent of the managers who responded. Although historically there has been a clearer separation between home and the workplace, the dysfunctions of the former have begun to spill over into the latter. Many women are victims of "intimate partner violence," incidents in which a husband or boyfriend follows her to the workplace. Indeed, the workplace often serves as a targeting mechanism: the batterer knows the shift hours, room number, and desk location of the intended victim. Recognition of the potential harm to both intended and unintended victims has caused a sea change in employer attitudes toward domestic violence.

The third major cause of workplace violence, according to survey respondents, is work-related stress (24 percent). This result can be viewed as a remarkable admission against interest, because it is managers who organize the work and thus create the stresses that may give rise to violence. The finding calls into question the effort devoted to perfecting screening mechanisms. Those devices presume that newly recruited employees may arrive with a proclivity for violence, whereas the SHRM survey suggests that employees are not born with aggressive propensities but acquire them on the job through subjection to stress. A prudent manager thus would ensure that unbearable stress levels are not imposed on workers.[4]

The sources of stress are manifold. The demands of production deadlines and quality standards may be compounded by uncertainties caused by rapid technological change, restructuring, downsizing, outsourcing, off-shoring, and other aspects of rampant globalization. A feeling that the workplace is essentially unfair and unsupportive may also stimulate disaffection. Aggression is much less likely when psychologically healthy employees work in a psychologically healthy organization.

Further details about the prevalence of workplace violence have come from the U.S. Bureau of Labor Statistics. Its *Survey of Workplace Violence Prevention, 2005* found that there had been 350,000 incidents nationwide over a twelve-month period.[5] Size of the workplace appeared to be a key variable. About half of all large establishments—defined as employing more than 1,000 persons—had been the scene of an incident. An even greater proportion of large state work sites (65 percent) had experienced violence. Almost one-third of all state facilities, regardless of size, suffered violent incidents, compared to only 5 percent of all establishments, private as well as public. Despite the high incidence rates, the vast majority of workplaces (about 70 percent) lacked a policy designed to prevent violence.

An even higher percentage—80 percent of employers—reported lacking a written policy in a survey taken in 2004 by the American Society of Safety Engineers. Nearly three-quarters of the organizations responding had not even conducted a formal risk assessment of the potential for violence.[6]

▌ Barriers to Reporting

It is noteworthy that the Bureau of Labor Statistics' conclusions were based on a sampling, rather than an actual count, apparently because there is no requirement to report incidents. Even if there were a requirement, it would probably be weakened by the well-known phenomenon of underreporting. Many employees do not report ominous events (such as threats) to responsible officials at their workplace even when they fear that their own safety may be in jeopardy. The reasons for the reluctance to report are complex. Some worry that there may be negative consequences for the reporter's career or personal safety. Sometimes the victim even worries about the perpetrator: there may be reluctance to cause a coworker to lose his job by "dropping a dime" on him. Victims often take pity on the perpetrator's dependents by minimizing the significance of a threat.

In some situations, victims may be reluctant to disclose a threat or even an assault because they feel ashamed and embarrassed by the incident. Moreover, some employees do not trust the employer to respond fairly and effectively. Others profess to be unclear about the kinds of incidents that are reportable—particularly when the workplace lacks a violence prevention policy. Finally, an employee may believe that violence or abuse is simply part of the job and must be endured.

▌ All the Rage

The concept of "road rage" entered the popular vocabulary in the 1990s, to be followed by similarly colorful terms for extreme behavior induced by frustration. "Air rage" and "rail rage" accounted for attacks on flight attendants and train conductors, and "queuing rage" was said to explain the behavior of those who exploded from impatience while standing in line at banks or motor vehicle offices.

Workers become enraged not only on the way to their jobs, research has shown, but also when they get there. An international survey of six hundred workers in 1999 found that 64 percent proclaimed themselves affected by workplace stress, whose symptoms were loss of sleep, sickness, and a tendency to have altercations with coworkers.

In a related study by Integra, Inc., a firm that tracks demographic trends, about one-fourth of the survey population reported that they had been driven to tears by work stress, and the same number recalled becoming so unhinged that they found themselves yelling. As many as 10 percent of workers acknowledged that, owing to job stress, they had damaged machinery and resorted to other acts of violence. The phenomenon was labeled "desk rage."[7]

An even more sobering study of the potential for outbursts was commissioned by the Yale School of Management in 1999. It hired the Gallup organization to explore a variety of attitudes among a broad swathe of the working population. One question was designed to elicit how often employees became angry at work. The answers were startling. Close to one-fourth of the workers surveyed reported that they felt angry all the time and not just at moments of high demand. The feeling ran so deep that the investigators labeled it as a new pathology: "chronic anger syndrome." Chronically angry workers painted a disturbing portrait of their workplaces—hostile environments completely lacking in loyalty, shared values, or respect for human dignity. In addition, promises—such as the alluring offer of a fast-track career—went unfulfilled.[8] Given such a vast seedbed of dissatisfaction, it seems inevitable that at least a few persons seek revenge.

▌ Rampage Killers

Work-related rage may be influenced by larger social forces. At the turn of the millennium, the *New York Times* looked back at a half-century of "rampage killings," defined as multiple murders in public places. During the 1990s, the newspaper discovered, their rate of occurrence had increased, as had the number of deaths per incident. Moreover, there was evidence of "social contagion," which meant that each event seemed to incite imitators.

Fully one-third of rampage killers found their victims in the workplace. Far from acting impulsively, the killers carefully planned their vengeance. Although explicit warnings or threats were lacking, the behavior of perpetrators had clearly been deteriorating in advance of the shootings. Nevertheless, no intervention, by an employer or others, had been attempted. A life-altering event—perhaps loss of employment or divorce—typically precipitated the carnage. Suicide or "suicide by cop" often marked the finale to the bloody episode.[9]

Almost a decade after the *Times* survey, the murder of thirty-two persons on the Virginia Tech campus in April 2007 became the worst rampage shooting in the United States. That event, too, ended with the killer—a student—taking his own life, thereby obscuring the motive. Deducing causation lay in the realm of "psychological autopsy," although it is known that the shooter legally obtained a gun despite having been judged mentally ill by a state court. Information recovered after the shooting suggests that the killer had stopped attending classes and spent weeks preparing for that day—purchasing guns, ammunition, and clothing, as well as photographing and videotaping himself in a pathological attempt at postmortem self-justification.

A review panel appointed by Virginia's governor to investigate the shooting faulted Virginia Tech for ineffectiveness "in connecting the dots or heeding the red flags," largely due to passivity and lack of coordination, in a report summarizing its findings.[10] The report suggested that risks posed by individuals like Seung Hui Cho, the student responsible for the shootings, could be reduced by carefully integrating mental health care, law enforcement resources, and crisis intervention strategy. The panel also found that efforts to confront the potential of violence may be hobbled by porous gun laws, confusing privacy regulations, and other factors beyond the workplace.

Mental health is often suspected as a possible extraneous cause of workplace violence. Indeed, it has been speculated that a seldom-studied brain malfunction known as intermittent explosive disorder (IED) may be the origin of many incidents. Sudden, impulsive attacks, grossly disproportionate to the social or work stresses that trigger them, characterize IED. Sufferers, according to the National Institute of Mental Health (NIMH), "overreact to situations with uncontrollable rage, feel a sense of relief during the angry outburst, and then feel remorseful about their actions."[11]

IED is recognized by the *Diagnostic and Statistical Manual IV* (DSM IV), the bible of the mental health profession, as a member of the family of personality disorders; kleptomania and pyromania are in the same family. But research sponsored by NIMH has shown that the illness is more common than previously believed: as many as 16 million Americans may be affected. A typical sufferer may experience as many as forty-three attacks of the illness in a lifetime, each one resulting in almost $1,400 in property damages and injuries or threats to others. Yet few persons who manifest IED are ever treated.[12]

▌ Varieties of Workplace Violence

To understand workplace violence, it is necessary to comprehend the various forms it may take. A standard taxonomy has been devised by state-level occupational health officials that has been largely accepted by researchers and policy planners nationwide. Under this system of categorization, on-the-job violence is divided into four types, depending on the source of harm to the employee and the perpetrator's connection to the workplace.

Type I Violence

Type I violence entails aggressive acts committed by strangers to the workplace, such as armed robbers and other intruders. The distinctive feature is that the perpetrator has no legitimate reason for being there. In most cases, Type I violence is a variant of invasive street crime and largely a matter for community law enforcement, although an organization obviously can take measures—such as installing metal detectors at entrances—to reduce its vulnerability. The late-night retail sector has been identified as a business activity that is particularly at risk and is one of only two sectors (the other is health care) to be the subject of federal safety guidelines.[13]

Type II Violence

Type II violence is committed by customers or clients of the establishment where the victim works. The perpetrator is often an unhappy consumer of services provided by state and local governmental agencies, social service organizations, or professional offices (e.g., legal, financial, real estate). In December 2006, for example, three persons were killed in the downtown office of a Chicago law firm by a frustrated inventor, who believed that a patent attorney had stolen his idea. According to his pastor, the inventor had "exhausted all his means and got so involved in this that it became a passion to correct it."[14] Despite the threat posed by dissatisfied clients, only 50 percent of organizations even have established procedures for notifying management about threats from clients or the public, according to the survey taken by the American Society of Safety Engineers.[15]

College students who assault professors—as in the Virginia Tech massacre—and patients (or relatives) who attack nurses are engaged in Type II violence, as well. Indeed, the health care sector, which has also benefited from federal guidelines,[16] is particularly affected by Type II incidents. Nurses are victimized at a much higher rate than other workers, according to the U.S. Bureau of Justice Statistics, suffering 24.9 nonfatal assaults per thousand, compared to 14.8 per thousand for all occupations combined.[17] Vulnerability arises from the intimate contact between patient and nurse, as well as the strains that are caused by an acute health care crisis. The effects of grief, drugs and alcohol, mental disabilities, and the ease with which guns and other weapons are smuggled into hospitals and emergency rooms are also factors. Here are few examples of Type II violence in the health care setting:

February 1996—An arbitrator reinstated a New York State hospital orderly who was discharged for allegedly striking a patient. The evidence indicated that the orderly was actually defending himself against the patient, an HIV-positive woman who had attempted to bite him on the back of the neck.

July 2000—The state of Washington conducted an investigation into the murder of a senior physician in a Seattle hospital by a medical school graduate who was training as a resident in pathology. Investigators sought to determine whether the hospital had adopted adequate plans for managing potentially explosive situations.

May 2002—Stones River Hospital, near Nashville, Tennessee, was evacuated after a patient sprayed the emergency room with a noxious chemical.

March 2006—Brian Ling, M.D., a nationally known kidney specialist, was gunned down in Asheville, North Carolina, by the father of a twenty-five-year-old patient who had died while under treatment. Colleagues noted that doctors often deal with end-of-life issues but are not trained to handle unstable family members. "Oftentimes the ones that may be the most concerning are ones that do not display any grief initially," observed a doctor who worked with the victim.[18]

Public sector employees are particularly affected by Type II violence because many interact with citizens in the course of their duties in such facilities as licensing bureaus, voter registration centers, and social service agencies. In an era of fiscal restraint, those who distribute social benefits may be especially vulnerable to IED or other rage reaction. As one union safety official has commented:

> More depressed, unstable, and desperate people are waiting in longer lines to talk to fewer workers who have less time to dispense dwindling services and reduced benefits. The result is frustrated clients—clients who may already be unemployed, depressed, homeless and possibly mentally ill.[19]

It is difficult to create barriers that ensure safety without detracting from the public's access. In 1992, a "deadbeat dad" who owed child support murdered four employees of a social service unit in the Schuyler County courthouse in rural upstate New York, apparently because his wages had been garnished. The warning signal, which was not appreciated at the time, was his reappearance in the county after an absence of more than twenty years.

Unescorted social workers and case managers are often subjected to ambush attacks when they investigate allegations of child abuse in private homes, try to take children into protective custody, or seek to help clients. Teri Lea Zenner, a twenty-six-year-old social worker, was killed in 2004 when she visited the home of a teenage mental health patient in Overland Park, Kansas, to make sure he was taking his medication.[20] Commenting on a similar incident in Texas two years later, a social worker lamented, "We don't have weapons, we don't have training in self-defense, we didn't go through a police academy and we're dealing with the same people they [law enforcement] are."[21]

A 2002 survey taken by the National Association of Social Workers found that about one in five of its members had been victims of violence and about three in five had been threatened. In a larger survey, published in March 2006, 55 percent of five thousand licensed social workers reported facing safety issues on the job, and most of those complained that employers had not adequately addressed their concerns. Unfortunately, many social workers fail to report incidents or threats, because they regard the behavior as nonserious or accept the "part of the job" rationalization. This is another manifestation of the underreporting phenomenon, which handicaps violence prevention planning.[22]

Moreover, inmates of state and municipal custodial facilities, such as prisons and mental hospitals, as well as outpatients, may pose extreme hazards for employees of those institutions. In New York, the Public Employees Federation (PEF) and other unions have campaigned effectively for heightened security measures, such as escorts, cell phones, panic buttons, and global position satellite (GPS) locators. A PEF member, Judith Scanlon, was murdered in November 1998 by a psychiatric outpatient who wielded a hammer and butcher knife. Scanlon was making a home visit to the patient, a diagnosed schizophrenic, as a member of an intensive case management unit in the Buffalo region. The patient was sentenced to twenty-five years to life for the crime.

Although the unit's clientele lived outside an institution, more than 80 percent of them suffered from psychoses, 60 percent had frequent contacts with the police, and nearly all were noncompliant with their doctor's orders to take prescribed medication. Almost one-third of them were described as self-mutilators. In the years before the Scanlon tragedy, fellow members of her unit had suffered head, neck, hip, shoulder, and arm injuries as a result of visits to patients' homes—an ominous series of warning signals.[23]

Type II violence can be difficult to deter because customers and clients have a legitimate reason to interact with employees; they cannot be screened out. Moreover, the employer lacks disciplinary sanctions, as would be available in the case of a hostile employee. Nevertheless, some organizations have taken steps to deter unduly aggressive behavior by warning customers that abusing the staff will result in suspension of privileges. Unions have generally argued that employers have a duty to protect workers against abuse—or at least abandon the maxim that the customer is always right.

The risk of Type II violence to employees is particularly acute when the "customers" are defendants in the criminal justice process. Maintaining security at courthouses has become difficult because of the need to afford access to the public while assuring safe custody for those who are on trial. The danger inherent in this volatile mixture was illustrated by a series of murders committed during a trial for rape in an Atlanta courthouse in March 2005. A sitting judge, a deputy sheriff, and a court reporter were killed during an escape in which the criminal defendant overpowered a guard and seized her weapon. A U.S. Customs agent was killed later the same day. Subsequent investigation revealed a number of lapses in the security arrangements.

Type III Violence

Type III violence is that which employees commit against their coworkers. Type III has tended to attract the most publicity, probably because headline readers are horrified by the notion that a person sitting beside you at work for years may suddenly turn on you and threaten your life. Moreover, Type III incidents are often exceedingly vengeful and bloody, perhaps because the aggressors are venting feelings of frustration that have been accumulating over time. Consider these episodes:

September 1997—A former employee of a plant that made lawn-mower ignition devices in Aiken County, South Carolina, took out his revenge by shooting to death four persons who (he believed) caused his firing several weeks earlier. Among the victims is the plant's human resources director. The intruder waited until the targets gathered at a shift change. Unlike many perpetrators, who commit suicide or die at the hands of the police, the Aiken County shooter was executed by lethal injection in a state prison eight years later.[24]

November 1999—A copier repairman killed six members of his work group and a supervisor in a Honolulu warehouse. The perpetrator, a 15-year employee, discharged his Glock 9-mm semiautomatic handgun as the coworkers gathered to discuss distribution of the workload. He apparently believed that they were conspiring to increase his burden.

January 2006—Six workers at a mail sorting facility near Santa Barbara, California, were shot to death by Jennifer San Marco, a former U.S. Postal Service employee who took disability retirement in 2003 due to a psychological condition. "She seemed to be having conversations, and there wasn't anyone around her," according to a work acquaintance. "It was pretty unsettling."[25] Before returning to the post office with a 9-mm handgun, San Marco, who had relocated to New Mexico, tried to found a publication titled "The Racist Press." The dead included minorities. Before arriving at the postal facility, San Marco killed a former neighbor. After shooting her former coworkers, San Marco turned the gun on herself.

January 2007—An assembly line worker at an Indianapolis manufacturing facility wounded an office manager and three fellow workers. The 24-year-old gunman told arresting officers that "it was over respect" and that he had specifically targeted the four victims. His mother explained that he had "endured a lifetime of taunting and was being teased at work." Witnesses sensed that a confrontation was brewing and that the culprit began shooting when "he got fed up."[26]

September 2006—A teenage supermarket food handler in suburban San Diego laced doughnuts with pins and needles, placing a tray of the tampered treats in an employee break room. An unsuspecting coworker who bit into the doughnuts had to seek medical treatment for a needle embedded in a cheek. Police arrested the food handler.[27]

Type III violence entails the type of incidents that gave rise to the dubious expression "going postal." The multiple shootings that took place at the mail sorting facility in Royal Oak, Michigan, in 1991, is a prime example. An arbitrator sustained the discharge of Tom McIlvane, an employee and former U.S. Marine. He returned to the facility through a loading dock, carrying several firearms, which he used to kill coworkers who had testified against him at the arbitration hearing. There were four fatalities and five wounded victims. A Congressional investigation revealed that the poor state of labor-management relations at the facility prevented timely measures from being taken to confront the danger that McIlvane clearly posed.[28]

Despite such carnage, research by the Califano Commission, a blue-ribbon body representing both organized labor and management, found in 2000 that the rate of violence within the U.S. Postal Service is the same as the national workforce as a whole. The link in the public mind between post offices and Type III violence is thus, in the words of the commission, a "myth."

The commission, which included persons who had held national positions as a cabinet secretary, a union leader, and a U.S. trade representative, also made the following recommendations:

- Assure that warning signals are heeded.

- Screen applicants more carefully.

- Train managers in interpersonal skills.

- Repair the dispute resolution process.

The commission noted that "a small industry of arbitrators" (about three hundred) heard 6,300 grievance cases annually for the postal service. The system cost more than $200 million each year, yet the arbitrators left a huge backlog: 126,000 cases. The backlog itself negatively affected safety, the commission concluded, inasmuch as it hinders the appropriate use of discipline, while allowing inappropriate discipline to go uncorrected. Some managers . . . have given up trying to apply discipline to behavioral problems. This is a risk factor for violence, because managers may overlook danger signs such as threatening or intimidating behavior.[29]

The commission recommended enhancing the process by resolving disputes at the lowest possible level in the hierarchy, expanding the use of mediation to settle grievances, and intensifying joint, long-term planning to improve the climate. Type III violence may manifest itself as a delayed response to a perceived affront in the workplace, often long after there has been a separation from employment. In October 2005, a former factory employee used a .38-caliber handgun to kill an office manager and wound two co-owners at a plant in Newburgh, New York. The perpetrator lost his job when he was arrested in 2004 for storing child pornography on a company computer. Pleading guilty, the former employee was sentenced to probation but continued to harbor a grudge against his bosses for the conviction. Being accused of a probation violation prompted him to seek revenge.[30]

If hatred can spur Type III violence, so too can love. Office romance frequently leads to marriage, but there is potential for a volatile reaction if the relationship ends unhappily. In September 2001, a security firm employee in Sacramento, California, shot and killed three coworkers, including his former girlfriend. The shooter had been suspended for vandalizing the girlfriend's car following the couple's breakup, which left him despondent. To prevent disastrous consequences from a love affair gone bad, some employers discourage romantic liaisons among coworkers, either through written policies or unwritten understandings.[31]

Perhaps the most publicized example of Type III violence linked to a love triangle occurred in February 2007, when astronaut Lisa Marie Nowak, who had operated the robotic arm of a space shuttle, was arrested for attacking a female rival for the affection of a male space shuttle commander. "We failed as an institution to recognize that she was very troubled," acknowledged National Aeronautics and Space administrator Michael Griffin.[32] Such turmoil among an elite corps of earth-orbiting scientists and military aviators demonstrates that even highly selective recruiting, thorough psychological screening, and constant monitoring are no guarantee against violence stemming from an employee's emotional instability.

Type IV Violence

Harm that is inflicted by a nonemployee who has a personal or domestic relationship with a worker, such as a spouse or other intimate partner, constitutes Type IV violence. Here are some examples:

> January 2001—Robin Kilmer's estranged husband, wielding a five-inch hunting knife, burst into a medical center in suburban Dutchess County, New York, where she worked as a cleaner. He stabbed his wife in the neck and chest, leaving her to be airlifted to a hospital in critical condition. Speeding from the scene, the assailant died after colliding with a utility pole, which police believed was a deliberate act.

> July 2001—Twenty-year-old Lisa Atkins fled by car from her boyfriend, who was armed with an automatic handgun. She sought refuge in a former place of employment: a building materials emporium in metropolitan Atlanta. The boyfriend followed Lisa inside "with guns blazing," according to a witness, killing her and the head of the hardware department before taking his own life.

> April 2003—Tacoma police chief David Brame, who was embroiled in a tumultuous divorce proceeding, encountered his wife, Crystal, and their two young children in a shopping mall. Drawing his .45-caliber service weapon, he mortally wounded his spouse and turned the gun on himself. The incident led to the resignation of city officials who had kept Brame at his post, despite danger signs.

September 2004—An employee of Elmhurst Hospital in Queens, New York, was abducted at gunpoint from the emergency room by her husband. In the course of the kidnapping, he shot and nearly killed a coworker who came to her aid. The escapade ended two days later, when the kidnapper was stopped by police in North Carolina, still holding a gun to his wife's head.

Episodes like these demonstrate that domestic violence, once confined to the home, now often spills onto the workplace floor, blurring the boundary between one's personal life and job. Although gruesome accounts of murder and suicide in a work setting most often bring to mind unstable employees and vindictive customers, all too often the offender is a battering boyfriend, an enraged former spouse, or a partner-turned-stalker. The possibility that an intimate partner may injure an employee challenges employers and unions to devise strategies for protecting the workplace while preserving a zone of privacy for workers. Equally important is protecting the targets of violence from being doubly victimized—by having to sacrifice their livelihoods as well as their safety.

The scope of Type IV violence is illustrated in a 2004 study sponsored by Handgun-Free America, a group that advocates greater restriction of firearms.[33] The study, which examined news stories published during a ten-year period, found that at least 13 percent of the incidents in which a gun had been used to wound or murder a worker could be classified as domestic violence—usually "men killing their current or former wives and girlfriends" or "a person thought to be having an affair with their significant other." Federal crime statistics indicate that females are the victims in the vast majority of violent events involving an intimate partner. Physical aggression is typically part of a pattern of coercive behavior. Offenders also engage in verbal, emotional, and sexual abuse, and may use fear and intimidation to isolate the victim from coworkers, friends, and family members.

In a hypothetical but typical stalking case, a telephone service representative receives a call at work from an angry boyfriend. She tells coworkers that he is considering visiting the office—and that he may be armed. Understandably frightened, the coworkers scramble to avoid encountering him. Owing to a series of similar incidents, revealing disarray at home, the employee is eventually discharged. The penalty is sustained in arbitration, because there seems to be no end in sight to the office disruption attributable to the woman's personal life—an outcome that is all too common.

Battering by partners may cause poor attendance, tardiness, and excessive sick time use. Some targets of violence are terminated because they leave work without authorization in response to threats against their children. Susan Lander, an attorney with the American Federation of State, County and Municipal Employees (AFSCME), which represents 1.3 million workers, supports "programs to make sure that problems stemming from domestic violence don't result in the woman losing her job at the time when she most desperately needs it."[34]

One promising strategy is to prevent batterers and stalkers from using the workplace as a convenient targeting mechanism. Too often, the predator easily finds his prey. A survey reported by the Maine Department of Labor in February 2004, discovered that nearly three-fourths of convicted domestic violence offenders had enjoyed easy access to a partner's workplace; they often caused embarrassment or created a distraction that prompted discipline.[35] At their own job, offenders were "likely to use work time and workplace resources to contact the victim for manipulative and abusive purposes," the survey revealed. Some offenders even suffered accidents with industrial tools because of their preoccupation with planning retaliation against a partner.

★   ★   ★

The intended targets are not the only persons at risk. Unsuspecting coworkers may become indirect or secondary casualties of domestic hostility and may confront aggressors who are in the latter stages of an elaborate suicide attempt. In the Dutchess County, New York, attack, an intervener was wounded as he struggled to restrain the perpetrator. In the Atlanta shooting, one of the two fatalities was a bystander. In August 2006, a man armed with a handgun sought his former girlfriend, a teacher, in her elementary school in Essex, Vermont. When he did not find her in the building, he fatally shot another teacher, evidently from sheer frustration.[36]

Adopting a laissez-faire approach, employers traditionally have drawn a clear line between work and the nonwork sphere. Arbitrators have consistently ruled that employers lack contractual authority to regulate an employee's off-duty conduct, including their domestic arrangements. But the specter of armed intruders at the employer's front door has forced a reconsideration of traditional policies that distance the employer from domestic dysfunction. There is a growing awareness that safety—for both the direct and indirect victims—is enhanced by forewarning that a spouse or domestic partner may commit mayhem on the job. In addition, employers are learning that more technically advanced batterers sometimes resort to "cyberstalking"— abusing the employer's communication system by sending threatening or harassing e-mail to their partners at work.

Some employers now try to thwart target-seeking intrusions by offering potential victims reasonable accommodation. In 2001, a policy drafted by a committee of management and union officials at the Higher Education Services Corporation (HESC), a New York State agency, pledged to "help create alternative work arrangements . . . when necessary to protect an employee." For example, a desk location or room assignment can be changed on request, obstructing an intruder's search for the victim. Shift hours can be adjusted or made flexible. Calls and visitors can be screened, and guards may be posted in parking areas. The agency also offers to help obtain training for battered spouses and to link them to other community resources through the Employee Assistance Program.

HESC recognizes that victims may be reluctant to divulge personal problems spontaneously, even though the joint labor-management origin of the program should offer reassurance and encourage candor. Consequently, employees are trained to remain alert to signs that coworkers are being abused. Among the common symptoms are:

- Increased number of absences

- Unexplained absences

- Bruises or other injuries

- Disturbing phone calls or harassing visits

Watching and listening for worrisome signals has been endorsed by the FBI's National Center for the Analysis of Violent Crime. When the threat is from a person close to an employee, the center reported, "there is a much greater chance that some warning sign will have reached the employer in the form of observable behavior. That knowledge, along with the appropriate prevention programs, can at the very least mitigate the potential for violence or prevent it altogether."[37]

Legislative remedies also are being pursued. The AFSCME and other unions have called for federal legislation that would provide the following:

- Emergency leave to address domestic or sexual violence issues

- Unemployment insurance for those who leave work due to violence

- Protection from employment discrimination against violence victims

- Tax credits for employers who create safe workplaces

Unions have argued that victims should benefit from the Family and Medical Leave Act as well as the Americans with Disabilities Act. In some states and cities, they are protected by law or executive order against discrimination.

When a violent husband threatens a woman, she often turns to the police. But what happens when the husband is himself a police officer? The victim may discover, as Crystal Brame did, that law enforcement authorities are often slow to respond to domestic violence committed by one of their own employees. "I strongly fear for my personal safety," Crystal presciently wrote just before she died. Yet she was unable to obtain protection, largely because her husband was the police chief.

The Washington State attorney general concluded that other officers chose to "dismiss Crystal Brame's troubling reports" of threats. A female senior aide to the chief even facilitated his harassment by serving as an emissary to the wife. Crystal's survivors have claimed that official misconduct contributed to her death. They point to a fateful meeting, held the day before the shooting, in which administrators decided not to strip Chief Brame of his gun and place him on leave, even though his obsessive behavior had been apparent to others.

According to the Texas-based Institute for Law Enforcement Administration, nearly half of all police departments "have no specific policy guidelines for dealing with this issue," suggesting that "officer-involved" domestic assault is not taken seriously.[38] In 2004, the Tacoma police department belatedly adopted a detailed written policy requiring that when a domestic violence complaint is made against the chief of police, the matter must immediately be referred to the county prosecutor. The widespread adoption of such a policy may prevent the blue wall of silence from obscuring another potential tragedy.

Is a Type V Needed?

A fifth category in the violence classification system has been proposed: harm inflicted by employees on themselves. In many instances, employees have wounded or killed themselves with a knife or a gun on the employer's premises. The meaning of such incidents is unclear, although presumably the suicide has ritualistic or symbolic significance for the victim because the workplace was deliberately chosen as the scene. In the public sector, suicide by law enforcement officers is particularly disturbing because the employer may have supplied the weapon. In February 2007, a corrections officer killed himself with a department-issued firearm while on duty in the guard tower of a New York State prison.

▌ Bullying

Violence in the workplace may be psychological as well as physical. Words can be an instrument of aggression, especially when used by a bully. Bullying has been given various definitions, each emphasizing a different aspect of this harmful phenomenon. Sociologist Loraleigh Keashly of Wayne State University in Detroit describes bullying as "repeated hostile verbal and nonverbal behaviors . . . such that the target's sense of self as a competent worker and person is negatively affected." The description focuses on the effects of bullying on the employee's self-confidence. Hostility that takes the form of unfair criticism, sabotage of work product, deliberate humiliation, or persistent, unwelcome teasing may undermine the victim's confidence, possibly leading to loss of employment.

Professor David Yamada of Suffolk University Law School in Boston defines bullying as: "Deliberate, hurtful, repeated mistreatment of an employee, driven by a desire to control that individual . . . [a] combination of overt and covert behavior that inflicts severe emotional pain." The Yamada definition emphasizes that the goal is to dominate the victim and force submission to the will of the bully. The latter typically resorts to intimidation, reinforced by efforts to "ice out" or isolate the victim and exclude him from the supportive social network of the workplace.[39] Laws against stalking and similar forms of harassment might become a model for legislative efforts to limit such behavior.

Bullying became a salient issue in Europe long before it achieved recognition in the United States, and the courts on that continent have begun issuing substantial judgments against employers who allow it to continue. For example, a secretary was awarded the equivalent of about $2 million in 2006 by a British court, which found that the employer failed to protect her against a group of coworkers who subjected her to a "relentless campaign of mean and spiteful behavior"—for example, insinuating that she gave off an offensive odor.[40]

To some, bullying necessarily involves superiors and subordinates. However, research conducted by the U.S. National Institute for Occupational Safety and Health (NIOSH) in 2004 suggests that the phenomenon is more complex. According to the NIOSH findings, the largest single source of bullies were coworkers (reported by 38 percent of victims), followed by customers (25 percent). Only 15 percent of victims named a boss as the bully.[41]

▌ Policy Issues

Promulgating a violence prevention policy is one of the most effective steps to reduce the risk, especially if management can cooperate with the employees' collective bargaining representative. A jointly framed policy typically gains employee "buy-in," whereas a unilateral policy may be received warily as an extension of the employer's disciplinary power. The goal of a policy document should be to raise the preparedness level of the workplace. It must help transition the organization from the vulnerable status of crisis-prone—lacking any prevention or intervention strategy—to the status of crisis-prepared, which entails readiness to respond at the earliest stage to a perceived risk.

Phases of Policy Development

A sound policy generation process generally entails five phases. First, there should be an assessment of the nature of the risk in the workplace based on actual experience, such as injury or incident reports, and on the perceptions of the workforce, as ascertained through surveys or interviews in randomly selected focus groups. The temptation to adopt another organization's policy off the shelf should be resisted, because conditions vary greatly among work-places.

The second phase involves drafting written rules with positive, as well as negative, features. The rules should not only set forth prohibitions but also affirm that each employee enjoys the right to perform his or her duties free of intimidation, threats, or harassment. Such a commitment by the employer is likely to convince employees to see benefit in an antiviolence program and to take "ownership" of it, thereby overcoming the tendency toward underreporting.

In the third phase, the employer alters the structure of the organization by adopting prevention and intervention mechanisms. An ombudsman may be designated or a special office created to receive reports of threats or chronic conflict. The employer might recruit a cadre of employees or outside volunteers who possess at least basic interpersonal mediation skills[42] and form a crisis response team that prepares itself for emergencies. The team is often a multidisciplinary assemblage that includes representatives of the human resources, security, health, and legal departments. The team formulates a protocol for dealing with incidents and practices its response.

Good coordination is essential to team effectiveness. In April 2007, a female employee of the University of Washington, in Seattle, was shot to death in her office by a stalker, even though she had alerted the campus police and submitted photographs of the individual. The police, regrettably, neglected to alert the university's crisis response team.[43] In the Virginia Tech shooting, similarly, the campus police neglected to lock down the campus for two hours after the first victims were discovered in a dormitory; the perpetrator had time to attack a classroom building.

The structural changes also may extend to building a capability for dealing with the aftereffects of a violent attack, particularly traumatic stress. Traumatic stress is a devastating psychological blow that overwhelms the individual's ability to function effectively. Among the symptoms are nightmares, insomnia, and depression. Employers may need to retain professional counselors, much as they do when natural events, such as earthquakes or storms, leave the workforce emotionally drained. All 10,000 employees of the Johnson Space Center in Houston were offered psychological counseling as they returned to their jobs in April 2007, after a popular supervisor was gunned down by a subordinate who had received a poor performance review. "Recovery from a tragedy can be a slow process," observed a spokesperson for the center. "The most important thing to do is talk."[44]

In addition, it is advisable to plan for restoration of relationships with customers, clients, and vendors. In the aftermath of a notorious scene of horror, it also may be necessary to rebuild relationships with the neighboring public.

In the fourth policy generation phase, the culture of the organization is changed. Employees are encouraged to take responsibility for reducing conflict and reporting potentially dangerous conduct. The goal should be creating a kind of civic consciousness that motivates employees to recognize a personal stake in their surroundings and to stop ignoring risk factors.

The fifth and final stage calls for an intensive training program, designed to impart the concepts and skills needed for violence prevention. A useful approach—the "bystander empowerment" model—teaches employees how to intercede in low-level conflict that might escalate into violence.[45] Intrinsic to the model is Interactive Crisis Simulation (ICS), a style of learning that was developed by Workplace Solutions, a not-for-profit organization.[46] It recreates realistic conflicts in the classroom so that employees can try their hand at intervening. ICS combines the analytical depth of a case study with the spontaneity of improvisational drama. The aim is not to graduate professional mediators but to empower bystanders to intercede constructively or summon more expert help when chronic conflict disrupts the workplace.

Many employers are being advised or mandated by federal and state authorities to train employees periodically in order to protect them against aggression by coworkers, clients, domestic partners, and others. The New York State Workplace Violence Prevention Law, signed into law in June of 2006, is one such enactment. Bystander empowerment through ICS could satisfy that mandate in an imaginative and stimulating manner.

Zero Tolerance and Other Policies

One of the most common policies deployed against workplace violence is "zero tolerance." It has been espoused by many employers, who vouch for its effectiveness. On the other hand, there is a growing critique of zero tolerance, whose popularity is at least partly attributable to the belief that it is a blunt instrument, relieving managers of the responsibility for making fine distinctions in evaluating conduct.

To begin with, zero tolerance carries unfortunate baggage as a concept borrowed from the war on drugs. In some workplaces, the policy became a mere slogan, a form of posturing for public consumption and a cynical substitute for genuine efforts to reduce substance abuse. Although it seemed to signal determination to uproot drug use, zero tolerance often coexisted with widespread availability of drugs. By transferring a largely discredited brand name to violence prevention, the employer risks seeming more interested in appearances than in effectiveness.

Owing to its ostensibly reflexive, automatic quality, zero tolerance is often taken to suggest a harsh and inflexible attitude toward employee conduct. For that reason it may exacerbate underreporting: fellow workers worry that alerting management to a dangerous situation could lead to draconian consequences, including discharge, regardless of the severity of the offense. The policy indeed may lead to overzealous enforcement. In the school context, at least, "zero tolerance has become a one-size-fits-all solution," according to a 2001 resolution of the American Bar Association House of Delegates, which warned that disproportionate penalties may ensue.[47]

Zero tolerance implies rough justice. It may not conform to the due process requirements to which most public employees are entitled. Judgments about conduct that fail to take into account mitigating and aggravating factors, as well as intent, would not conform with the principle of just cause. Moreover, an arbitrator could conclude that the employer did not take the time to determine what penalty would have been most appropriate for the particular offense because zero tolerance policies foster an automated response to misconduct.

Finally, zero tolerance may not be well understood by employees as a guide to behavior. In the postal service, the Califano Commission discovered, "[t]here is confusion about what the zero tolerance policy means and what the consequences are for different acts." One reason for the confusion is that zero tolerance may be applied to Type III violence but not Type II, in keeping with the notion that the customer is always right.

Some employer policies attempt to deal with mental health issues. Employees who take prescribed psychoactive drugs may receive doses daily from the company nurse to ensure continuity of treatment. In several incidents discontinuing prescribed medication has been linked to employee violence. Just before the Indianapolis factory shooting, for example, the culprit apparently had stopped taking the antidepressant medication he had been prescribed. Additionally, a fitness-for-duty examination might be required of those returning from leave due to a psychiatric illness. In 1998, the head of the Connecticut state lottery was murdered by an employee who had recently rejoined the workforce after such a leave.[48] The employer had not, however, required a fitness-for-duty exam upon his return, leaving the agency with little information about his condition.

Employers have also enacted policies designed to deal with customers who are abusive to employees (Type II violence). For example, a federally chartered credit union announced that it would take the following actions against abusive customers:

- Denial of all services other than account maintenance

- Denial of personal contact with staff

- Denial of access to premises

■ Any other action not precluded by federal law or the institution's bylaws

Classifying Behavioral Risk

Some policies equip employees with guidelines for evaluating ominous behavior, thereby helping to remedy underreporting. Employees gain a set of standards to discipline their perceptions, giving them confidence to come forward with their observations. The need for such guidelines was underscored by a survey taken by the American Association of Occupational Health Nurses. It found that most employees were unable to recognize in their coworkers behavioral symptoms that might suggest they were at risk for committing violence.[49]

One approach is to apply a four-point scale of dangerousness. On the low end of the scale is obnoxious behavior: annoying but not necessarily harmful. Next highest on the danger scale are emotionally hurtful acts: accusations, cursing, and screaming. Higher still are physically hurtful acts, including shoving, hitting, biting, or throwing objects. At the summit are potentially life-threatening attacks with weapons or injurious force.

Guidelines also may help to evaluate the degree of risk in a pattern of behavior. A crisis response team might apply a risk assessment protocol as a yardstick in deciding how to respond to a reported incident. Here is an example of a protocol that incorporates three ascending levels of risk:[50]

Level One

The employee may:

■ Show signs of increasing stress, involving negative changes in behavior

■ Reject all criticism, refuse to take responsibility, and seek to displace blame

■ Spread rumors and gossip to harm others

- Argue and act belligerently with customers and coworkers

- Constantly swear

- Hold unreasonable expectations

- Ignore the effect of his or her behavior on others

- Show obsessive involvement with the job, excluding outside interests

- Seek to displace blame and avoid responsibility for errors

- Make unwelcome sexual comments

- Show performance deficits

- Allow physical appearance to deteriorate

- Show signs of distress over personal or workplace problems

- Seem unusually confrontational, argumentative, and belligerent

- Exhibit impulsive, secretive, or unpredictable behavior

Level Two

The employee may:

- Become isolated emotionally from fellow workers

- Flout policies and regulations

- Make veiled threats of harm

- Become chronically irritated, inflexible, or intemperate

- Engage in intimidating behavior

- Harbor an excessive sense of entitlement and justifiable anger

- Reveal an obsession with weapons and acts of violence

- Express hopelessness, desperation, or thoughts of self-harm

- Show signs of depression or abuse of alcohol and other drugs

- React with hostility to changes in policy or working conditions

- Profess paranoid beliefs or panic easily

- Make menacing jokes and comments

- Appear sullen, angry, or lacking in empathy

- Judge others harshly

- Talk of settling a score or taking care of a "problem"

Level Three

The employee may:

- Make blatant threats to harm others and destroy property

- Engage in aggressive verbal abuse or physical "in your face" posturing

- Sabotage equipment and remove property for revenge

- Engage in destructive behavior (e.g., pound the wall when upset)

- Dwell obsessively on notorious incidents of workplace violence, expressing praise or sympathy for the perpetrators

- Act depressed, withdrawn, or preoccupied with suicidal ideas

- Talk about a specific target or specific plans to do harm

- Display a weapon or carry one to work

- Appear fascinated or preoccupied with firearms, particularly assault weapons, or explosives

- Frequently display intense anger

- Make recurrent suicide threats

- Engage in physical fights

- Destroy property

- Utilize weapons to harm others

- Commit overt acts of violence or out-of-control behavior

- Cause physical harm

Although each incident has its unique features, being able to benchmark extreme behavior against an accepted standard should add weight to the crisis response team's assessment. Moreover, the three-level system encourages the team to take into account a general pattern rather than a single act, assuring that the assessment is not unduly narrow. In the public sector, such standards can be promulgated statewide, ensuring a uniform safety standard at all state and municipal facilities.

★　　★　　★

The chapters that follow in this volume deal in further detail with the manifold issues raised by the phenomenon of workplace violence in the public sector. Although the authors present a diversity of approaches and viewpoints, each imparts his or her expertise based on years of practical experience in the field. Those who read this book as a guide to policy and practice should be better able to address workplace safety issues when they arise.

Notes

1. "Everybody Remain Calm: Looking for Clues on Workplace Violence," CNN, May 1, 2001.

2. Pinkerton, Inc., *Top Security Threats Facing Corporate America*, 1999.

3. Society for Human Resource Management, *2006 Job Satisfaction Survey Report*, June 2006.

4. Society for Human Resource Management, Nov. 1999. The percentages total more than 100 because some managers reported more than one incident.

5. U.S. Department of Labor, Bureau of Labor Statistics, *Survey of Workplace Violence Prevention, 2005*, Washington, D.C., Oct. 27, 2006.

6. "Workplace Violence Concerns Not Being Addressed: Survey," *Business Insurance*, Aug. 9, 2004.

7. "Longer Hours, Job Stress Propel Rise of 'Desk Rage,'" Gannett News Service, Dec.10, 2000.

8. Donald Gibson, "The Experience of Anger at Work: Lessons from the Chronically Angry," Yale School of Management, 1999.

9. "The Well-Marked Roads to Homicidal Rage," *New York Times*, Apr. 9, 2000.

10. *Mass Shootings at Virginia Tech: Report of the Review Panel*, Richmond, Va., Aug. 2007, p. 52, at http://www.governor.virginia.gov/TempContent/techPanelReport.cfm.

11. "Under-Diagnosed Rage Disorder More Prevalent Than Previously Thought," *Research Matters*, Harvard Medical School, June 5, 2006. See also "Intermittent Explosive Disorder Affects up to 16 Million Americans," National Institute of Mental Health, June 5, 2006; "Study: 16 Million Might Have Road Rage Disorder," Associated Press, June 5, 2006. The condition is also known as militant episode disorder (MED).

12. The disorder is caused by inadequate production of serotonin, a mood-regulating brain chemical. Psychiatrists often treat IED by targeting serotonin receptors in the brain with antidepressants and behavior therapy. Early detection of the disorder, especially in school-based programs, could contribute to workplace safety. Other research indicates that serotonin levels may be controlled by genetic factors, which would open the possibility for gene-based treatment of aggressive disorders. "Missing Gene 'Increases Aggression,'" BBC, Jan. 26, 2003.

13. "Recommendations for Workplace Violence Prevention Programs in Late-Night Retail Establishments," U.S. Department of Labor, Occupational Safety and Health Administration, 1998.

14. "Gunman Obsessed About Getting Even, Friends and Family Say," *Chicago Tribune*, Dec. 11, 2006.

15. "Workplace Violence Concerns Not Being Addressed: Survey," *Business Insurance*, Aug. 9, 2004.

16. U.S. Occupational Safety and Health Administration, *Guidelines for Preventing Workplace Violence for Health Care and Social Service Workers*, 1996.

17. U.S. Department of Justice, Bureau of Justice Statistics, *Criminal Victimization in the United States*, 2005.

18. "Something So Awful," *Asheville Citizen-Times*, Mar. 11, 2006.

19. Jordan Barab, "Workplace Violence: How Labor Sees It," *New Solutions* (AFSCME), 1995.

20. "Safety Sought for Social Workers," *Kansas City Star*, Oct. 19, 2004.

21. "Killing in Texas Spotlights Attacks on Social Workers," Associated Press, Mar. 20, 2006.

22. *Assuring the Sufficiency of a Frontline Workforce*, National Association of Social Workers, Center for Workforce Studies, 2006.

23. "Fatality Investigation Narrative: Buffalo Psychiatric Center Employee Judith Scanlon," New York State Department of Labor, Public Employee Safety and Health Bureau, May 18, 1999.

24. "Man Who Killed 4 in Aiken County Plant Put to Death," Associated Press, Nov. 4, 2005.

25. "Postal Worker Rampage Death Toll Rises," Associated Press, Feb. 2, 2006.

26. "Gunman Wounds 4 on Far Eastside," *Indianapolis Star*, Jan.11, 2007; "Mom: Teasing Led Son to Shoot 4 Co-Workers," *Indianapolis Star*, Jan.12, 2007.

27. "Vons Worker Arrested in Food Tampering," *San Diego Union*, Sept. 15, 2006.

28. Richard V. Denenberg and Mark Braverman, *The Violence-Prone Workplace*, Cornell University Press, 1999.

29. *U.S. Postal Service Commission on a Safe and Secure Workplace*, Aug. 2000. The commission members were Joseph Califano, Douglas Fraser, B. Hamburg, M.D., D. Hamburg, M.D., John E. Robson, and Robert Zoellick.

30. "Woman Who Was Shot Dies; Killer's Letter Blames Bosses for Conviction," *Poughkeepsie Journal*, Oct. 2005.

31. "SHRM Survey Finds Office Romances Are Often Frowned Upon by Employers," press release, Society for Human Resource Management, Alexandria, Va., Jan. 28, 1998.

32. "NASA Chief: We Didn't Recognize Nowak Was Troubled," CNN, Mar. 1, 2007.

33. *Terror Nine to Five: Guns in the American Workplace, 1994–2003*, Handgun-Free America, May 2004.

34. Richard V. Denenberg, "Domestic Violence Comes to the Workplace," *Perspectives on Work*, Labor and Employment Relations Association, Winter 2005.

35. *Impact of Domestic Offenders on Occupational Safety & Health: A Pilot Study*, Maine Department of Labor and Family Crisis Services, Feb. 2004.

36. "Essex Shootings: Tragedy Began with a Cry for Help," *Burlington Free Press*, Aug. 27, 2006.

37. *Workplace Violence: Issues in Response*, Critical Incident Response Group, National Center for the Analysis of Violent Crime, FBI Academy, Quantico, Va., 2004.

38. *Domestic Assault Among Police: A Survey of Internal Affairs Policies*, Institute for Law Enforcement Administration, Plano, Tex., 1994.

39. The views of Keashly and Yamada are summarized in "Combating Workplace Bullying Pays Dividends," *Minneapolis Star Tribune,* Jan. 12, 2003.

40. "City Secretary Driven to Breakdown by Bullies Gets £800,000," *The Telegraph* (London), Feb. 8, 2006.

41. "Most Workplace Bullying Is Worker to Worker, Early Findings from NIOSH Study Suggest," *NIOSH Update,* July 28, 2004.

42. Richard V. Denenberg, "Needed: Barefoot Mediators," *Perspectives on Work,* Labor and Employment Relations Association, Summer, 2005.

43. "UW Cites Failures on Griego; School's Protection Policies Not Followed by Employees," *Seattle Post-Intelligencer,* Apr. 6, 2007.

44. "NASA Workers Begin Road to Recovery: Shaken JSC Employees Are Urged to Talk About Tragedy," *Houston Chronicle,* Apr. 24, 2007.

45. Richard V. Denenberg, "Bystander Empowerment," *Perspectives on Work,* Labor and Employment Relations Association, Winter 2007. See also Tia Schneider Denenberg and R.V. Denenberg, "The Future of the Workplace Dispute Resolver, *Dispute Resolution Journal,* June 1994.

46. The authors of this chapter are the codirectors of Workplace Solutions.

47. "ABA Recommends Dropping 'Zero Tolerance' in Schools," Associated Press, Feb. 21, 2001.

48. "An Unlucky Day at the Lottery," in Richard V. Denenberg and Mark Braverman, *The Violence-Prone Workplace,* Cornell University Press, 1999.

49. "Critical Warning Signs of Violence Not What Employees Expect," American Association of Occupational Health Nurses, Dec. 1, 2003.

50. Adapted from the violence prevention policy drafted by New York State HESC in 2001.

CHAPTER 2

Basic Principles and Concepts in Threat Assessment Evaluations

Alan F. Friedman, Ph.D.

▌ Overview

Threat assessment (TA), sometimes referred to as violence risk forecasting, is a term for a process used to make predictions and recommendations regarding the potential for violence in an identified individual or individuals. Threat assessment is considered a core responsibility and important skill set of mental health professionals, such as forensic psychologists and psychiatrists, and other individuals charged with evaluating the potential for violence in workplace and nonwork settings.

The public expects mental health providers and individuals responsible for hiring, training, and supervising others in the workplace to identify those persons who pose a danger to others and to intervene when possible to prevent violence. However, it should be noted that the literature on this subject has taught us to move away from trying to predict specific dangerous acts or violence in an open-ended time frame.[1] Instead, we have come to think in terms of evaluating the *probability* (risk assessment) of an individual perpetrating an act of violence in a brief and defined window of time, with the knowledge that many factors influence the propensity for violence and that these factors can shift or change rapidly. Accordingly, all substantive threats need to be addressed in a timely manner, and decisions regarding how they should be handled must be determined expeditiously.

From the outset, it should be noted that there is no single model or approach to use in assessing individuals who are at risk to commit violence in the workplace or elsewhere. However, empirical findings from violence research and sound clinical approaches from the experiences of clinicians, threat assessment professionals, and others, when taken together, constitute a best practices approach to threat assessment. This chapter provides an overview of findings from both empirical studies of risk assessment or violence forecasting, and clinical judgment about violence prediction, together with practical recommendations for understanding and implementing a TA and risk management approach in public sector workplaces. The terms TA and risk assessment are used interchangeably.

▮ Classifying Workplace Violence

Threat assessments are aimed at preventing violence in the workplace. According to U.S. Occupational Health and Safety agencies, workplace violence incidents can be classified according to the relationship of the perpetrator to the victim. This classification scheme allows prevention specialists to study different types of workplace violence.

Type I

This category includes violent acts committed during the course of a crime by an individual with no connection to the workplace such as a homicide during a robbery. A terrorist attack in a work setting would be included as a subcategory under this type.

Type II

This category of violence primarily includes aggression aimed at employees by customers, clients, patients, students, inmates, or any others for whom an organization provides services. An example would be a psychiatric patient assaulting a psychologist or an angry client shooting his or her attorney.

Type III

This category refers to worker-on-worker violence. The employment relationship may be current or past. The relationship may be between employees of equal or unequal rank.

Type IV

This category describes aggression in the workplace stemming from a personal relationship, such as a spouse or former intimate partner who comes onto the work site to assault the employee. This category would also include employees who were once romantically involved.

▌Defining Threats

Identifying what constitutes an actual threat is one of the many challenges facing professionals making risk-management assessments and decisions. The definition of a threat as an expressed intention to hurt or punish another individual leaves open for interpretation when exactly a threat has been made and how serious it is. Threatening communications can be classified in a multitude of ways. The classification scheme developed by Eugene A. Rugala and James R. Fitzgerald, former and current FBI supervisory special agents, is one of the more comprehensive systems for organizing and understanding threats.[2] They explain that a

> communicated threat is a verbalized, written, electronically transmitted statement, or a combination of some or all of these methods that states or suggests that some potentially harmful incident or event will occur that negatively will affect the recipient, someone or something associated with the recipient, or specified or non-specified other individuals.[3]

They classify communicated threats into three behaviorally based categories: (1) direct threats—clear statements of an intent to commit harm without any conditions or recourse for the intended victim to avoid this harm; (2) veiled threats—indirect, vague, or subtle statements suggesting potential harm, again without conditions stated to avoid the danger; and (3) conditional threats—threatening statements which portend harm but with conditions that can avoid a violent outcome. Conditional threats use qualifiers like "if," "if not," "unless," and "or else." The threats may be signed or unsigned and sent by mail, voice mail, or e-mail, or otherwise left where the recipient is certain to receive it.

TA has two basic components: (1) evaluating the threat itself and its credibility or viability as an expression of an intent to do harm; and (2) evaluating the threatener regarding the threat itself. A textual analysis, often resulting in a linguistic profile, evaluates the perpetrator's personality or character traits, and his or her level of psychological adjustment. This can help differentiate an individual who is only making a threat from an individual who is actually posing one. Robert A. Fein, Ph.D., and Bryan Vossekuil, a U.S. Secret Service special agent, provide the following important distinctions:[4]

1.   Some individuals who make threats ultimately pose threats.
2.   Many individuals who make threats do not pose threats.
3.   Some individuals who pose threats never make threats.

It should be noted that even when the threat is simply expressive in nature with no intention to do harm, the perpetrator may cause psychological harm to others, causing fear and the avoidance of work and/or distress.

The TA will focus on the exact nature and context of the threat and/or threatening behavior as well as the identified target. If the threatener is known, their apparent motivation and ability to carry out the threat should also be analyzed as well as their work history, criminal record, mental health and military history, and past behavior on the job. When identification is possible, the following questions compiled at the FBI Academy's National Center for the Analysis of Violent Crime are useful to address to individuals familiar with the offender's behavior, both prior to and after any alleged threat or actions.[5] Answers to many of the following questions can help forecast the risk for violence and suggest possible interventions:

■ Why has the offender threatened or made comments which have been perceived by others as threatening, or taken this action at this particular time? What is happening in his or her own life that has prompted this?

■ What has been said to others (i.e., friends, colleagues, coworkers, etc.) regarding what is troubling him or her?

■ Has the offender identified a specific target and communicated with others his thoughts or intended places for violence?[6]

■ Does the person feel that he or she has been wronged in some way?

■ Does the person feel that he or she is being treated fairly or unfairly by the organization?

- Does the person accept responsibility for his or her own actions?

- How does the offender cope with disappointment, loss, or failure?

- Does the individual blame others for his or her own failures?

- How does the offender interact with his or her coworkers?

- Does the individual have problems with supervisors or management?

- Is the individual overwhelmed by job responsibilities?

- Has the individual received unfavorable performance reviews or been reprimanded by management?

- Is the individual experiencing personal problems such as divorce, death in the family, health problems, or other personal losses or issues?

- Is the individual experiencing financial problems, high personal debt, or bankruptcy?

- Is there evidence of substance abuse, alcoholism, or mental illness/depression?

- Has the individual shown an interest in violence through movies, games, books, or magazines?

- Is there a preoccupation with violent themes; interest in publicized violent events; or fascination with and/or recent acquisition of weapons?

- Is there evidence of obsession with others or any stalking or surveillance activity?

- Has the offender spoken of homicide or suicide?

- Does the individual have a past criminal history or history of past violent behavior?

- Does the individual have a plan for what he or she would do?

- Does the plan make sense, is it reasonable, is it specific?

- Does the offender have the means, common knowledge, and capacity to carry out the plan?

Threat Assessment Process

TA teams are often designated in a workplace violence prevention program. Team members vary across organizations but typically include departmental representatives from human resources, security, legal, management, and outside mental health experts. Frequently, team members receive special training in risk assessment (i.e., simulations), but the team itself does not typically conduct a TA, instead seeking the assistance of outside TA professionals who collaborate with the team. Typically, TAs are conducted by a psychologist or psychiatrist who is specifically trained to evaluate the potential risk of violence. Both legal concerns and practical limitations often render it inadvisable to seek a TA evaluation from an employee assistance program (EAP), security professionals, or even mental health professionals who lack training in this area.

In the typical work situation, a coemployee or supervisor either observes or learns about questionable, threatening, or outright bizarre verbal or physical behavior by an employee or third party either in or outside the workplace. This creates a concern and sometimes a palpable fear that the employee or third party is about to engage in some type of behavior that may result in a self-inflicted injury to the individual (including suicide) or injury to others (threats, hostile acts). The frightened (or concerned) coemployee or supervisor then brings this information to the employer's attention and asks management to respond to the perceived threat. Of course, in some situations, the problem individual may be a supervisor or even a senior executive, in which case the opportunities for subordinates to make a complaint may be limited or complicated. Or, the instigator of threats may be a spouse or former disgruntled significant other of an employee. Hopefully, the employer has a written workplace violence policy in place, and managers have been trained to be attentive and receptive to receiving and responding to this disturbing information. At this stage, the employer must begin an expedited process of assessing whether there may be a substantial threat and, if so, what response is necessary or appropriate.[7] This response may include a fitness-for-duty evaluation (discussed later in this chapter).

A word of caution is in order at this point. Because of heightened reactions by the media to spectacular and tragic workplace violence incidents, some employers may tend to react in an impulsive, knee-jerk fashion by immediately terminating the suspected employee or imposing significant disciplinary measures. Such vigilante-style justice may be proven to have no foundation when the employer's subsequent investigation reveals the actual context in which the conduct occurred or the comments were made. Such an investigation may find that the conduct or statements were ambiguous or misquoted or, worse yet, that the threat complaints made against the employee were fabricated by other employees with an ulterior purpose.

If this were to happen, the potential for employment-related litigation would be substantial. It is important to stress that just as coworkers are entitled to a workplace free of violence and threats, so too is an accused employee entitled to a right to privacy, fairness, and an equitable hearing. As addressed elsewhere in this book, public employees also may have constitutional due process rights and rights under union contracts that cannot be ignored. The accused employee who is later found innocent of improper conduct, but whose name has been mentioned in staff meetings and within the workplace in memos and in e-mails, can be expected to seek legal redress for constitutional liberty interest violations or defamation if he or she has sustained damage to his or her career and reputation.

Without question many instances warrant immediate termination, but in other circumstances doing so in the heat of the moment, without any time for thorough investigation, evaluation, or preparation, may be exactly the wrong thing to do. By removing the potentially dangerous employee from observation, an employer may possibly bring on a violent act instead of preventing one.[8]

Predictive Factors of Violence

Because behavior is complex, its prediction is difficult. An array of personality traits, situational circumstances, and motivational and biological factors all interact to produce specific behavioral acts. Important factors that should be considered in all TA include the evaluation of static and dynamic factors, base-rate phenomena, the relationship between mental health and violence, and clinical versus actuarial risk assessment considerations. These factors are discussed in greater detail in the following sections.

Static versus Dynamic Factors

A competent threat assessor recognizes that numerous factors influence individuals to think and behave in a violent manner. Reid Meloy, a clinical psychologist, suggests that violence risk factors can be organized into static and dynamic categories.[9] A static factor is defined as something that does not change, or changes very slowly, and is not usually amenable to an intervention. One's disposition or temperament (e.g., being an extrovert) or gender and age are examples of static factors. On the other hand, dynamic factors can change, do so quickly, and are subject to intervention. Dynamic risk factors that influence an individual to think and behave in a violent manner include, but are not limited to, changes in personal circumstances such as a loss of support from significant others, intense grievances with a coworker, a supervisor, or one's employer, or the exacerbation of severe psychiatric symptoms such as hearing voices that command violent actions. Other examples of dynamic factors include intolerable depressive symptoms with severe agitation or alcohol and/or drug intoxication. These dynamic factors can be influenced through direct psychiatric treatment and interventions such as hospitalization, the administration of medications, and the provision of emotional support. There are risk-management implications in recognizing the important differences between static and dynamic factors.

Base Rates

Dangerousness is a state, not a trait. Therefore, violence potential should not be treated as a fixed level of risk as it can vary with time, symptoms, and situations.[10] Of crucial importance to the understanding and management of violence potential is the concept of base rates. The term base rate refers to the frequency in a given setting of a specific act or behaviors. There are three basic aspects of base rates: (1) a behavior (i.e., violent actions, psychotic symptoms); (2) a group of people (i.e., psychiatric patients, criminals); and (3) a time frame. For example, the FBI's Annual Uniform Crime Report illustrates base rates for specific crimes by different geographical areas. When conducting a threat assessment, base rates provide an idea of the probability (or likelihood) that the threatening behavior will take place. Oftentimes base-rate knowledge tells us that predicting the likelihood that the threatened behavior will take place will be difficult. For example, predicting suicidal behavior is difficult because it is characterized by a low base-rate phenomenon. In other words, it occurs with a very low frequency in almost all settings and populations. When a behavior has a low base rate of occurrence, there are significant difficulties in predicting its likelihood of occurring.[11] Not only do low base rates decrease the predictability of the behavior but they also can result in "a large over-prediction of the behavior if it is attempted."[12] This phenomenon is referred to as a "false positive prediction." Therefore, one can expect, given the low base rate of violence in most work settings—even those occupations or settings associated with higher risks like law enforcement or late-night convenience stores—that there will be a high degree of false positive predictions given how infrequently violence occurs in these work settings.

Clinical versus Actuarial Prediction of Violence

The previous year's crime reports provide a general picture of what types of violence occur in specific types of work settings. This information is helpful in planning and prevention efforts such as learning to detect and recognize indicators of potential violence for managers and supervisors who work in high-risk environments. However, mental health professionals typically do not rely on base-rate data alone to make a threat assessment, in part because the data have certain inherent limitations with respect to predicting future behavior. Typically, a threat assessment relies on human judgment and decision making. Traditionally this has been referred to as the *clinical approach* and involves data gathering about the instigator, the situation, and, frequently, the evaluator's knowledge of risk factors for violence and reasoning about the relationship between mental illness and violence, if relevant.

In contrast to the clinical decision-making approach to predicting dangerousness is the *actuarial approach*. This approach expresses a probability estimate that violent behavior will be perpetrated by an individual. The actuarial approach basically estimates that a specific kind of violence will occur in a specific time frame in a particular situation. These predictions are based on empirical studies examining violence across specific populations. Insurance companies typically rely upon this approach for creating the risk category in which an individual should be placed given the specific lifestyle characteristics (i.e., smoker versus nonsmoker, etc.) of that person. In a clinical assessment the same data is collected as in the actuarial assessment, but reasoning rather than a mathematical equation leads to the decision-making conclusion.

Advocates for the actuarial versus the clinical approach rely upon studies that demonstrate deficiencies in human reasoning.

People typically assume that they have more information than they actually possess and, therefore, are willing to make more extreme judgments than are justified. They also have more unfounded confidence in their judgments. Individuals charged with making a prediction of dangerousness are inclined to make a judgment of dangerousness versus nondangerousness, as the stakes are higher for a missed prediction of violence.

The superiority of actuarial over clinical risk assessment in the behavioral sciences has long been established and recognized. However, the actuarial risk data on predicting dangerousness pertains primarily to criminal and psychiatric populations. Workplace environments require more of these actuarial risk studies to assist in TAs. There is much to support an actuarial research effort for violence forecasting in employment settings despite the methodological challenges in collecting reliable data. Important findings from actuarial studies that can be applied in a nonactuarial, workplace TA may include, for example, the knowledge that psychopaths commit a disproportionately large number of violent crimes. With respect to predicting violence in psychopaths from actuarial research, early developmental markers that have been identified are factors such as conduct disorders and elementary school maladjustment.[13]

In my opinion, a combination of both clinical assessment and actuarial research findings will lead to more accurate and useful TAs in the workplace. The recommendations in this chapter are based upon a blending of best practices from both approaches. At this time actuarial instruments are best used as aides in clinical decision making.

▌ Violence and Mental Health

The relationship between violence and mental illness has been extensively investigated with the research focused primarily on psychiatric and forensic patients, as well as criminals. There is almost no empirical literature investigating those at risk for workplace violence.

Many misconceptions abound regarding the propensity for violence among individuals with psychiatric histories. A prevailing stereotype is that if a person has any psychiatric diagnosis at all, he or she is more likely to be at higher risk for behaving in a violent fashion. While it is true that mental disorders significantly contribute to the risk of violence, it is usually small.

However, when dual diagnoses coexist—such as an active psychosis and/or certain personality disorders *and* alcoholism and/or substance abuse—the combination of factors exponentially increases an individual's risk for violence. As recounted in Meloy,[14] an important 1990 epidemiological study looked at the relation between violence and mental disorder.[15] The study included participants who were selected through a random probability community sampling with controls in place to allow for generalizability to the U.S. population. One of the study's critical issues focused on the participant's self-reported, noncriminal violence in the past year (such as hitting another person or throwing an object at someone) and its relationship to whether or not the person had a legitimate psychiatric diagnosis. The study's findings revealed that 2 percent of the people without a mental disorder self-reported being violent during the past year. But individuals who were diagnosed with a panic disorder, major depression, or schizophrenia, self-reported being violent in the previous year at considerably higher rates: 11.5 percent, 12 percent, and 13 percent, respectively. Thus, while the study reflects that the majority of individuals with a mental disorder did not engage in violent behavior, they experienced a much higher rate of violent behavior than those who did not have a psychiatric diagnosis.

The MacArthur Violence Risk Assessment Study took ten years to plan and execute, and to analyze the research data collected over a period of five years. The results were so important that more than five hundred researchers have reviewed the original data and written articles about the study's findings. A major objective of the study was to produce an actuarial risk assessment tool with practical application and without the inherent limitations in previous studies. The

MacArthur study expanded the range of risk factors studied, widened the populations examined, used multiple sites, and included both patient's self-reports and collateral information from police and hospital records. The research included a wide array of risk factors including gender, prior violence, histories of childhood physical abuse, race, diagnoses, delusions, hallucinations, violent thoughts, and anger. Men and women were both studied and the research was conducted at several sites.

Over one thousand subjects were sampled from acute civil psychiatric inpatient facilities in Pennsylvania, Missouri, and Massachusetts. English-speaking participants between the ages of eighteen and forty were selected and were of white, African American, or Hispanic ethnicity. Their chart diagnoses consisted of one (or more) of the following: a thought or affective (mood) disorder, substance abuse, or personality disorders. Patients were interviewed in the hospital to assess them on specific risk factors. Others who were familiar with the patients were also interviewed. Violence toward others was defined as acts of battery, sexual assaults, weapon assaults, or threats with a weapon in hand.

Many of the important findings from the MacArthur study are reported and summarized by John Monahan in a 2006 article in the *Virginia Law Review*. The violence forecasting variables he identifies are applicable to TAs conducted in any workplace setting.[16] In fact, in my opinion, the risk factors that he identifies should be ascertained in all TA evaluations. Monahan usefully organizes these risk factors into four categories: (1) what the person *is*; (2) what the person *has*; (3) what the person has *done*; and (4) what has been *done* to the person.

What the Person Is

Factors that constitute someone as an "individual" are age, gender, race or ethnicity, and personality. Regarding age, arrests for violent crimes and sexual offenses decreased by age cohorts (grouping), with older individuals committing less violent and less sexual offenses.

Generally speaking, arrests for violent crimes peak at age eighteen and decline after that.[17] Individuals with mental disorders also commit less violence as they age. Monahan observes that for people between "eighteen and forty years old who were in psychiatric facilities, for every one-year increase in a patient's age, the odds that the patient would commit a violent act within the first several months after discharge decreased by twenty percent."[18] Gender, as a risk factor, has long been known to correlate with violence, as males are generally more aggressive (physically and verbally) than are females. Monahan cites research showing that gender is one of the most powerful demographic correlates of violence, with males experiencing significantly higher arrest rates for homicide, rape, robbery, and assault. He states that "of the 418,964 persons arrested for a violent crime in the U.S. in 2003 (the latest year for which data are available), 344,435 (82 percent) were men and 74,529 (18 percent) were women."[19] It should not be surprising that for sexual offenses, the strong majority of offenders are male. In 2003, 18,446 individuals were arrested for forcible rape and 99 percent of the offenders were men.[20]

Race appears to be a risk factor in violence studies, but courts have held that race cannot be used as a basis to deprive an individual of employment. Statistics reveal that African Americans are at a greater risk for being arrested for a violent crime. In 2003, African Americans represented about 12 percent of the U.S. population but accounted for a disproportionate number of the violent crime arrests: 37 percent. The MacArthur study states that "the odds that a patient who is African American would commit a violent act within several months after discharge from the hospital were eighty-five percent higher than the odds that a patient who was white would do so. Since the vast majority of this violence came from the patient's own self-report, official bias in arrest or hospitalization practices cannot account for this difference."[21] Because the factor of race in crime statistics is complicated by the role racial profiling may play in who is targeted for arrest, Monahan and others have removed race from their predictive models. Moreover, the risk software that was generated from the MacArthur Violence Risk Assessment Study no longer records race.

Two broad areas of personality trait constellations appear linked to violence. The first area involves hyperactivity, risk taking, impulsivity, and concentration difficulties, which are commonly seen and diagnosed in school settings as attention deficit disorders, with and without hyperactivity. These characteristics are predictive of conduct disorders and later potential antisocial activities. Monahan cites a Swedish investigation linking restlessness and concentration difficulties at age thirteen with later violent crime by age twenty-six.[22] It appears that the factors described here are activators, not inhibitors, regarding violence potential and that their presence in a threat assessment—whether currently active or as part of the person's history—should not be overlooked.

The second dimension of personality associated with violence is anger intensity and control. Individuals with the capacity to employ inhibition or restraint over their aggressive impulses are more likely to refrain from violence than those individuals for whom urges override their restraints. *Intensity* of violent fantasies or of anger expression is an important personality factor to assess, along with its *frequency* of occurrence. An individual in a highly aroused emotional state is less likely to engage in problem-solving thinking and more likely to be action prone, especially if under the influence of alcohol or other disinhibiting substances. Paranoid individuals, for example, who perceive a person as threatening them, while under the influence of an amphetamine are at greater risk for committing violence. In that condition, the individual's cognitive processing capabilities are impaired, and it is difficult to differentiate benign signals from provocative cues.

In contrast to the angry, highly emotionally aroused individual is the individual who overcontrols any expression of anger whatsoever. "Overcontrolled hostility" is a construct well studied in psychology and basically reflects an individual who accumulates and stores frustrations and, only after much provocation, blows up in either a verbal tirade or in explosive hostile aggression.[23] Typically, people later describe their behavior as "out of character" as they were never seen to have expressed any anger whatsoever. Therefore, frustration tolerance and patience are factors that threat assessors must always evaluate in the personality make-up of the individual being assessed.

What the Person Has

The clinical risk factors that increase the probability for committing violence include major mental disorders, personality disorders, and substance abuse disorders. Major mental disorders include schizophrenia, major depression, and bipolar disorders. Regardless of how these disorders are considered, a consensus of opinion holds that there "appears to be a greater-than-chance relationship between mental disorder and violent behavior." Therefore, major mental disorders should be considered in threat assessments as a recognized risk factor for the occurrence of violence.[24] One caveat is in order here. Because much anecdotal evidence exists for the relationship between violence and mental disorders, especially schizophrenia, it is

> important, however, to consider relative rather than absolute rates. For example, people with the diagnosis of schizophrenia may have a *lower* rate of violence than people with other diagnoses, yet have a *higher* rate of violence than people with no diagnosis at all. Indeed, this is exactly what was found in the MacArthur Study: 8.7% of the patients who had a diagnosis of schizophrenia committed at least one violent act during the first ten weeks after discharge, a figure lower than the 10.7% violence rate of the patients with a diagnosis of major depression, but higher than the 4.6% violence rate of a comparison group of people without mental disorder living in the same communities.[25]

Psychopathy has been empirically linked to the commitment of violence. Psychopathy is considered to be a personality disorder involving a pattern of traits that are relatively fixed and that lead to distress or impairment through a pervasive influence on a person's inability to flexibly adapt to situations. The *Diagnostic and Statistical Manual IV* (DSM IV) does not list psychopathy as a personality disorder but identifies a closely related construct: antisocial personality disorder.[26] People who had been diagnosed with an antisocial personality disorder, versus those who had not, were at much greater risk (three times) to behave in a violent manner within months after leaving the hospital. The cardinal personality traits involved in psychopathy consist of impulsivity, feeling deficits, lack of empathy, and manipulative behavior. The Psychopathy Check List–Revised (PCL–R) has been extensively studied in both prison inmates and mentally disordered offenders.[27] Monahan reports strong correlates between elevated scores on this instrument measuring psychopathy and the commitment of violence within months after discharge from a hospital.

Other disorders that have been associated with violence include narcissistic, borderline, and paranoid personality disorders. Narcissistic types have the potential to react to rebuffs and rejections with rageful retaliation, feeling diminished and devalued by those who have offended them. Borderline personality disorders have unstable emotions and also react very strongly to rejection and perceived abandonment. They have a tendency to idealize significant others but can quickly devalue individuals who disillusion them. Because they are impulsive, they can decompensate (become upset or agitated) quickly and act out violently, either against themselves in self-injurious acts and/or against others.

Individuals with a paranoid personality disorder can also have delusional disorders that impair their ability to accurately interpret reality. For example, they can misperceive the intentions or motives of others, overpersonalize another's actions, and believe that they are being attacked. In response, they can feel justified in committing acts of violence. In my experience, many employees who make threats suffer from paranoid traits or disorders. Additionally, they are hypersensitive to criticism and/or are acutely sensitive to empathic failures by others. They often harbor a long list of grievances or a specific intense grievance, remember exactly when and where the grievance occurred and the exact words used to hurt their feelings or to impose perceived injustice upon them.

The base rates for violence are very high when paired with substance abuse and alcohol. Therefore, threat assessors must carefully focus on these variables. "Thirty-eight percent of all people serving a jail sentence in the United States for the commission of a violent crime were drinking alcohol at the time they committed the crime, and thirty-six percent were under the influence of illegal drugs."[28] Alcohol is a disinhibitor and causes aggressive impulses to become unleashed, as do substances such as cocaine or amphetamines. This is supported by the MacArthur study. Data showed that individuals carrying a diagnosis of alcohol or drug abuse or dependence were 2.7 times more likely than someone without such a diagnosis to behave violently within months after release from the hospital.

What the Person Has Done

Historical risk factors concern violent or criminal acts that the person has previously committed. The most thoroughly investigated risk factor for predicting violence is a history of past violence. It has been shown repeatedly that a past history of violence is the strongest predictor for future violent behavior. This predictive pattern applies to both criminal and psychiatric populations. In the case of such a history, it is important to identify the number of prior arrests and convictions, incarcerations, and self-reported incidents of violence. However, the challenge often faced by professionals conducting TAs in work settings is the employee who has allegedly made a threat but has no history of violence. The past history risk factor, despite its reliability as a predictor of violence, does not contraindicate the possibility of violence in its absence. Many workplace homicides are committed by individuals with no prior criminal record or history of violence.

What Has Been Done to the Individual

Risk factors for violence as an adult, as indicated by Monahan, concern what has been *done to* the individual. Pathological family environments and a history of physical abuse are important contributory background factors to future violence. Pathological or toxic family environments vary greatly but usually consist of defective parenting.

> Violent offenders tend to have experienced poor parental child-rearing methods, poor supervision and separations from their parents when they were children . . . they tend to have alcoholic or criminal parents, and they tend to have disharmonious parents who are likely to separate or divorce.[29]

Family is the oldest and most enduring of all institutions, so common sense dictates that one's family becomes the reference point through which a child gains a sense of who he or she is and how to cope with the expanded life space of community and society. Family dynamics can influence later violence in family members and is documented in the MacArthur study.

In that investigation, individuals with fathers who were regular drug abusers while the individual was growing up had nearly a 2.5 times greater probability of committing a violent act soon after release from the hospital than those individuals with fathers who were not drug abusers. Similar findings, albeit slightly less probable, were found in connection with drug-abusing mothers. If a child's mother or father was arrested, this also increased the probability of a violent incident later in adulthood. "The MacArthur study showed that patients who had suffered serious childhood abuse were fifty-one percent more likely than those who had not been abused to commit a violent act within several months after discharge from the hospital."[30]

Individuals with histories of childhood abuse, in the form of neglect and physical and sexual abuse, are at higher risk for having arrests as either juveniles or as adults and for being involved in violent crime. Researchers Joan Kaufman and Edward Zigler, as reported in

Monahan's article, reviewed the research on the effects of child abuse on later aggression toward one's own offspring and stated the following:

> The best estimate of the rate of intergenerational transmission of violence appears to be 30% ± 5%. This suggests that approximately one-third of all individuals who are physically abused, sexually abused, or extremely neglected will subject their offspring to one of these forms of maltreatment, while the remaining two-thirds will provide adequate care for their children . . . the rate of abuse among individuals with a history of abuse . . . is approximately six times higher than the base rate for abuse in the general population (5%).[31]

This data underlines the importance of learning about an individual's personal family history when conducting a TA, given the weight of the described risk factors in contributing to potential violent behavior.

Fitness for Duty Evaluations

Once an employer has received information that an employee has engaged, or threatened to engage, in physical or verbal conduct with the potential to cause physical or emotional harm to coemployees or third parties, the employer must determine what action should be taken.[32] The use of a fitness-for-duty evaluation (FFD) typically arises where the employee's conduct raises the following questions:

- Given the employee's mental or emotional state of mind, is he or she qualified to continue performing his or her job?

- Does the employee pose a direct threat to his or her own safety or to the safety of a coemployee or a third party?

Clearly, there are situations where an FFD evaluation does not need to be conducted because the employee's conduct is sufficiently egregious to warrant termination or other significant disciplinary action. Where the employee's conduct is less clear, an employer confronted with these questions may want to send the employee for an FFD evaluation. The right to send an employee for an FFD evaluation is subject to certain limitations that are imposed by the following laws:

■ Americans with Disabilities Act (ADA)

■ Family and Medical Leave Act (FMLA)

■ Federal and state workers' compensation laws

The application, scope, and limitations of these laws are, in many aspects, both complementary and conflicting. Employers should be aware of what constraints these laws place on seeking an FFD evaluation.

An FFD evaluation is an individualized assessment of an employee's mental or physical ability to safely perform his or her essential job functions without any limitations. Where there are questions about an employee's mental fitness, employees may be interviewed by an appropriate professional, such as a clinical psychologist with forensic experience, a forensic psychiatrist, or a psychologist specializing in occupational matters. The interview can be conducted at the work site or at an off-site location. It is prudent to identify a provider before the need arises to conduct a fitness evaluation.

Because an FFD evaluation may result in an employee's removal from his or her job, the evaluator should be experienced and as well-credentialed as possible. It is important for an employer to be in as strong a position as possible to support and defend an evaluator's credentials in the event that the evaluation findings or recommendations are challenged. For this reason, a doctoral-level evaluator who is licensed to perform mental health evaluations is strongly recommended. When the employee has made threatening statements or displayed threatening behavior, it is even more important for the FFD evaluator to have a forensic risk assessment background.

A fitness evaluator typically will consult with the employee's supervisors, the referral source, and often someone from human resources. If the employee is receiving psychological treatment *and* has given permission for that information to be released, it is useful to interview the practitioner who is treating the employee. Supervisors should remember that the employee must provide written permission to all parties to discuss his or her case, unless the employee is deemed a direct threat to the safety of others or to him or herself, in which case the "duty to warn" becomes paramount.

In these kinds of situations, the professional who is treating the employee is generally compelled by law to alert potential targets of any threats that have been made against them. While employee privacy is critical, the evaluator must balance the need for confidentiality against the organizational needs of the employer. Moreover, written FFD evaluations should not be placed in an employee's personnel file but should be maintained in a separate medical file kept under lock and key. Access to this file should be limited to appropriate personnel on a "need-to-know" basis. Normally, employees (and patients) are given access to their medical records. However, in the case of FFD evaluations, the regulations of the Health Insurance Portability and Accountability Act (HIPAA) provide that "patients do not have the right of access to information compiled in reasonable anticipation of, or for use in, a civil, criminal, or administrative action or procedure."[33]

The "need-to-know" basis of a particular FFD finding could be exemplified by the following: An employee may have been evaluated for repeatedly losing his or her temper at work and was diagnosed as having severe marital problems. It is recommended that the employee undergo marital counseling. This recommendation might necessitate that the employee take time off from work to attend counseling sessions. The fact that the employee attends counseling sessions should only be made known to those individuals who have a need to know, that is, his or her supervisor and human resources.

When a referral is made for an FFD evaluation, personnel records are often shared directly or indirectly with the evaluator. If the records are not directly shared, the information may be communicated to the evaluator for review. Information pertaining to past behavioral problems such as absenteeism, fighting, or more serious problems, such as threats or irrational behavior, is very important for the evaluator to be aware of so that a composite picture of the employee can be constructed. Observations giving rise to the referral are always important to identify early in the referral process.

Ordinarily, the employer bears the financial cost of an FFD evaluation. Although the number of individuals expected to have access to the report is small, an FFD evaluation should be written with sensitivity so as to avoid inflaming, humiliating, or otherwise offending the subject employee. Evaluators writing reports should be aware of the debate over how detailed an FFD report should be. At least one court has addressed at length what information should be included in an FFD report.

In *Pettus v. Cole*,[34] the California appellate court was asked to address the question of whether two FFD reports contained unnecessary or inappropriate personal information about an employee that violated the state's law prohibiting the unauthorized disclosure of a person's medical information. In this case, two psychiatrists were asked to evaluate the plaintiff's mental fitness in conjunction with his request for leave under the employer's short-term disability plan. The plaintiff had requested disability leave for what he claimed was a work-related stress condition. The psychiatrists submitted detailed reports to the employer regarding the plaintiff's fitness that included extensive information about his medical and social history. Neither psychiatrist obtained the employee's consent to release his medical information.

Initially, the trial court ruled in favor of the psychiatrists, holding that the employer was entitled to detailed, narrative reports, even in the absence of the plaintiff's consent to the release of his medical information. On appeal, however, the appellate court found that the plaintiff had a reasonable expectation of privacy in the information he provided to the psychiatrists, even though he knew they would be communicating their findings and conclusions to his employer. The appellate court was critical of the fact that the reports contained far more personal and medical information than was needed by the employer to accomplish its legitimate objective, which in this instance was to determine whether the plaintiff was entitled to short-term disability leave.

One conclusion the appellate court reached was that the information an employer obtains should be related to the employee's functional limitations and whether or not his injury was work related. The court's finding underscores the conflict between an employee's privacy rights and an employer's need to know.[35] As one commentator stated about the *Pettus* case, the decision "suggests the courts do not necessarily agree that employers are entitled to or require a high level of personal detail in fitness for duty and other reports addressing the mental health of employees."[36]

While the ruling in *Pettus* was decided under California's Confidentiality of Medical Information Act (CMI) and the state constitution (which recognizes a constitutional right to privacy), and, therefore, has no legal force and effect in courts outside of California, I believe that it is prudent for all FFD evaluators to exercise great care and discretion in selecting what details to put into an FFD report. At the same time, FFD evaluators need to include sufficient detail to convey the appropriate depth of the problem and, thus, enable the employer to take appropriate personnel action when warranted. Clearly, providing a limited report poses a danger; such a report can lead an employer to draw inappropriate conclusions about a person's potential dangerousness.

If an employer relies on an FFD report that involves a threat assessment, the report must contain sufficient detail to help the employer reach a decision. A basic principle governing the content of an FFD report is that the report should articulate the findings or details framed by the context in which the employer sought the evaluation. Therefore, the report content must be clear and unequivocal. At a minimum, the FFD report should contain a statement regarding the probability that the employee will commit violence, along with other relevant details (such as the diagnosis, if known). A word of caution: under the CMI, California employers are prohibited from receiving medical diagnosis information unless the employee has consented to its disclosure. In most cases, an FFD report should set forth the bases for its conclusions and refrain from including extraneous information that could in any way be construed as defamatory toward the employee, or anyone else.

▌ Benefits of an FFD Evaluation

An FFD evaluation offers a number of insights:

1. An evaluation reduces an employer's liability and vulnerability by fulfilling the legal obligation to provide a safe workplace. The General Duty Clause of the Occupational Safety and Health Act of 1970 (OSHA) makes the employer directly responsible for exposure of employees to recognized workplace hazards likely to cause serious injury or death to an employee. Thus, an employer is potentially liable for failing to correct a known or foreseeable danger in the workplace. OSHA has asserted that workplace violence is a hazard likely to cause serious injury or death, and it has issued citations to employers with monetary penalties. In other words, an employer can be held responsible for failing to properly identify, manage, and communicate information about a threatening employee. An FFD policy, while not needed to conduct an FFD evaluation, communicates a strong message to employees about the employer's concern for, and commitment to, their safety; it is also a solid risk-management strategy to have in place.

2. An FFD evaluation may provide key information about the duration of a potential leave of absence for a psychological condition. It can also identify when such leaves may be justified. If an employee is seeking paid leave under an employer's

short- or long-term disability plan, the employer is entitled to determine whether the employee satisfies the plan's criteria for a covered disability.[37] Additionally, the evaluation can be helpful in assessing the effects of the physical or mental impairment on the employee's ability to work effectively, and the possible side effects of treatment (i.e., medications) on productivity and safety to others.

3. A last chance agreement could be crafted as a result of the FFD evaluation, giving the employer permission to monitor the employee's compliance with a treatment plan following his or her return to work.[38] Knowledge of an employee's noncompliance could serve as a red flag that the employee is not acting or thinking rationally and could potentially place others at risk for their safety.

4. An FFD evaluation can also identify what accommodation(s), if any, would be useful to maximize an employee's productivity on the job. For example, most accommodations are inexpensive and reasonably easy to implement, such as adjusting an employee's work schedule or providing brief rest periods during the course of the work day. Changing the employee's supervisor, however, is not considered a reasonable accommodation, even if it is believed a toxic relationship exists between the supervisor and the employee. If implementing such an accommodation places an undue burden on the employer, the employer is not obligated to continue to employ the individual, particularly if the employee may represent a direct threat of harm if the supervisor is not changed.

▍ Americans with Disabilities Act

The concept of "direct threat" comes from the Americans with Disabilities Act (ADA) and has been interpreted by the Equal Employment Opportunity Commission (EEOC) to mean that a "significant risk of substantial harm exists to the health or safety of the individual or others that cannot be eliminated or reduced by reasonable accommodation."[39] An employee who is determined to be a "direct threat" to the health or safety of individuals in the workplace does not qualify as an individual with a disability.[40] In other words, the employee is not entitled to any of the protections provided for by the ADA.

Determining whether someone poses a "direct threat" must be made on the basis of an *individualized* assessment of the employee's present ability to safely perform the functions of his or her job, considering a reasonable medical judgment and relying on the most current medical knowledge and/or the best available objective evidence. In determining whether an individual presents a direct threat, the EEOC requires that the following factors to be considered:

1. The duration of the risk;
2. The nature and severity of the potential harm;
3. The likelihood that the potential harm will occur; and
4. The imminence of the potential harm.

Such considerations must be based on objective, factual evidence and not on subjective perceptions, irrational fears, or stereotypes about the nature or effect of a particular medical or psychological condition. Just because someone is making threats and behaving in a menacing fashion does not automatically make them a direct threat. Even if an employee is mentally impaired, immediate dismissal may be an inappropriate response.

The burden of proving that an employee poses a "direct threat" rests with the employer since the concept serves as an affirmative defense, thereby shielding an employer from liability for a claim of discrimination based on a disability. An FFD evaluation would be an example of the kind of objective evidence an employer could use to establish that an employee poses a "direct threat." The purpose of such an evaluation is to determine if the employee is likely to behave in an unsafe manner in the near future. This suggests that the FFD evaluator must be well-versed in threat assessment. The process usually requires an ongoing risk evaluation and monitoring, given that a person's risk factors are constantly changing and, as such, will increase or decrease the person's probability for committing violence.

▌ Family and Medical Leave Act

The employer's right to require that an employee submit to an FFD evaluation is limited in scope and time under the FMLA. Briefly, the FMLA allows employees who are otherwise eligible for FMLA coverage (having previously worked a minimum of twelve months for the employer, which need not be consecutive, and 1,250 hours in the preceding year), and are suffering from a "serious health condition," to take up to twelve weeks of unpaid, protected leave with a right to job reinstatement.[41] Essentially, an employer may require that an employee *returning from* FMLA leave submit an FFD *certification* from his or her health care provider before being allowed to return to work, provided that: (1) the employer has a uniformly applied practice or policy that requires such certification of all employees returning from a medical leave of absence (without regard to whether the leave was FMLA-protected); (2) notice of the FFD certification requirement is contained in the employer's employee handbook and in the employer's FMLA response form; (3) the certification is limited to the health condition causing the need for FMLA leave; and (4) any clarification of the FFD certification can only be obtained by the employer's health care provider, with the employee's consent.

An FFD certification does *not* include a medical or psychological exam. Unlike the ADA, employees may not be required to undergo a FFD evaluation before returning from FMLA leave unless one of two conditions are present: (1) it is required by state or local law; or (2) it is required pursuant to the provisions of a collective bargaining agreement.

Thus, unless required by law or contract, an employer may only request an FFD certification that an employee is able to resume work and no longer represents a threat to coworkers or to him or herself.

A few courts have recognized one other instance in which an employer may order that an employee submit to an FFD examination without violating the FMLA. Borrowing from the ADA, some courts have held that an employer can require that an employee submit to further examination *once* he or she has been reinstated if the employer can demonstrate that it has a sufficient "business necessity" to examine the returning employee. An employer can show that it has a "business necessity" to send an employee for further medical evaluation if it has reason to believe that the employee's ongoing health limitations interfere with his or her ability to work.

In one case, a sawmill employee who took medication to control a seizure disorder was prohibited from returning from FMLA leave (which he took to have his medication levels readjusted) because he refused to submit to his employer's request for an FFD evaluation. The court held that the employer had violated the FMLA by refusing to reinstate the employee, who provided an FFD certification from his physician. The court, however, recognized that the employer lawfully could have required the employee to submit to an examination if it, first, had permitted the employee to return to work and, second, been able to establish that the employee continued to experience limitations from his antiseizure medication that interfered with his ability to perform his job safely.[42]

Other conditions that the FMLA imposes on requests for an FFD certification include the following:[43]

1. The employee bears the cost of obtaining an FFD certification.
2. The employer may not require an FFD certification from an employee returning from intermittent leave.
3. The employer may not seek a second or third opinion on an FFD certification.
4. The employee's return to work cannot be delayed pending the employer's efforts to obtain clarification of the FFD certification by its health care provider.

Workers' Compensation Statutes

An employer may also have the right to conduct an FFD evaluation after the employee has sustained (or claims to have sustained) a work-related injury or illness. An FFD evaluation may be permitted upon an employee's return to work from workers' compensation leave, but this requirement can vary under state law. In addition, most state workers' compensation statutes require that any medical information sought be restricted to the injury or illness and the employee's ability to work as a result of the injury or illness.

Under state law, varying restrictions are placed on an employer's ability to contact an employee's treating physician and on obtaining a second or third opinion regarding an employee's ability to return to work. Finally, the employer must avoid taking adverse action against an individual who has been on workers' compensation leave, lest its action be seen as retaliatory. Even if an employee's discharge does not violate the ADA or FMLA, it could constitute a retaliatory discharge claim under state law.[44]

Potential Consequences of Not Pursuing an FFD Evaluation

If an employer is aware of an employee's potential for violence and does not have the individual evaluated, an employer could be held liable under a negligent retention or supervision theory.[45] Also, in some jurisdictions, an injured employee can potentially assert, subject to potential workers' compensation preemption issues, a separate claim for intentional or negligent infliction of emotional distress if an employer is aware of an unstable employee's harmful conduct to a specific employee and takes no action to protect the potential victim from this known risk.

Concern about one's potential tort liability should not, however, lead an employer to ignore the requirements of the ADA and act on mere suspicion without first evaluating the presence of significant, objective evidence of an employee threat. Nevertheless, it is noteworthy that the damages under available state law for negligent conduct are potentially higher than those available under the ADA, which are subject to statutory caps. Finally, in addition to tort liability, if an employer has a specific written policy against violence in the workplace but fails to enforce it, the employee could arguably assert a claim in the nature of breach of contract for any resulting damages.

A Legal Look at Threat Assessments

Previously, I stated that a TA team should not be a replacement for a qualified threat assessment professional. Once a decision has been made to conduct a TA, it is necessary to identify three steps in the process:

1. Identification of the employee or third party who poses the actual threat;
2. Determination of the immediacy of the risks of violence posed by the employee or third party; and
3. How to manage, if possible, the employee or third party and the risks that he or she represents to a particular target (other employee or group of employees).

At the outset, before requesting a threat assessment, the TA team (or its designees) must secure detailed information about the employee's behavior and conduct which led other employees or third parties to become concerned. For example, information pertaining to:

- Specific language and physical acts engaged in by the employee;

- Information about actions or comments made by the employee which may indicate the employee's motivations or intentions toward a target; and

- Information which may indicate the employee's capacity to engage in violence (e.g., information about ownership of weapons or participation in activities such as martial arts, military record, prior criminal history, etc.).

In addition, the assessment should attempt to obtain information about behavior which may indicate that an attack may be imminent, such as:

- Comments or actions expressing an interest in potential target employees;

- Information indicating that the employee has communicated with, or spoken to other employees about, the target employee;

- Information which indicates that the employee has either expressed or attempted to harm him or herself or other employees;

- Whether the employee has obtained a weapon and/or has indicated that he or she has been practicing with a weapon; and

- Whether the employee has focused on, followed, or approached the potential target employee on prior occasions, with or without a weapon.

Once this information is assembled, the employer must decide whether or not to directly approach the problem employee and conduct an interview. Unfortunately, this is frequently a delicate judgment call because the interview may cause the employee to react in a defensive and potentially violent manner. Moreover, the employer should be prepared for such a negative response and may wish to consult with a threat assessment professional, legal counsel, human resources, and security personnel concerning whether, where, and when such an interview should occur and who should be present.

In addition to considering the responses of the potentially violent employee, the employer needs to assemble information about the potential target employee or groups of employees that includes:

- Determining whether a target has been identified, who the likely targets may be, and whether and how to communicate concerns to potential targets;

- The nature of the relationship between the employee and the targets;

- How familiar the employee is with the target individual's daily work and personal activities and habits;

- The extent to which the target individual is vulnerable to an attack, and, if so, what changes in that person's life, work, and living arrangements would make it more difficult for the employee to succeed in harming the target individual; and

- Whether the target individual, family members, or coworkers expressed fear of the employee and the factual bases for such fear.

In order to obtain this information from the target individual, the employer must conduct a detailed interview and should share with such individual all the information that has led to a concern about the potential for violence against the target individual.

After this information is obtained, the employer must proceed to the next step of the analysis: What steps, if any, can be taken to manage the threat? Depending upon the nature of the information, the employer may be able to manage the threat by issuing a simple warning to the targeted employee. Or, the situation may be so acute that immediate intervention by the police, the courts (e.g., issuance of a restraining or protective order), and other third parties are necessary because the threatened hazard has moved beyond the employer's control. Whether one should seek a protective order is not without certain risks because, in some cases, their use can actually escalate the potential for violence. Domestic violence research studies generally show restraining orders to be effective, but enforcement by local police is a strong determiner of their effectiveness. Also, it is crucial to obtain information pertaining to an individual's reactions to previous orders.[46] In developing a strategy, the employer should rely upon its TA team, augmented, if necessary, by a qualified threat assessment professional.

The Role of Mental Health Professionals

Where information gathered by the employer indicates that an employee has engaged in threatening conduct, serious consideration should be given to contacting a competent mental health professional to participate in the TA. By engaging such a professional, particularly where the employee has a history of mental or emotional impairments, the employer will undercut any contention that it relied upon speculation, inferences, or stereotypes. Also, reliance on professional assistance will hopefully undercut any charge that the employer violated the ADA owing to the manner in which it assessed the employee.

The selection of the mental health care professional is of crucial importance. Health care professionals who have had no experience with workplace violence cannot provide meaningful assistance. Further, should a violent event occur (or litigation ensue over the handling of the event) and the employee is terminated or disciplined, an unqualified professional will be vulnerable to being discredited and could jeopardize the employer's entire course of action.

Before engaging a mental health professional, the following information should be obtained from the individual: (1) whether he or she has received training in, and studied, workplace violence; (2) whether he or she has ever conducted a TA; (3) which methodologies he or she utilizes; (4) how prior TA and case management incidents were resolved; and (5) references that can be contacted to confirm his or her experience and past performance.

Again, employers are cautioned about using a mental health care professional who is a member of the employer's Employee Assistance Program (EAP) to conduct the TA. Several commentators have recommended that EAP professionals not be utilized for this purpose because of the potential loss of trust in the EAP professional's assurances of confidentiality if they are perceived as instruments of the employer. Employees will be less inclined to utilize the EAP if they do not believe EAP counselors have their best interests at heart.

Workplace Hazards

The workplace itself may be a potential site of violence because of the nature of the business conducted or where it is located. For example, health care providers, particularly those who work in mental health facilities, are a frequent target of violence because of the interaction between staff and patients. The staff must be trained in how to deal with such incidents and be equipped with security devices to restrain patients, if necessary.

Other workplace violence incidents may occur because the workplace is located in a high-crime area. Unfortunately, gangs have infiltrated certain workplaces and frequently utilize threats of violence to extort money from coemployees and to intimidate supervisors.[47] In this case, a security consultant should be contacted regarding steps which can be taken (e.g., video surveillance, secure entry procedures, computer identification systems, employee escorts, etc.).

Finally, the workplace is frequently the site of violence because of the presence of hostile outsiders, such as former spouses or significant others, who know that their former spouse or lover can be found at work during certain hours of the day. The potential problem can be heightened further if the individual, a former employee, continues to have physical access to the workplace (e.g., failed to return security badge, has knowledge of breaches in employer's security system). Many incidents have occurred where such individuals have stalked the employee outside the premises or have entered the workplace (forcibly or not) and injured or killed the former spouse, oftentimes along with other coworkers who happened to be in the right place at the wrong time.

Once the employer becomes aware of such activity, it should consider prompt involvement of the police—and potentially the courts—to keep such outsiders off its premises. An employer who, in good faith, engages law enforcement and/or the judicial process in such incidents should be protected from liability. It is worth repeating the earlier caution that when involving the police or the courts, such action may prompt the problem employee to react in an explosive or otherwise unpredictable manner.

Thus, the entire phenomenon of workplace violence is a dynamic one that makes it impossible for the employer to develop one strategy that meets every situation. If employers develop policies within the framework of existing laws, enforce the policies in a consistent manner, and provide appropriate training to managers to help them recognize and defuse preincident indicators of violence, they will be able to reduce or eliminate the potential that these tragic events will occur. TAs, when conducted competently and on a timely basis, are invaluable aids in this process.

Notes

1. A.F. Friedman, R.P. Archer & R.W. Handel, *Minnesota Multiphasic Personality Inventories and Suicide, in* Assessment, Treatment, and Prevention of Suicidal Behavior (R. Yufit & D. Lester eds., John Wiley & Sons, Inc. 2005); American Psychological Association, Violent Offenders: Appraising and Managing Risk (V.L. Quinsey, G.T. Harris, M.E. Rice & C.A. Cormier eds., 1998).

2. E.A. Rugala & J.R. Fitzgerald, *Workplace Violence: From Threat to Intervention,* 3 Clinical and Occupational Medicine 775–789 (2003).

3. Id. at 778.

4. R.A. Fein & B. Vossekuil, U.S. Department of Justice, Protective Intelligence and Threat Assessment Investigations: A Guide for State and Local Law Enforcement Officials (1998).

5. E.A. Rugala & J.R. Fitzgerald, U.S. Department of Justice, Workplace Violence: Issues in Response (E.A. Rugala & A.R. Issacs eds., 2004).

6. Research into recent school violence by the Secret Service shows that in more than 75 percent of the incidents investigated, a number of other students *knew* about the attacks *before* they occurred. See K. Mohandie, *School Violence Threat Management* (Specialized Training Services 2000). In more than half the cases, more than one person previously expressed concern to others; over half of the attackers develop the idea to hurt the victims at least weeks prior to the incident. See T.B. Feldman & P.W. Johnson, Pacific Institute for the Study of Conflict and Aggression, *Workplace Violence: A New Form of Lethal Aggression, in* Lethal Violence 2000: A sourcebook on fatal domestic, acquaintance, and stranger aggression 311–338 (H.V. Hall ed., 1996). Because these findings are often also seen in adult violent incidents at work, it is important for the threat evaluator to

speak with coworkers and others who may have heard the individual expressing resentments or even direct threats, as these behaviors may represent early warning signs that the person is unable to contain his or her emotions and behaviors. Additional findings demonstrate that adult workplace violence perpetrators communicated their intentions in advance about 86 percent of the time, usually to friends, coworkers, and acquaintances, and less frequently to intended victims. See supra note 2.

7. See supra note 5.

8. Id.

9. J.R. Meloy, Violence Risk and Threat Assessment (Specialized Training Services 2000).

10. E.P. Mulvey, *Assessing the Evidence of a Link Between Mental Illness and Violence*, 45 Hospital & Community Psychiatry 663–668 (1994).

11. The problems related to the prediction of low base-rate phenomena have been discussed at length by authors such as P.E. Meehl and A. Rosen, and J.S. Wiggins. See P.E. Meehl & A. Rosen, *Antecedent Probability and the Efficiency of Psychometric Signs, Patterns, or Cutting Scores*, 52 Psychological Bulletin 194–216 (1955); J.S. Wiggins, Personality and Prediction: Principles of Personality Assessment (reprint 1988, Krieger Publishing Co.) (1973).

12. See supra note 9, at 7.

13. The reader interested in learning about appraising and managing risk from a strictly actuarial approach should consult the excellent text by Vernon L. Quinsey and his colleagues. See American Psychological Association, supra note 1. The interested reader should also consult psychologist Robert D. Hare. Hare has created a powerful actuarial instrument for identifying psychopaths entitled *The Psychopathy Checklist–Revised (PCL–R)*. See R.D. Hare, *Psychopathy: A Clinical Construct Whose Time Has Come*, 23 Criminal Justice and Behavior 25–54 (1996). In fact, this actuarial instrument blends clinical data derived from in-depth interviews focusing on personality traits such as superficial charm, narcissism, empathy deficits, and manipulativeness.

14. See supra note 9.

15. J.W. Swanson, C.E. Holzer, V.K. Ganjv & R.T. Jono, *Violence and Psychiatric Disorders in the Community: Evidence from the Epidemiologic Catchment Area Surveys*, 41 Hospital Community Psychiatry 761–770 (July 1990).

16. J. Monahan, *A Jurisprudence of Risk Assessment: Forecasting Harm Among Prisoners, Predators, and Patients*, 92 Va. L. Rev. 391–435 (2006).

17. R.J. Sampson & J.L. Lauritsen, *Violent Victimization and Offending: Individual-, Situational-, and Community-Level Risk Factors in Understanding and Preventing Violence*, in Social Influences 1, 18 (A.J. Reiss & Jeffrey A. Roth eds., 1994).

18. See supra note 16, at 415–416.

19. Id. at 415.

20. Id. at 391–435.

21. Id. at 418.

22. Id. at 391–435.

23. A.F. Friedman, R. Lewak, D.S. Nichols & J.T. Webb, Psychological Assessment with the MMPI-2 (Erlbaum 2001); E.I. Megargee, P.E. Cook & G.A. Mendelsohn, *The Development and Validation of an MMPI Scale of Assaultiveness in Overcontrolled Individuals,* 72 J. of Abnormal Psychol. 519–528 (1967).

24. See supra note 16, at 391–435.

25. Id. at 420.

26. American Psychiatric Association, Diagnostic and Statistical Manual of Mental Disorders (4th ed. 2000).

27. R.D. Hare, Manual for the Revised Psychopathy Checklist (2d ed., Multi-Health Systems 2003).

28. See supra note 16, at 422.

29. Id. at 425.

30. Id. at 427.

31. Id. at 426.

32. A.F. Friedman, *When and How to Evaluate Fitness for Duty,* 2723 Security Management Bulletin 1–3 (Dec. 10, 1998).

33. 45 C.F.R. §§ 164.508, 164.524[a][1].

34. 49 Cal. App. 4th 402, 57 Cal. Rptr. 2d 46 (1996).

35. A.V. Stone, Fitness for Duty: Principles, Methods, and Legal Issues (CRC Press 2000).

36. Id. at 183.

37. Id.

38. Id.

39. EEOC Guidance on the Americans with Disabilities Act and Psychiatric Disabilities (Mar. 1997), available at http://www.eeoc.gov/policy/docs/psych.html.

40. Daughtery v. City of El Paso, 56 F. 3d. 695, 696 (5th Cir. 1995).

41. 29 U.S.C. §§ 2612–2614. At the beginning of 2008, two new leave provisions were added to the FMLA specifically addressing the needs of servicemembers and their families. One provision provides up to twenty-six weeks of leave in a twelve-month period to care for an injured servicemember. The other provision provides up to twelve weeks of leave in a twelve-month period due to any "qualifying exigency" arising out of the fact that an employee's family member has been notified of an impending call or order to active duty or is already on active duty.

42. See Underhill v. Willamina Lumber Co., 1999 U.S. Dist. LEXIS 9722 (D. Or. June 19, 1999) (citing Albert v. Runyon, 6 F. Supp. 2d 57 (D. Mass. 1999) with approval).

43. 29 C.F.R. § 825.310.

44. See, e.g., Heldenbrand v. Roadmaster Corp., 277 Ill. App. 3d 664, 660 N.E.2d 1354 (5th Dist. 1996) (affirming $1 million verdict for employee discharged for asserting rights under Illinois Workers' Compensation Act).

45. See, e.g., Foster v. Loft, Inc., 26 Mass. App. Ct. 289, 526 N.E.2d 1309 (Mass. App. 1988) (employer's knowledge of disorder on the part of the employee is generally sufficient to forewarn employer that employee may commit assault); Garcia v. Duffy, 492 So. 2d 435 (Fla. Dist. Ct. App. 1986) ("Negligent retention . . . occurs when, during the course of employment, the employer becomes aware or should have been aware of problems with an employee that indicated his unfitness, and the employer fails to take further action such as investigating, discharge or reassignment.").

46. S.G. White & J.S. Cawood, *Threat Management of Stalking Cases, in* Psychology of Stalking: Clinical and Forensic Perspectives (J. Reid Meloy ed., Academic Press 1998).

47. J.S. Barber, *Workplace Violence: An Overview of Evolving Employer Liability*, 83 Ill. B.J. 462 (Sept. 1995).

CHAPTER 3

State Legislation Addressing Workplace Violence

Lynn Jenkins, Ph.D.,
Matt Bowyer, M.S.,
and John Howard, M.D.

▌ Introduction/Background

Although certain occupational groups, such as law enforcement, corrections, and health care—particularly psychiatric care—have long recognized the risk of violence associated with their jobs, it is only in recent decades that workplace violence has been recognized as a critical occupational safety and health issue across all employment sectors.[1]

The first national data on the incidence of workplace homicide were published by the National Institute for Occupational Safety and Health (NIOSH) in 1989.[2] This publication demonstrated, on a national basis, that homicide was the third leading cause of occupational injury death, exceeded only by motor vehicle crashes and machine-related deaths. This study also documented that homicide was the leading cause of injury death for women in the workplace.

Prior to this publication, homicide had not been seriously regarded as an occupational safety and health issue. In the early 1990s, data on the magnitude of nonfatal workplace violence began to appear in the literature, including information from the U.S. Bureau of Labor Statistics (BLS) Survey of Occupational Injuries and Illnesses, indicating that, in 1992, approximately 22,000 private sector workers experienced on-site assaults serious enough to require at least one day away from work.[3] The U.S. Bureau of Justice Statistics, examining data from the National Crime Victimization Survey for the period 1987 to 1992, found that approximately one million workers annually were victims of a crime while at work or on duty.[4] Although these estimates varied significantly, due to differences in definitions and the scope of coverage of the two data systems, it was clear that the number of nonfatal workplace violence incidents was markedly greater than the number of workplace homicides that had first captured the attention of researchers and policy makers. In the early-to-mid-1990s, spokespersons representing government and labor, as well as safety and health professionals and others, began asking that greater attention be given to workplace violence risk factors and potential prevention strategies.[5]

In 1992, the Occupational Safety and Health Administration (OSHA) stated in a "letter of interpretation" that the General Duty Clause of the Occupational Safety and Health Act provides a mechanism to address new or previously unrecognized hazards for which no OSHA standards exist. In this important interpretation of the scope of an existing statute, OSHA wrote that preventing workplace violence could be considered a component of the requirement for all employers to provide a workplace free from recognized hazards.[6] In 1996, OSHA published guidelines for the prevention of violence in health care and social service settings.[7] These were followed in 1998 by recommendations for the prevention of violence in late-night retail settings[8] and in 2000 by a fact sheet on violence prevention in taxicab services.[9]

As professional and general interest in the topic grew, it became clear that the term "workplace violence" meant different things to different people. Rather than being a single issue, it encompassed incidents across a range of circumstances and relationships between victims and perpetrators. For example, it was recognized that the violence that may occur during the course of a robbery of a taxicab driver or a convenience store was distinctly different from that which might occur when a distraught patient lashes out at a health care provider, when a worker attacks his or her coworker, or when a boyfriend assaults his girlfriend at work.

In an effort to facilitate discussion of research and prevention needs and strategies, a typology of workplace violence has been developed over the last decade that categorizes the range of workplace violence incidents. Specifically, the types are:

- Type I: criminal intent incidents in which the perpetrator has no legitimate relationship to the business and is usually committing a crime in conjunction with the violence;

- Type II: customer/client incidents in which the perpetrator has a legitimate relationship with the business and becomes violent while being served by the business;

- Type III: worker-on-worker incidents in which the perpetrator is an employee or past employee of the business and attacks or threatens another employee; and,

- Type IV: personal relationship incidents in which the perpetrator does not have a direct employment relationship with the workplace, but has a personal relationship with the intended victim-employee.[10]

Over time, the field has also come to recognize that the continuum of workplace violence includes not only incidents of direct physical harm or the threat of physical harm but also bullying and psychological aggression.[11] In a 2002 survey of key informants across a sample of U.S. workplaces, researchers found that about one-fourth of companies or agencies reported some degree of bullying in the twelve months prior to the survey. Bullying was defined as "repeated intimidation, slandering, social isolation, or humiliation by one or more persons against another."[12]

▮ The Magnitude of the Problem

During an eight-year period from 1997 to 2004, the Census of Fatal Occupational Injuries documented a total of 5,336 workplace homicides among private and public sector U.S. workers. Of these, 642 (12 percent) of the victims were public sector employees—that is, at the time of their murder, they were working for federal, state, or local government agencies. The vast majority of these workers (74 percent) were employed at the local governmental level. Another 17 percent were employed by state governments, and 8 percent were federal government employees (see Table 3.1).[13]

With regard to nonfatal workplace victimizations, the National Crime Victimization Survey for the seven-year period from 1993 to 1999 documented a total of 1,743,400 U.S. workplace victimizations among private and public sector workers. Of these, 612,800 (35 percent) occurred among governmental workers. In this survey, employees of state, city, and local governments could not be analyzed individually because they were grouped into a single category.

Table 3.1 Homicides of government workers by agency type, Census of Fatal Occupational Injuries, 1997–2004

Agency Type*	Number of workplace homicides	Percent of public sector homicides
Federal government	55	8
State government	111	17
Local government	472	74

*There were four cases for which agency type was unknown.

Ninety-one percent (559,000) of the victimizations of public sector workers occurred among these individuals. Eight percent (53,800) occurred against federal government. Notably, the victimization rate per 1,000 workers was three times higher for state, city, and local governmental workers than for employees in the private sector (33 per 1,000 versus 9.9 per 1,000).[14]

▌General Legislative Initiatives by Typology

A number of states have crafted legislation or developed other administrative procedures related to various aspects of workplace violence prevention. It is useful to think of these in terms of the typology of workplace violence. Clearly, Type I (criminal intent) violence prevention initiatives may not be as relevant to the public sector as Type II (patient, client, customer) and Type IV (intimate partner) initiatives. Notably, however, a few states have addressed workplace violence prevention in the public-sector context. This section provides an overview of existing state-based efforts based on the type of violence involved.

Type I: Criminal Intent

Florida

In 1992, the Florida legislature passed the Convenience Business Security Act (CBSA)[15] to protect convenience businesses from violent crimes. The CBSA requires that certain security devices and standards be established at all convenience businesses open any time between 11 p.m. and 5 a.m. The minimum security standards include: (1) training in robbery deterrence and safety for each retail employee conducted through an approved curriculum; (2) a drop safe or cash management device that is secured to the floor or counter or that weighs at least 500 pounds; (3) lighted parking lots; (4) notice at the entrance that the cash register contains $50 or less;

(5) height markers at the entrance; (6) window sign placement allowing an unobstructed view of the sales transaction area from inside and outside the building; (7) a written cash management policy, kept on the premises, that limits cash on hand between the hours of 11 p.m. and 5 a.m.; (8) a security camera system that is capable of retrieving an identifiable image of an offender, including annual test photos and a maintenance log showing maintenance every four months; and (9) a silent alarm.

Convenience businesses that experience a murder, robbery, sexual battery, aggravated assault, aggravated battery, kidnapping, or false imprisonment in connection with the operation of the business must also implement one of the following: (1) at least two employees on the premises at all times; (2) a secured safety enclosure made of transparent polycarbonate; (3) a security guard or off-duty law enforcement officer on the premises; or (4) locked premises, with business conducted through an indirect pass-through, trapdoor, or window. The additional security measures must be in place for a minimum of twenty-four months after the date of the most recent crime.[16]

Washington

In 1990, the Washington Industrial Safety and Health Services Agency adopted measures to protect convenience store workers. The Washington State Administrative Code 296-24-10203 applies to retail establishments, except restaurants, hotels, or taverns, that operate between the hours of 11 p.m. and 6 a.m. This regulation focuses on the environmental design of stores and the training of workers. With regard to store safety, employers are required to have a drop safe on the premises, to post signs stating that a safe is in use, that staff do not have access to the safe, and that limited amounts of cash are kept on hand. With regard to training, employers must instruct their employees in safety, security, and crime avoidance measures. The employer must emphasize the importance of maintaining a clear view of the cash register from outside of the store and maintaining only minimal cash levels in the register. This training must be provided before an employee works a shift from 11 p.m. to 6 a.m. Additionally, refresher training must be provided annually.[17]

New Mexico

In October 2004, the New Mexico Environmental Improvement Board approved standards related to occupational safety and health of convenience store employees. Convenience stores are defined as businesses "primarily engaged in the retail sale of convenience goods, or both convenience goods and gasoline; it does not include gasoline service stations, grocery stores, or supermarkets." These standards include security requirements including exterior lighting, limits on store window signage, security cameras, security alarms, depository or time-lock safe, cash management, signs regarding the security measures in place (e.g., safe, security alarm, and security camera system), and employee training. This legislation also includes specific security measures to be taken in convenience stores operating from midnight to 5 a.m. Stores operating during these overnight hours must utilize at least one of the following security measures: two employees on duty; controlled access area; pass-through window(s); or alternative operation (defined as being closed to all sales transactions but allowing employees to stock shelves or to perform cleaning or maintenance tasks). This option requires that signs be "conspicuously posted" that the store is closed.[18]

Type II: Patient, Client, Customer

California

In 1998, the California Department of Industrial Relations, Division of Occupational Safety and Health (Cal/OSHA) published *Guidelines for Security and Safety of Health Care and Community Service Workers.*[19] This document described the problem of workplace violence in health care settings and stated that health care and community service organizations must comply with Title 8 of the California Code of Regulations (CCR), Section 3203, that requires an injury and illness prevention program and that the program, in these high-risk settings, must specifically address prevention of assaults against workers. The guidelines include general and program development provisions that must be adopted by all high-risk industries and specific work setting guidelines for three types of work sites: (1) inpatient psychiatric hospitals and psychiatric units; (2) hospital and emergency rooms; and (3) outpatient facilities and community workers.

Furthermore, California's Health and Safety Code, Section 1257.7, stated: "By July 1, 1995, all hospitals licensed pursuant to subdivisions (a), (b), and (f) of Section 1250 shall conduct a security and safety assessment and, using the assessment, develop a security plan with measures to protect personnel, patients, and visitors from aggressive or violent behavior." Hospitals in subdivisions (a), (b), and (f) are "general acute care hospitals," "acute psychiatric hospitals," and "special hospitals," respectively. Precise definitions for these facilities are found in Section 1250 of the California Health and Safety Code.

Specific components of Section 1257.7 require the reporting of assaults against hospital personnel to local law enforcement within 72 hours of the incident and training for all hospital employees regularly assigned to the emergency department. Training should address the following topics: (1) general safety measures; (2) personal safety measures; (3) the assault cycle; (4) aggression and violence predicting factors; (5) obtaining patient history from a patient with violent behavior; (6) characteristics of aggressive and violent patients and victims; (7) verbal and physical maneuvers to diffuse and avoid violent behavior; (8) strategies to avoid physical harm; (9) restraining techniques; (10) appropriate use of medications as chemical restraints; and (11) any resources available to employees for coping with incidents of violence, including, by way of example, critical incident stress debriefing or employee assistance programs.

Washington

In 1999, the Washington State Legislature passed Substitute Senate Bill 5312.[20] This law requires "health care settings" to develop and implement plans "to reasonably protect employees from violence." Health care settings are defined as including hospitals, home health, hospice, and home care agencies, evaluation and treatment facilities, and community mental health programs. Nursing homes and other long-term residential care facilities are not included in the definition of a health care setting. This law requires health care facilities to conduct a safety and security assessment and, based upon the findings, to develop and implement a workplace violence prevention plan that includes consideration of issues such as physical site security, staffing, reporting of incidents, and employee training.

The law has specific requirements with regard to training all affected employees. Topics to be addressed in training include: (1) general and personal safety procedures; (2) the violence escalation cycle; (3) violence-predicting factors; (4) obtaining patient history from a patient with violent behavior; (5) verbal and physical techniques to de-escalate and minimize violent behavior; (6) strategies to avoid physical harm; (7) restraining techniques; (8) appropriate use of medication as chemical restraints; (9) documenting and reporting incidents; and (10) the process for debriefing and the resources available to employees in the event of an incident of workplace violence.

The law also specifies requirements for record keeping with regard to violent incidents comprising a list of minimum variables that includes, but is not limited to: the date, time, and specific location where an incident occurred; information on the employee victim in terms of occupation and department; the nature of the injury; a description of any weapons used; and a description of actions taken by the employee(s) and employer in response to the event.

In the subsequent legislative session, the Washington State Legislature passed additional legislation to address violence prevention in state psychiatric hospitals.[21] Like the previous law, this legislation requires that safety and security assessments be conducted and that workplace violence prevention plans be developed and implemented based on the information gleaned from those assessments, along with input from the state hospital's safety committee. Like the general health care law, the instant law specifies that the plan should include issues such as physical site security, staffing, reporting of incidents, and employee training.

In 2007, the Washington State Legislature passed substitute House Bill 1456, also known as the "Marty Smith law."[22] The law, which relates to home visits by mental health professionals, adds several new sections to Chapter 71.05 RCW. These new sections provide that (1) no designated mental health professional or crisis intervention worker shall be required to respond to a private location alone; (2) providers of mental health and crisis intervention services must have a written policy that describes their plan for training, staff backup, information sharing, and communication for crisis outreach staff who respond to private homes or nonpublic settings; (3) mental health professionals who make home visits to clients must be supplied with a cell phone or other device for emergency communications; (4) mental health professionals doing home visits shall have prompt access to information regarding the client's history of violence or dangerousness; and (5) all mental health staff who work directly with clients shall be provided annual training on safety and violence prevention.

Type III: Worker on Worker

David Yamada, professor of law and the director of the Project on Workplace Bullying and Discrimination at Suffolk University Law School, in Boston, argues that as awareness of the impact of workplace bullying, intimidation, and interpersonal conflict has grown, it has become clear that existing laws are inadequate to address these issues. To remedy this, he has proposed draft model legislation— termed the Healthy Workplace Bill—to specifically deal with bullying and abusive/hostile work environments.[23] Between 2003 and the present, bills based upon this model legislation have been introduced at least once in thirteen different states (California, Oklahoma, Hawaii, Washington, Oregon, Massachusetts, Missouri, Kansas, New York, New Jersey, Montana, Connecticut, and Vermont). At the time this book went to press, three states were actively considering the bill: Washington (HB 2142), Vermont (H. 548), and New York (A7801-A, A492, S2715).[24] The full text of the model Healthy Workplace Bill can be found in the Appendix.

Type IV: Intimate Partner Violence

As of July 2007, there are ten states—Arizona, Arkansas, California, Colorado, Georgia, Indiana, Nevada, North Carolina, Rhode Island, and Tennessee—in which an employer may seek a temporary restraining order to prevent violence against one of its employees. The laws vary with regard to the employer's burden of proving the existence of imminent danger. Most of these laws require only that a credible threat of violence need exist. The laws also vary with regard to whether the employer may request protection on its own behalf, or on the employee's behalf, and whether the threatened employee must be notified that protection is being sought.[25]

Since 2003, another nine states—Florida, Hawaii, Kentucky, Maryland, New Jersey, New York, North Dakota, Oklahoma, and Washington—have considered legislation related to an employer's ability to seek a temporary restraining order.[26] At least fourteen states—Florida, Idaho, Indiana, Kentucky, Maine, Maryland, Massachusetts, New Hampshire, New York, North Carolina, Oregon, Utah, Vermont, and Washington—have developed policies or training materials specific to domestic violence awareness and prevention for employees working in state government.[27]

▌ Legislative Initiatives Specific to Public Sector Employees

One state, New York, has passed legislation requiring all public sector workplaces to address the risk for workplace violence through the conduct of risk assessments, the implementation of feasible prevention measures, and the provision of staff training. Specifically, this legislation requires that all public sector workplaces conduct a risk evaluation with specific attention to risk factors for workplace violence that have been identified in the literature on the issue.

For all public sector employers with at least twenty full-time, permanent employees, the law requires the development and implementation of a written workplace violence prevention plan. The plan should address the risk factors for workplace violence identified during the risk evaluation, as well as the prevention measures in place to address those risks. Such strategies may include, but are not limited to, making high-risk areas visible to more people, installing good external lighting, using drop safes where cash is handled, and providing training in conflict resolution and nonviolent self-defense. The plan should include a mechanism for reporting incidents of workplace violence.

The law also contains specific requirements for training for those employers who satisfy the twenty-employee threshold. This training should provide information on the law, the employer's written workplace violence prevention plan, and the specific prevention measures in place based on that plan. Training must be provided at the time of the employee's initial assignment and include annual refresher courses. New York State law outlines the process for reporting and resolving violations of a workplace violence prevention plan or imminent danger due to workplace violence.[28]

On July 28, 2005, the Illinois General Assembly passed the Health Care Workplace Violence Prevention Act.[29] This act requires a two-year pilot test of workplace violence prevention efforts in state mental health care facilities. The pilot effort is slated to run from 2006 to 2008 in five sites. The law establishes a six-member task force to evaluate the pilot's efforts and make recommendations for the implementation of the legislation in all health care workplaces.

Similar to other state-based legislation that addresses violence in health care settings, the Illinois law includes provisions for a security and safety assessment, development and implementation of a workplace violence prevention plan, employee training, and record keeping with regard to workplace violence incidents. The Illinois law specifically requires that the security and safety assessment include a review of workplace violence incidents occurring at the facility during the previous five years. This law also emphasizes that the workplace violence prevention plan—including issues such as physical security, personnel policies, employee training, and incident reporting— should be tailored to the hazards identified and the specific needs of individual health care facilities.

Several states have issued executive orders or other administrative guidance regarding workplace violence prevention policies or training with respect to state government employees. For example, Connecticut Executive Order Number 16 requires that all state agencies comply with a violence in the workplace prevention policy as described in a September 1999 policy and procedures manual.[30] The manual includes a copy of the executive order, definitions of terms, background information and guidance on the development of a threat assessment team, a statewide security management council, various prevention strategies, response procedures, and other organizational and management issues.

In Louisiana, Executive Order No. MJF 97-15 requires the Division of Administration to develop a workplace violence prevention plan to "create a safe and secure work environment free of violence, aggressive acts, verbal and non-verbal threatening behavior and harassment toward or by its employees or the public they serve."[31] This policy includes definitions as well as the procedures for assembling a workplace violence assessment team, conducting workplace analysis, implementing prevention strategies, and responding to and evaluating incidents. In Oregon, workplace violence prevention for employees in the state is addressed in a policy issued by the Division of Human Resources regarding a violence-free workplace.[32]

In Pennsylvania, Management Directive 205.33 contains "policy, responsibilities, and procedures on preventative measures and responses to violence in the workplace."[33] In Oklahoma, the Department of Human Services has had in place for more than a decade a workplace violence prevention policy so that "employees may safely function and clients may safely obtain services."[34] The policy includes guidance on local response plans, reporting of incidents, and a departmental crisis management team. The specific examples provided here are not exhaustive, and other states have developed various guidance documents and requirements specific to preventing workplace violence against employees of state agencies. In addition to the states discussed, the following states have issued materials on workplace violence prevention: Colorado, Indiana, Iowa, Kansas, Massachusetts, Ohio, South Carolina, and Wyoming.

▌ Other Resources

The Occupational Safety and Health Act of 1970, Section 18, encourages states to develop and operate their own job safety and health programs. The federal Occupational Safety and Health Administration (OSHA) approves and monitors state plans and provides up to 50 percent of the funding for a state program. At the present time, there are twenty-one states that have comprehensive state plans covering employees in both the private and public (state and local government) sectors. They include: Alaska, Arizona, California, Hawaii, Indiana, Iowa, Kentucky, Maryland, Michigan, Minnesota, Nevada, New Mexico, North Carolina, Oregon, South Carolina, Tennessee, Utah, Vermont, Virginia, Washington, and Wyoming. Another three states—Connecticut, New Jersey, and New York—operate state plans that cover only public sector employees. The legislation specific to workplace violence that has been developed under these plans has been previously described in this chapter. Additionally, there may be other general occupational safety and health requirements in these states that may have some bearing on, or include consideration of, workplace violence prevention issues.

As already described, there are no federal OSHA regulations specific to workplace violence prevention, but OSHA has published guidelines and recommendations for the prevention of workplace violence in high-risk settings (i.e., health care, late-night retail, and taxicab services). In addition, the U.S. Office of Personnel Management developed a document entitled *Dealing With Workplace Violence: A Guide for Agency Planners*, that was published in October 1997. The document includes chapters on program and policy development, prevention strategies, investigation and threat assessment, employee relations, employee assistance programs, security, and organizational recovery after an incident. These topic-specific chapters are followed by a chapter containing sixteen case studies that provide details of actual workplace violence scenarios and relevant questions to address in developing and implementing a workplace violence program to address similar situations. Although the guidance was developed with federal agencies in mind, the concepts and approaches are fairly universal and serve as a useful guide for any employer developing and implementing workplace violence prevention programs.[35]

▌ Conclusion

It is clear that workplace violence is a significant safety and health issue for public sector employers and employees. Limited legislative efforts have created specific requirements for employers in some states. It is prudent for public sector employers to consider the risks for workplace violence in developing their overall safety and security plans.

Notes

1. Eleanor Lynn Watson Jenkins. 2006. Active Inaction: Symbolic Politics, Agenda Denial or Incubation Period: Twenty Years of U.S. Workplace Violence Activity. Dissertation. West Virginia University.

2. National Institute for Occupational Safety and Health (NIOSH). 1989. National Traumatic Occupational Fatalities Surveillance System, 1980–1985. Morgantown, W.Va.: U.S. Department of Health and Human Services (DHHS), Public Health Service, Centers for Disease Control and Prevention, National Institute for Occupational Safety and Health. DHHS (NIOSH) Publication No. 89-116.

3. Bureau of Labor Statistics (BLS). 1994. Violence in the Workplace Comes Under Closer Scrutiny. Issues in Labor Statistics. Washington, D.C.: U.S. Department of Labor, Bureau of Labor Statistics, Summary 94-10.

4. Ronet Bachman. 1994. Violence and Theft in the Workplace. U.S. Department of Justice Crime Data Brief. Washington, D.C.: U.S. Government Printing Office, NCJ-148199.

5. Dawn N. Castillo. 1993. NIOSH Alert: Request for Assistance in Preventing Homicide in the Workplace. Cincinnati, Ohio: U.S. Department of Health and Human Services, Public Health Service, Centers for Disease Control and Prevention, National Institute for Occupational Safety and Health. DHHS (NIOSH) Publication No. 93-109; E. Lynn Jenkins. 1996. Current Intelligence Bulletin No. 57: Workplace Violence—Risk Factors and Prevention Strategies. Morgantown, W.Va.: U.S. Department of Health and Human Services, Public Health Service, Centers for Disease Control and Prevention, National Institute for Occupational Safety and Health. DHHS (NIOSH) Publication No. 96-100.

6. Robert C. Barish. 2001. Legislation and Administrative Regulations Addressing Workplace Violence in the United States and British Columbia. *American Journal of Preventive Medicine* 20(2):149–154. (Citing Cynthia L. Atwood, associate solicitor for occupational safety and health, U.S. Department of Labor, Criminal Violence in the Workplace, May 13, 1992; OSHA Integrated Management Information System.)

7. Occupational Safety and Health Administration (OSHA). 1996. Guidelines for Preventing Workplace Violence for Health Care and Social Service Workers. OSHA Publication 3148. Washington, D.C.: U.S. Department of Labor.

8. Id. 1998. Recommendations for Workplace Violence Prevention Programs in Late-Night Retail Establishments. OSHA Publication 3153. Washington, D.C.: U.S. Department of Labor.

9. Id. 2000. Risk Factors and Protective Measures for Taxi and Livery Drivers. Washington, D.C.: U.S. Department of Labor.

10. John Howard. 1996. State and Regulatory Approaches to Preventing Workplace Violence. *Occupational Medicine: State of the Art Reviews* 11: 293–301; University of Iowa, Injury Prevention Research Center. 2001. Workplace Violence: A Report to the Nation. Iowa City, Iowa: Injury Prevention Research Center, University of Iowa.

11. Paula L. Grubb, Rashaun K. Roberts, James W. Grosch, and W. Stephen Brightwell. 2004. Workplace Bullying: What Organizations Are Saying. *Employee Rights and Employment Policy Journal* 8(2):407–422.

12. Id.

13. BLS. 2005. Census of Fatal Occupational Injuries. Special BLS data tabulation, homicides, 1997–2004 by selected characteristics.

14. Detis T. Duhart. 2001. Violence in the Workplace, 1993–1999. Bureau of Justice Statistics Special Report. NCJ 190076.

15. Convenience Business Security Act. Florida Statutes (Crimes) Title 46 § 812.1701-812.175 (1990 and 1992).

16. Id.

17. The requirements of the original legislation have been moved to Washington Administrative Code 296-832: Late Night Retail Workers Crime Prevention.

18. New Mexico Environmental Improvement Board. Title 11, Chapter 5, Part 6. Occupational Health and Safety—Convenience Stores.

19. Cal/OSHA. 1996. Guidelines for Preventing Workplace Violence for Health Care and Social Service Workers. San Francisco, Cal.: Division of Occupational Safety and Health, California Department of Industrial Relations.

20. Washington Workplace Violence Prevention Law. Chapter 49.19 RCW. Safety—Health Care Settings.

21. Washington Workplace Safety Plan. Chapter 72.23.400 RCW. Violence Prevention in State Psychiatric Hospitals.

22. Marty Smith Law. Chapter 360, Laws of 2007. Creates new sections to Chapter 71.05 RCW.

23. David C. Yamada. 2004. Crafting a Legislative Response to Workplace Bullying. *Employee Rights and Employment Policy Journal* 8(2): 475–521.

24. The history and status of legislative activity relative to the Healthy Workplace Bill may be viewed at http://workplacebullyinglaw.org/hwbgrid .html.

25. Legal Momentum. 2004. State Law Guide: Workplace Restraining Orders (updated July 2007), available at http://www.legalmomentum.org/ site/DocServer/restraining.pdf?docID=534.

26. Id.

27. Legal Momentum. 2006. State Law Guide: Domestic and Sexual Violence Workplace Policies (updated Feb. 2008), available at http:// www.legalmomentum.org/site/DocServer/Dv_Workplace_Policies_Feb_08 .pdf?doc1D=1242.

28. New York State Workplace Violence Prevention Act, N.Y. Labor Law § 27-b (2006).

29. 30 ILCS 5/3-2 (2005).

30. The State of Connecticut. Violence in the Workplace Policy and Procedures Manual for Human Resource Professionals, available at http:// www.opm.state.ct.us/olr/wpv/manual.pdf.

31. State of Louisiana. Division of Administration Policy No. 9. Workplace Violence. State of Louisiana Executive Order No. MJF 97-15, Violence in the workplace, available at http://doa.louisiana.gov/OHR/policies/ DOAPolicy09.pdf.

32. State of Oregon. Department of Administrative Services. Human Resources Services Division. State Policy: 50.010.02 Violence-Free Workplace. Reference ORS 240.306; 240.321; 240.555; 240.560, available at http://egov.oregon.gov/DAS/HR/docs/advice/P5001002.pdf.

33. Commonwealth of Pennsylvania Governor's Office. Management Directive 205.33—Workplace Violence. Personnel, OA, (717) 787-8575, available at http://www.portal.state.pa.us/portal/server.pt/gateway/PTARGS_0_2_785_711_0_43/http%3B/ENCTCAPP099%3B7087/publishedcontent/publish/global/files/management_directives/management__administrative_support/205_33.pdf.

34. Oklahoma Department of Human Services. OKDHS:2-15-52. Workplace Violence, available at http://www.okdhs.org/library/policy/dhs/002/15/0052000.htm.

35. U.S. Office of Personnel Management. 1997. Dealing with Workplace Violence: A Guide for Agency Planners. Washington, D.C.: U.S. Office of Personnel Management Document No. OWR-037.

CHAPTER 4

Due Process Rights for Public Employees Charged with Workplace Violence

Michael H. LeRoy

▌ What Is Due Process, and Why Is It Important in the Context of Public Employment?

For over a century, government employees have enjoyed more employment rights than their private sector counterparts, who, in most cases, are subject to the legal doctrine of employment-at-will. This bedrock principle permits an employer to terminate an employee at any time, without notice, with or without cause, provided that the termination is not for a discriminatory reason (i.e., race, sex, age, etc.). In contrast, federal, state and local civil service codes variously provide employees protection from arbitrary termination.

Beginning in the 1970s and 1980s, state and federal courts further expanded employment rights to include constitutional forms of due process. The U.S. Constitution prohibits government entities from depriving a person of life, liberty, and property without due process of law. Appearing in the Fifth and Fourteenth Amendments, these restrictions on government authority apply, respectively, to federal and state governments and their political subdivisions. In the employment setting, an employee cannot be deprived of a property or liberty interest without first being provided certain procedural due process safeguards—notice and hearing (an opportunity to respond to the employer's allegations).

When a public employer terminates an employee, or imposes some other penalty, the action may involve liberty or property rights—or both. However, before an employee can claim a right to procedural due process when an adverse personnel action occurs, the individual must have a property interest in his or her job, unless the individual is claiming a liberty deprivation. In *Board of Regents v. Roth*,[1] the U.S. Supreme Court explained that property interests can to be found in "existing rules or understandings that stem from an independent source such as state law—rules or understandings that secure certain benefits and that support claims of entitlement to those benefits." A local ordinance or a contract—for instance, a collective bargaining agreement with a just cause provision—may create a property interest in employment. Alternatively, a civil service code or statute that provides for tenure may create a property interest in a job.

When employees do not possess these legal rights and safeguards, they do not have a property interest in their jobs. In other words, they are at-will employees and are subject to discipline—including termination—without the right to a hearing or even the courtesy of an explanation for their employer's decision.

The Supreme Court has treated liberty and property as different types of employment interests. While an individual must have a property interest in a job to qualify for procedural due process rights, as previously noted, this is not a requirement for one who is asserting a violation of his or her liberty interest. In the employment setting, "liberty" means the freedom to change jobs without a current employer stigmatizing the individual through its actions (e.g., publicly terminating the employee), thus making it difficult for the employee to find work elsewhere. The case *Goetz v. Windsor Central School District*[2] illustrates the distinction in due process between liberty and property interests. A school janitor was arrested on the job for theft but was not provided a hearing to clear his name before the public school district fired him. Because he lacked tenure, the court ruled that he did not have a property right in his job. But his visible arrest in a small town presumably had a stigmatizing effect on him. Even without tenure, he was entitled to a pretermination hearing because he had a liberty interest in clearing his name of wrongdoing.

The Supreme Court has ruled that the right to liberty includes a name-clearing hearing when an employer disseminates false *and* defamatory information about an employee in connection with a personnel action (e.g., termination).[3] The purpose of the hearing is to prevent false and stigmatizing information from limiting the employee's ability—in constitutional terms, his or her "liberty"—to make a living without forcing the individual to move to a new city to avoid the harmful effects of defamatory information.

Procedural due process encompasses one's right to notice and a hearing before an employee can be deprived of his or her interest in employment. In this context, it does not matter whether the underlying property interest is created by a state legislature or a common law ruling, or is something more fundamental (i.e., appears in a constitution). However, this distinction is crucial for substantive due process, which protects only fundamental interests under the Constitution. When a public employer administers a routine physical exam but also tests for such conditions as pregnancy, venereal disease, or sickle cell anemia, without the employee's knowledge and consent, this violates an individual's substantive due process rights. But these violations seem to occur rarely, partly because substantive due process affords only those protections "so rooted in the traditions and conscience of our people as to be ranked as fundamental."[4] The Supreme Court explained in *Regents of the University of Michigan v. Ewing*:[5]

Even if one assumes the existence of a property right, however, not every such right is entitled to the protection of substantive due process. While property interests are protected by procedural due process even though the interest is derived from state law rather than the Constitution, substantive due process rights are created only by the Constitution.[6]

The application of due process principles to public employment began in 1972 with the U.S. Supreme Court's decision in *Board of Regents v. Roth.*[7] The employee in this case, David Roth, was hired for a one-year teaching term that was renewable. Toward the middle of the academic year, the university timely notified Roth of its decision not to renew his contract. The university gave Roth no reason for its decision not to renew his employment contract.

Roth challenged the university's decision on procedural and substantive grounds. He alleged that his employer had punished him for his outspoken criticism of the university. This, he claimed, violated his freedom of speech. He also said that the university failed to notify him of the reasons for his nonretention or provide him with a hearing. In Roth's view, the lack of notice or hearing was a violation of his procedural due process rights. Although Roth did not allege that his due process claim was based on a deprivation of his liberty rights, both the trial and appellate courts ordered the university to provide Roth with an explanation for its nonrenewal and a hearing on the grounds that Roth's nonretention would limit his future employment opportunities (a liberty interest deprivation). The Supreme Court disagreed.

In a 5–3 ruling, the Court's majority reasoned that the university did not make any charge that was damaging to Roth's reputation and standing in the academic community. In other words, the university did not create a stigma or other disability that would hamper Roth's pursuit of similar employment opportunities in the field based on its decision not to renew Roth's contract—since it gave no explanation for its action. Additionally, the Court found that because Roth's one-year appointment created no right of continued employment, he had no property deprivation claim under the due process clause.

While the employee in *Roth* was unsuccessful in establishing that he had suffered a liberty interest deprivation, the existence of such a claim was not in doubt at the time the case was decided. Following *Roth*, the Supreme Court clarified that an employee is not deprived of a liberty interest in the public employment context unless he or she can establish (1) that he or she suffered an injury to name or reputation through the publication of false and defamatory information, and (2) that this injury occurred in the course of (or in connection with) the individual's termination from employment.[8]

One aspect of this claim that courts continue to wrestle with today is what constitutes "publication" of false and defamatory information.[9] Depending on where one resides, publication has been defined variously and inconsistently. For example, some courts define "publication" literally, requiring that false and defamatory information actually be disseminated to a potential employer to satisfy this element of a liberty deprivation claim. Those courts who do not define "publication" quite so literally have embraced several differing interpretations: (1) the information has been placed in an employee's personnel file and is *available* for viewing by a potential employer; (2) the information has been placed in an employee's personnel file, which is treated as a public record under state or local law; or (3) the information has been placed in an employee's personnel file and is *likely* to be disclosed to a potential employer.[10]

The Supreme Court has taken a flexible approach in defining such key procedural due process terms as "notice" and "hearing." In *Mathews v. Eldridge*,[11] the Supreme Court observed that due process is not a "technical conception with a fixed content unrelated to time, place and circumstances."[12] The Court allows the requirements of due process to vary based on the specific circumstances of the case. For example, the Court has said that due process varies, depending on the private interest that is affected by an official action. In practical terms, a hearing may be needed as a prerequisite to termination, but not to issuing a written reprimand of an employee. The Court has also said that due process should balance both the individual's and employer's interests: the employee should be protected from an error, but a fact-finding procedure should add actual value to protect an employee from erroneous discipline.

Practically speaking, this means that due process may require that an employee be given an opportunity to tell his or her side of a story to a supervisor. However, if discipline appears to be related to an employee's whistle-blowing activities against the superior who imposes discipline, courts may require an alternative hearing procedure—for example, a hearing before a neutral person or body within the employer's organization—to satisfy due process. The Court has also said that due process must take into account the public employer's financial and administrative capabilities. This may mean that an employer is not obligated to keep an accused employee on the job until the name-clearing hearing occurs—for instance, in the case of an employee who stands accused of using excessive force against a suspect or a prisoner.

In 1986, the U.S. Supreme Court laid out with greater specificity what procedural due process safeguards a public employee is entitled to when his employer is contemplating disciplinary action. In *Cleveland Board of Education v. Loudermill*,[13] the Supreme Court ruled that certain procedural safeguards must be implemented before disciplinary action can be taken against an employee. The Court said that "some form of [a] pre-termination hearing" must be made available to the individual.[14] The purpose of this hearing is to be "an initial check against mistaken decisions—essentially, a determination of whether there are reasonable grounds to believe that the charges against the employee are true and support the proposed action."[15] However, this need not entail an elaborate hearing.

Rather, procedural due process afforded at the pretermination/disciplinary stage simply means that the employee be given oral or written notice of the charges, a statement of what evidence the employer has in support of its decision to take disciplinary action, and that it provide the employee with an opportunity to respond to the charges.[16] The formality of the pretermination hearing varies depending on the importance of the interest at stake. The Court in *Loudermill* added that to "require more than this prior to termination would intrude to an unwarranted extent on the government's interest in quickly removing an unsatisfactory employee."[17]

Westbrook v. City of Omaha[18] provides a helpful illustration of the procedural due process requirements enumerated in *Loudermill*. A police officer was accused by a suspect of taking cash from his pockets at the time of his arrest and using the money for gambling. The city investigated the allegations against the officer by taking witness accounts from both the suspect and the officer. The city then communicated its findings to the police officer. The officer was informed that the suspect's polygraph test results showed truthful responses and that his polygraph test results exhibited deception. The city concluded that the officer took the suspect's money. In a pretermination notice letter, the city explained what evidence it had and enumerated the various misconduct charges against the officer. A federal appeals court ruled that the city had provided the police officer with adequate procedural due process before it fired him. The court said that the officer was informed of the evidence and charges against him, and provided an opportunity to give his side of the story.

Conversely, *Cox v. Roskelley*[19] illustrates how an employer failed to comply with the procedural due process requirements of *Loudermill* where an employee's liberty interest was a stake. A county road resurfacing project resulted in damage to approximately eight hundred cars when the oil-and-chip mixture did not properly set. The county official responsible for handling damage claims was accused of steering business to a friend, who in turn was accused of overcharging the county for repairing the vehicles. The county conducted an investigation and detailed its findings and conclusions in a letter of termination it provided to the employee. A copy of the letter was placed in the employee's personnel file which, under state law, was treated as a public record. The termination letter was subsequently released to the media after a local newspaper filed a public records request seeking release of the letter. Neither prior to nor following his discharge did the county afford the employee a pre- or post-termination hearing to address the county's reasons for discharging him. Moreover, at no time did the employee concede that he had engaged in any wrongdoing or failed to meet his responsibilities.

A federal appeals court ruled that the county had violated the employee's procedural due process rights by releasing to the public stigmatizing information about him. While it may not have been the county's intention to disclose the contents of the termination letter to the public, once the county placed a copy of the letter in the employee's personnel file—a statutorily created public record—the county's actions constituted publication "sufficient to trigger [the employee's] liberty interest under the Fourteenth Amendment." Having failed to provide the employee with a name-clearing hearing and an opportunity to tell his side of the story, the county violated the employee's due process rights.

▌Due Process in Practice

A. A Sampling of Court Rulings Where Due Process Safeguards Were Held Adequate

Probationary Status

In *Turner v. Department of Interior,*[20] a police recruit was dismissed from a training program after an investigation confirmed that he had assaulted two fellow trainees. Due to his removal from the required training class, his employer provided Turner with notice of its intent to terminate him. After considering Turner's oral and written responses to the proposed removal, the National Park Service police force finalized its termination decision. On appeal, a federal court denied Turner's due process claim. A probationary employee is considered an at-will employee, and therefore lacks the requisite property interest to trigger procedural due process protections. The court observed that the due process clause does not by itself create a property interest in a job. Because this probationary employee had no entitlement to continued employment that was created by a statute, regulation, ordinance, or other rule, his due process claim failed.

At-Will Employment

In *Jackson v. Long*,[21] a jail guard was accused of raping a female prisoner. The sheriff suspended the guard with pay immediately after receiving the prisoner's complaint; an investigation into the prisoner's allegations was conducted by the state police. When the sheriff learned that the guard failed a lie detector test, he fired the employee. The sheriff justified his action by stating that jailers are at-will employees who serve at his discretion. The employee's at-will status meant that he had no property interest in his employment. A federal appeals court agreed with the sheriff, citing a state law that grants sheriffs exclusive power over employment decisions.

No Evidence of Bias by Hearing Officer

A supervisor was terminated by a regional transportation authority for breaching its policy against workplace violence in *Flynn v. San Francisco Bay Area Rapid Transit District* (BART).[22] The employee lost his temper in front of a female subordinate. The supervisor ordered the female employee into his office, yelled at her, and slammed his fists on the desk, frightening her. When she attempted to leave his office the supervisor grabbed the subordinate's arm and jerked her back, causing a visible bruise. The supervisor had a work history of temper tantrums but had never been disciplined for his earlier outbursts.

After BART placed the supervisor on paid leave, the employer notified the employee that a hearing would be held by a "district hearing officer," an individual whom BART exclusively employed in this capacity. The discharge was upheld and the ruling was affirmed by BART's human resources committee and the agency's general manager. A court denied the supervisor's contention that the hearing violated his due process rights because the hearing officer was a BART employee. Flynn did not object to this arrangement at the time of his hearing. In addition, the court concluded that there was no danger of bias on the part of the hearing officer due to his employment relationship with BART.

Ex Parte Communications Involving Neutral Decision Maker and Employer

A professor in *Marder v. Board of Regents of University of Wisconsin System*[23] was charged with sexual misconduct and other disruptive behavior involving both students and colleagues. Because of his conduct toward his faculty colleagues and departmental staff, the university provost moved the professor's office out of the building where his department was housed and adjusted his workload. After the professor was terminated for his conduct, he sued in state court. He alleged that his appeal to the state university system had been tainted by ex parte contacts between the campus and the system board that upheld his discharge. In particular, Marder alleged that improper communication occurred when a system board member and the campus president traveled together to the termination meeting. Marder also raised concerns about the fact that both the board and the university administration received legal guidance from the same group of attorneys.

The Wisconsin Supreme Court rejected Marder's argument, first reasoning that not every ex parte communication is so prejudicial that it undermines the guarantees of due process. Second, the court found no proof that ex parte communications took place which tainted the deliberative process (insofar as conveying new information about the case to the deciding official). Finally, the state supreme court concluded that an administrator is entitled to a presumption of honesty and integrity. In other words, the burden of proof in establishing a procedural due process violation is high in situations where an administrator has a professional relationship with attorneys who corepresent the administrator (campus president) and the neutral decision-making body (system board of trustees).

Interim Suspension Without Pay and Benefits

After a school district secretary alleged that the district superintendent touched her inappropriately in *Burger v. Board of School Directors of McGuffey School District*,[24] the employer retained an attorney to conduct an investigation. During this inquiry, the district suspended the accused with pay. The attorney interviewed several witnesses and, at an informal hearing, questioned the superintendent in the presence of his attorney. After completing his investigation for the school district, the attorney advised the employer that there was sufficient evidence to proceed with termination proceedings against the superintendent. To minimize the possibility that the board would prejudge the facts in advance of the termination hearing, the attorney submitted draft charges but did not reveal what evidence he had gathered against the superintendent. Citing the serious nature of the charges, the school district suspended the superintendent without pay or benefits.

Prior to the removal hearing, the superintendent sued to compel his immediate reinstatement or full restoration of his pay. He cited a state law that provided for removal of school officials only after a termination hearing. The trial court agreed and ordered the district to rescind the suspension and reinstate the superintendent with full compensation and benefits due under his employment contract. An intermediate-level court reversed the trial court's order, holding that the school board had the authority to suspend the superintendent without pay pending a due process hearing on the employee's dismissal.

A divided Pennsylvania supreme court ruled that although a school board may implement an interim suspension with or without pay, the employer must ensure that procedural due process rights are observed when implementing such measures. In the instant case, because the superintendent did not raise a procedural due process claim, the court could not rule on whether the board's procedures satisfied the requirements for due process. Nevertheless, the court observed, in dicta, that while the concept of due process is a flexible one and "requires procedural protections as each particular situation demands" when an employer's personnel decision is expected to have a "prolonged impact" on an individual's livelihood interests, that fact should be taken into account when assessing the adequacy of the due process procedures provided.[25]

Neutral Decision Maker Crucial at the Post-Termination Hearing Stage

In *Farhat v. Jopke*,[26] a school district fired a custodian who had a history of confrontational behavior involving coworkers and union and school officials. After being denied a position he applied for, the custodian contacted a coworker/union representative by phone and accused her of being responsible for his not getting the job. During the course of the conversation, the custodian allegedly threatened the female coworker: "When I get through with you, you won't be driving a bus or doing custodial work." The frightened coworker contacted both school officials and the police. As a result of the incident, the following day the custodian was suspended with pay and an investigation was commenced. Two predisciplinary meetings were held before the school district proposed that the employee be suspended. The first meeting ended prematurely owing to the employee's disruptive behavior. After being notified of the suspension, the custodian responded by letter, accusing the school district and the union of collusion and corruption. It is not clear from the court's decision whether the employee ever served the recommended suspension.

Concerned about the allegations contained in the letter, several months later the school board moved to terminate the employee. The employee grieved his termination and lost. He also asked the union to arbitrate the matter. During the arbitration proceedings, a settlement was reached by the parties, which the employee later disavowed, then filed the instant action. In his lawsuit, the employee alleged that his procedural due process rights had been violated because he had not received pre- and post-termination hearings before a neutral decision maker.

A federal appeals court ruled that Farhat had received ample
due process. Two due process meetings were held—though both
took place *before* the employer decided to terminate the employee. At
the post-termination stage (arbitration), the employee received a full
hearing before a neutral arbitrator. The court observed that a hearing before a neutral arbitrator at the post-termination hearing stage
satisfies the requirements of procedural due process, even if a neutral decision maker was not available at the pretermination hearing
stage. The outcome in this case conflicts with a case discussed below
in subsection B (see *Hrbek v. City of Bellevue Civil Service*).

Publication of Stigmatizing Information

A sheriff's deputy in *Cross v. Beltrami County*[27] was accused of sexual harassment and conduct unbecoming an officer with supervisory responsibilities. While the sheriff's deputy was cleared of the
sexual harassment charges, he was found guilty of the latter charges
and terminated. The accused officer complained that he was provided only categories of charges and that the information he was
provided was not specific enough. He also claimed that a published
news story linking him to discipline for "sexual improprieties" violated his liberty interest.

A state appeals court disagreed with Cross. It concluded that the
officer was provided a pretermination hearing when he and his attorney met with the county to discuss the charges. The appeals court
said that the guidelines articulated in *Loudermill* do not dictate that
an employee be advised of every charge against him or her prior to
the pretermination hearing. In this case, the accused was unable to
identify any information that he would have used in rebuttal if he
had been provided additional notice of the charges.

The officer also claimed a liberty interest violation of his reputation and integrity, because the sheriff's office caused damaging information to be published about him in the newspaper. Relying on a
highly placed source, the news story, titled "Sheriff Fires Chief
Deputy," reported that the case against the officer involved alleged
sexual improprieties. The officer argued that he was entitled to a

separate name-clearing hearing. The court disagreed, explaining that a pretermination hearing under *Loudermill* is sufficient to protect both one's liberty and property interests where it is followed by a full evidentiary hearing, provided that it occurs *after* the stigmatizing information has been published. Moreover, the court held that the deputy sheriff failed to establish a violation of his liberty interest because he was unable to show that representatives of the county were directly responsible for the publication of the news article.

Involuntary Psychiatric Examination Does Not Trigger Procedural Due Process Requirements

After several coworkers complained to prison administration officials that the plaintiff, a guard, had been threatening them with physical harm, the warden ordered the plaintiff to submit to a psychiatric examination in *Flynn v. Sandahl*.[28] The plaintiff objected, contending that the order violated his procedural due process and privacy rights. First a supervisor, and then later the prison warden, explained to the plaintiff that the order for the psychiatric evaluation stemmed from complaints that had been lodged against him. Nonetheless, the plaintiff refused two orders to be evaluated and was charged with insubordination. A hearing was scheduled to determine whether the plaintiff should be discharged for insubordination. The plaintiff filed the instant action to enjoin his employer from ordering him to submit to a psychiatric examination. His request was denied and the hearing on whether the plaintiff was insubordinate went forward. The employee review board concluded that the plaintiff had been insubordinate and recommended that he be suspended pending discharge. The warden accepted the findings of the employee review officer. In response, the plaintiff filed a second application for an injunction.

In support of his lawsuit, the plaintiff alleged that his procedural due process rights had been violated because he had been ordered to submit to the psychiatric examination without first being offered a hearing in which he could have challenged the order (to be evaluated). A federal appeals court disagreed with the plaintiff's contention, finding that he had been offered such a pretermination hearing in the form of a face-to-face meeting with the warden, which he refused to attend. The court additionally found that the employer had given the plaintiff a sufficient explanation for why it wanted him to submit to the examination and, in choosing not to meet with the warden, the plaintiff waived his opportunity to contest the merits of the order.

More importantly, however, was the court's conclusion that procedural due process requirements were never triggered in this case, because the request to submit to a psychiatric exam, by itself, did not jeopardize the plaintiff's property interest in his job. In other words, the order was neither tantamount to a notice of termination, a clear deprivation of a property interest, nor was there anything in the record to support "the assertion that the results of the examination would have had an adverse effect upon [the plaintiff's] job status."

B. A Sampling of Court Rulings Where Due Process Safeguards Were Held Inadequate

Incomplete Notice of Charges

In *Clipps v. City of Cleveland*,[29] Phillis Fuller Clipps was notified by her employer that a female coworker had filed a complaint against her alleging that she (Clipps) had groped the coworker's breasts. Although Clipps submitted a written apology to the coworker, the city nevertheless went ahead and scheduled a predisciplinary conference. At the conference, for the first time, Clipps learned that other coworkers had come forward with similar allegations of inappropriate touching. Following the predisciplinary conference, Clipps was suspended for five days and demoted.

On appeal, a court ruled that the city had failed to provide Clipps with complete notice of the charges against her—a violation of her due process rights. Although predisciplinary procedural requirements need not be elaborate, they must be sufficient to enable the accused to tell her side of the story. Clipps was denied this opportunity because the city led her to believe that there was only one accuser.

A similar situation occurred in *Hrbek v. City of Bellevue Civil Service Commission*.[30] A city administrator recommended that Tim Hrbek, a police officer, be discharged for a variety of offenses, including violent behavior. Hrbek wrongfully discharged his weapon and wounded an individual. On another occasion, Hrbek was disciplined for using pepper spray in an unauthorized manner. The chief of police recommended to the city administrator that Hrbek be terminated, alleging several rule violations, but did not identify any factual information to support the charges.

At a pretermination hearing, Hrbek complained that the chief of police had not adequately advised him of the grounds for his termination. The administrator agreed and rescheduled the hearing. Hrbek was provided with a more detailed list of incidents to support the chief's recommendation. Following the hearing, the administrator recommended termination and a civil service hearing was scheduled.

At this point, Hrbek received a packet of information from the commission which included all of the documents in the police department's investigative file. The officer complained that he had received only a portion of this information in advance of the pretermination hearing. The commission affirmed the termination discharge. Hrbek sued the city, claiming that his due process rights had been violated.

The trial court agreed that the city provided Hrbek with inadequate due process before and at the pretermination hearing. A state appeals court upheld the reinstatement and backpay rulings on the grounds that Hrbek was not afforded adequate due process because he was not given all the information that had been compiled during the internal investigation. This deprived him of the opportunity to rebut the chief's evidence at the hearing before the city administrator. The fact that such information was ultimately forwarded to him in advance of his appeal to the civil service commission (post-termination hearing) did not cure the due process defect.

As noted earlier, this case is at odds with the court's ruling in *Farhat v. Jopke*, discussed above in subsection A. In *Farhat*, the court held that procedural shortcomings at the pretermination stage did not give rise to a violation of the plaintiff's due process rights because there were adequate post-termination proceedings.

Untimely Notice of Charges

A corrections officer in *Morton v. Beyer*[31] was suspended after being charged with physically abusing an inmate with a baton. On the day of the alleged assault, prison investigators interviewed Morton about the incident. A month passed before the inquiry was completed, and six months elapsed between when the incident took place and when Morton was abruptly ordered to appear for a pretermination hearing.

At the pretermination hearing, Morton was handed various investigative reports. On his union representative's advice, Morton declined to offer his version of the incident other than to deny the charges lodged against him. He was suspended without pay, pending further investigation. The pretermination hearing lasted all of ten minutes.

Following his suspension and receipt of notice of disciplinary action (which included a summary of the allegations against him), Morton sued. The district court issued a preliminary injunction, concluding that the pretermination hearing had not met the requirements laid out in *Loudermill*. A federal appeals court agreed with the lower court that the state failed to give Morton meaningful notice of the charges against him but concluded on other grounds that Morton was not entitled to injunctive relief. As to its finding that the employer failed to provide Morton with an adequate pretermination hearing, the appeals court found that both the employer's notice and Morton's opportunity to respond to the charges against him were flawed, owing in part to the six-month delay between the events in question and the pretermination hearing. Although Morton had been provided with copies of the employer's various investigative reports within minutes of receiving notice of the charges, the appeals court explained that because of the lapse in time, Morton should have been provided sufficient time to recount the facts in his own mind in order that he could prepare an effective defense. An accused worker's opportunity to respond must be afforded at a meaningful time and in a meaningful manner.

Publishing Stigmatizing Information

The University of California fired its men's basketball coach after the athletic director concluded that the coach's treatment of his student athletes was harmful to their well-being in *Campanelli v. Bockrath*.[32] The university chancellor told a major newspaper that the coach intimidated players to the point of causing them to become physically ill. National media quoted the athletic director as saying that the coach was an "abusive bully" who perpetuated "a cycle of abuse."

A federal appeals court reinstated the coach's lawsuit on the grounds that post-termination interviews by the decision makers who fired the coach abridged his liberty interest. The news accounts, which charged the coach with engaging in morally reprehensible behavior, were likely to deprive the coach of future job opportunities.

The university argued that the due process clause did not apply in this instance because the news reports were published a week after he was fired. The statements were not made in the course of the coach's termination. The court disagreed. When an employer's potentially damaging public statements occur at roughly the same time the individual is terminated, the law recognizes the presence of a connection. The court observed that at least four other federal appellate circuits had previously adopted such a construction of the phrase "in the course of the termination."

Exclusion of an Employee's Evidence at a Post-Termination Hearing

In *Lucas v. Murray City Civil Service Commission*,[33] the city fired Edward Lucas, a police officer, for lying during an internal affairs investigation. Lucas was accused of using excessive force during an arrest, but he contended that the charges had been fabricated in retaliation for his having submitted an anonymous report to the Utah attorney general, wherein Lucas accused one of his coworkers of official misconduct. Specifically, Lucas alleged that a fellow officer routinely used excessive force against arrestees and had rigged bids involving vehicle repairs. Lucas claimed that the police chief knew that he was one of the authors of the report before recommending and later ordering that he be discharged for using excessive force. The charges detailed in the report to the attorney general infuriated the police chief, who demanded that they be withdrawn. Lucas also alleged that the police chief sought to uncover the identity of the whistle-blower. At the post-termination hearing, the city commission excluded the evidence supporting the employee's retaliation charge. The state court of appeals ruled that the exclusion of this evidence violated Lucas's due process right to a full and fair hearing.

Due Process Guidance from the Courts

Before the 1970s, public employers had a freer hand in dealing with workplace violence. Two separate trends have complicated a public employer's response to what has become front-page news: (1) the perception that workplace violence is on the rise; and (2) the right of certain employees to procedural due process.

Forty years ago, workplace violence was not a well-recognized concept, but today the term has widespread currency. Watershed events have caused employers to exercise a firmer hand against workplace violence. "Going postal," an expression coined in the 1990s after several deadly shootings by postal workers, is now understood by most to refer to someone who has lost his temper. More recently, mass shootings at secondary and higher education facilities—notably Columbine High School and Virginia Tech—have caused public employers to take employee threats seriously.

By erring on the side of caution, employers run an increasing risk of violating employee due process rights. As employers take a harder line in responding to both potential and actual threats of violence, they still need to abide by the due process principles set forth in *Roth* and *Loudermill*. In interpreting these cases, lower courts have recognized that public employers have an interest in administering discipline. At the same time, the courts have utilized the due process requirements to deter employer abuses—such as judgments that are colored by malice or prejudice, suffer from haste or misinformation, or are formed without adequate inquiry or investigation.

While the degree of due process required will vary depending on which employee rights are at stake, certain general principles can be drawn from the cases that can serve as a guide to employers seeking to navigate the procedural due process thicket without incurring liability. They include the following:

- As a general rule, discharge decisions will be subject to greater scrutiny because the loss of one's livelihood is viewed as a serious deprivation. That said, employers need not be deterred from terminating an employee it believes has engaged in a terminable offense but *should* be prepared to defend their actions in court.

- An employer should provide *written* notice of the charges against the employee. The notice should identify what work rules the employee is alleged to have violated, along with a statement summarizing the facts supporting each alleged rule violation. Employers should err on the side of providing as much information as possible to avoid an employee's claim that she or he was denied a meaningful opportunity to respond to the charges because of the adequacy of the notice.

- While courts have envisioned that employees subject to discharge will receive both a pre- and a post-termination hearing, in practice, they often only receive a due process hearing after they have been terminated. The lack of a pretermination hearing does not automatically result in a due process violation, provided that the employee is afforded an adequate post-termination hearing.

- Employees should always be suspended with pay (and benefits intact), pending a hearing or a determination of what disciplinary action, if any, shall be taken by the employer. By maintaining the status quo, employers avoid exposing themselves to needless due process violations.

■ Except in rare instances, employers should limit their public disclosure of personnel matters to avoid liberty interest violations. In those instances where the disclosure of this information is inevitable, employers must provide the employee with an opportunity to clear his or her name.

■ An employee who impedes the employer's disciplinary process by refusing to avail him- or herself of the employer's due process procedures (i.e., pre- and/or postdisciplinary hearing) cannot later claim that he or she was not given a meaningful opportunity to respond to the allegations of wrongdoing.

▌ Conclusion

When government employers take disciplinary action to enforce rules against workplace violence, they face challenges that do not apply to their counterparts in the private sector. Due process requires that employers do not deprive employees of their property or liberty rights. Additionally, their actions (firing a worker) are more likely to be the subject of public interest or scrutiny. Therefore, it is not surprising that courts do not rubber stamp these actions. Courts intervene on behalf of individuals when a charge of workplace violence coincides with an employee's whistle-blowing activities, as was the case in *Lucas*, or where there are defects in the employer's notice or hearing.

Public employers also encounter due process liability when they publicize their reasons for taking action against a worker who has been accused of workplace violence and then fail to provide the employee a hearing to clear his name. Injurious publications are not easily cured by a subsequent due process hearing. Like a fumble-fingered customer in a fine china store, an employer who damages a worker's reputation is likely to pay.

But if there is no appearance of scandal or wrongdoing in the employer's office, and no publication of a reason for acting against an employee, courts grant employers wide latitude in applying the principles laid out in *Loudermill*. Courts recognize that workplace violence can also stigmatize the employer and, within limits, try not to interfere with a public employer's effort to maintain its (good) image.

When all is said and done, one clear and constant lesson emerges: No employer pays a legal penalty for applying *Loudermill* procedures more carefully than the Supreme Court requires. The employer who aims for minimum compliance flirts with liability. Thus, no harm comes from providing an accused employee with too much process.

Notes

1. 408 U.S. 564, 577 (1972).
2. 698 F.2d 606 (2d Cir. 1983).
3. Paul v. Davis, 424 U.S. 693 (1976). Subsequent case law has referred to the test under which reputational liberty interest claims are analyzed as the "stigma-plus [a deprivation] test." The "stigma" portion of the test refers to the injury or harm done to the individual's reputation or good name, and the "plus" portion of the test refers to the individual's job loss. See, e.g., Hill v. Borough of Kutztown, 455 F.3d 225 (3d Cir. 2006).
4. American Federation of Government Employees v. U.S., 330 F.3d 513, 523 (D.C. Cir. 2003).
5. 474 U.S. 214 (1985).
6. Id. at 229.
7. See supra note 1.
8. *Paul*, supra note 3, at 701.
9. Sciolino v. City of Newport, 480 F.3d 642 (4th Cir. 2007).
10. Id.
11. 424 U.S. 319 (1976).
12. Id. at 334.
13. Cleveland Bd. of Educ. v. Loudermill, 470 U.S. 532 (1985).
14. Id. at 542.
15. Id. at 545–546.
16. Duchesne v. Williams, 849 F.2d 1004, 1006-07 (6th Cir. 1988).
17. See supra note 13, at 546.
18. 2007 WL 950165 (8th Cir. 2007).
19. 359 F.3d 1105 (9th Cir. 2004).
20. 2006 WL 3518691 (D.D.C. 2006).
21. 102 F.3d 722 (4th Cir. 1996).

22. 2005 WL 1415919 (Cal. App. 1 Dist. 2005).
23. 706 N.W.2d 110 (Wis. 2005).
24. 839 A.2d 1055 (Pa. 2003).
25. See also Gilbert v. Richard, 520 U.S. 924 (1997). Drawing a distinction between a termination and a suspension, the U.S. Supreme Court held that procedural due process does not require that an employer provide an employee with a pre-suspension hearing before suspending the employee without pay, provided that "the suspended employee receives a sufficiently prompt postsuspension hearing, the lost income is relatively insubstantial (compared with termination), and fringe benefits such as health and life insurance are often not affected at all." Id. at 932.
26. 370 F.3d 580 (6th Cir. 2004).
27. 2001 WL 1570382 (Minn. App. 2001).
28. 58 F.3d 283 (7th Cir. 1995).
29. 2006 WL 1705130 (Ohio App. 8th Dist.).
30. 2005 WL 1949498 (Neb. App. 2005).
31. 822 F.2d 364 (3d Cir. 1987).
32. 100 F.3d 1476 (9th Cir. 1996).
33. 949 P.2d 746 (Utah App. 1997).

CHAPTER 5

Discipline for Off-Duty Conduct

Steven Bierig, Michelle Camden, and Brian Clauss

Introduction

Historically, an employee's conduct while off duty and away from the workplace has not been subject to discipline by the employer, the underlying concept being that an employee's time belongs to the employee. In recent years, however, a slight shift has occurred in what is considered unacceptable off-duty conduct. This evolution has come about as employers have become more sensitive to such issues as workplace violence, employee security, and liability for workplace incidents.

While the principle still applies that employees' time "off the clock" is their own, certain types of jobs now involve higher levels of scrutiny. Public safety employees and teachers, for example, consistently have been held to a higher standard of conduct while off duty.

This higher standard is due to the nature of the work they perform and to the high degree of public trust inherent in their work.

The courts have upheld this higher standard for teachers and public safety employees because of the role such employment plays in society at large. For example, the United States Supreme Court observed:

> Within the public school system, teachers play a critical part in developing students' attitude toward government and understanding of the role of citizens in our society . . . a teacher serves as a role model for students . . . exerting a subtle but important influence over their perception and values.[1]

Because of this high degree of public trust in educational and public safety employees, allegations of off-duty misconduct present serious and significant challenges. Even where the public employee is not a public safety or educational employee, an allegation of off-duty misconduct can still present serious challenges for the employer.

Can an Employer Discipline an Employee for Off-Duty Misconduct?

When determining whether discipline for off-duty conduct is appropriate, courts have generally adopted a test that examines the relationship between the off-duty conduct and the employer. Referred to by various names or legal terms in different jurisdictions, the test, which originated in the field of labor relations, is most commonly known as the "nexus test."[2] Because public sector employees are often protected by a civil service system and/or a collective bargaining agreement, and any disciplinary action taken must be for "just cause" or "cause," an examination of the nexus test is both necessary and instructive for any employer confronted with an off-duty conduct issue. Meeting the requirements of the nexus test is the key to determining whether an employee can be disciplined for certain off-duty misconduct. In contrast, for those few public sector employees employed "at will" and the many private sector "at will" employees, their employers need not have cause to discipline such employees for off-duty conduct. While the nexus test may be largely inapplicable, demonstrating a nexus may defend against claims of discrimination or retaliatory discharge.

The Nexus Test

In the past, employers subject to "cause-based" discipline had no right to discipline employees for conduct that occurred outside of the workplace during nonwork hours. However, arbitrators and courts have recognized a limited number of exceptions to this general rule. These exceptions arise where there is some connection, or "nexus," between the off-duty conduct and its impact on the employer and the workplace.

In order to impose discipline for off-duty misconduct, there must be some connection between the off-duty conduct and the workplace. Without this relationship, the off-duty conduct would have no effect on employment and disciplinary action would not be warranted under most cause-based standards. The nexus test presents a number of inquiries that can determine whether the off-duty conduct is sufficiently related to the employer to warrant imposing discipline. If *one* of the following questions is answered in the affirmative, then the off-duty misconduct *may* be punishable:

1. Has there been an injury to the employer's business?
2. Does the misconduct render the employee unable to perform his or her duties?
3. Does the misconduct lead to a refusal by other employees to work with the offender?
4. Has the alleged off-duty misconduct harmed the relationship between the employer and the employee to the extent that it is no longer an acceptable relationship?"[3]

5. If the employee is a public sector employee, does the position occupy a position of public trust?

Each of these questions will be explored in further detail.

1. Has There Been an Injury to the Employer's Business? Actual Harm versus Harm to the Employer's Reputation

In the private sector, unlike the public sector, discipline for off-duty misconduct may only occur when there has been actual harm to the business. Harm is usually defined as *actual* business loss or damage to a company's reputation—not merely speculative harm.[4] For example, in *Eastern Airlines Inc.*,[5] the company discharged a flight attendant who was arrested for selling marijuana to another employee while in uniform but not on the clock. The flight attendant's conduct constituted "conduct on or off the job which was in conflict with the company's interest" and the discharge was upheld.

Differences exist between the public and private sectors regarding the way business is conducted. An actual business loss by a public sector employer often cannot be determined. However, this does not end the inquiry. For employers in the public sector, harm to their reputation may also justify discipline.

Determining whether an employer's reputation has been harmed is a much more difficult inquiry than the "actual harm" test described above. The considerations include the degree of adverse publicity, as well as the position of the employer in the community. Although a private sector case, *Trailways Southeastern Lines Inc.*[6] illustrates how an employee's conduct can harm the employer's reputation. In this case, an employee pled guilty to charges of breaking and entering his estranged wife's house with an intent to commit murder, as well as attempted residential arson of her house. The employee's behavior resulted in significant negative press coverage for the company: the employee was identified as a Trailways bus driver who had an alcohol problem. An arbitrator upheld the discharge because of the damage to the employer's reputation, stating:

> The very nature of grievant's job and the nature of the company business dictates that an employee must not either commit violent acts or have an alcohol problem because the company cannot afford to lose the confidence of the public.[7]

The same test for harm to the employer's reputation has been applied to public sector cases. In *Baltimore Transit Company*,[8] the company discharged a bus driver who was publicly identified as the acting grand dragon of the Ku Klux Klan. In upholding the discharge, the arbitrator identified a clear and present danger of physical violence involving patrons and property on the driver's bus. There was also a reasonable probability of an economic boycott and a threatened wildcat strike by other drivers. Further, the employee's public utterances were widely publicized, and the goals of the Klan made it clear that the employee was considering activities that potentially could threaten at least 50 percent of the company's patrons.[9]

It is important to note that there must be a public link between the employee's conduct and the employer. For example, in *City of Joliet and AFSCME*,[10] a public sector employee was convicted of arson and conspiracy—felony offenses—and the convictions were the subject of extensive newspaper coverage. However, there was no connection between the employer and the employee's off-duty criminal behavior, because the extensive newspaper coverage did not disclose the name of the employer. Because of the lack of a public connection between the conduct and the employer, there was no damage to the public employer's reputation. The employee was not in a position of public trust.

In order for off-duty misconduct to be actionable, an employer needs to be in a position to prove that it sustained an *actual* economic loss or harm to its reputation. Where the damage or harm to the employer is simply speculative, it is difficult, if not impossible for the neutral, either a court or an arbitrator, to uphold the discipline.

2. Does the Misconduct Render the Employee Unable to Perform the Job?

Employees who are absent from work and fail to perform their jobs may be subject to discipline. The analysis does not change because the absenteeism is caused by incarceration for off-duty misconduct. When an employee is incarcerated, the resulting discipline is not for the crime that led to incarceration but rather for the fact that the employee's actions have made it impossible to report to work.[11]

However, as with most general rules, there are exceptions. Arbitrators sometimes have accepted mitigating circumstances to avoid the imposition of this strict rule. For example, in *Metropolitan Transit Authority*,[12] a bus driver with nine years on the job and a good work record was incarcerated for about two and one-half weeks. During that time, he requested sick leave. The employer rejected the employee's request and discharged him. The arbitrator reinstated the bus driver, stating that mitigating circumstances called for giving him a second chance. The arbitrator observed that the jail sentence (the first one in the employee's life) was related to the employee's inability to accept his divorce and the recent separation from his wife and was not caused by alcohol or drug abuse. The employee did not have an excessive absenteeism record, he had made a sincere effort to notify his employer of his incarceration, he was suffering from a legitimate illness (depression), and his incarceration had an impact on his ability to perform his job.

Some arbitrators have gone even further and attempted to set up guidelines for determining whether incarcerated employees should be discharged. In *Sperry Rand Corporation*,[13] an employee was sentenced to thirty days in jail for abusing a police officer. The employee's request for personal leave while incarcerated was rejected and the employee was terminated. The contract provided that an employee who does not show up for work for more than five consecutive workdays without permission would be terminated. In upholding the discharge, the arbitrator relied on the language in the agreement, which stated that "unless a justifiable reason acceptable to the Company to justify the absence is given," the company has the right to deny permission for leave and terminate the grievant.[14]

Even if an employee can show up for work, a conviction might still render the employee unable to perform the job. For example, in *Scioto County Engineer and AFSCME Local 1354*,[15] a highway maintenance worker was discharged for an off-duty DUI conviction. The discharge was upheld because of the clear nexus between the off-duty conduct, which resulted in a loss of driving privileges for two years, and the employee's duties which entailed driving a county truck. Because of the conviction, the employee could not perform his job and was appropriately discharged. When employees' convictions keep them from performing their jobs, then discipline may be appropriate.

Thus, although the general rule is that an employee who is unavailable for work because of incarceration can be discharged simply for absenteeism, arbitrators will also balance a wide range of mitigating factors in the employee's favor against the employer's need for a stable workforce. Further, when an employee is convicted but not incarcerated, the employer should research the local law or consult with local counsel to determine whether the employee is prohibited from performing the job because of the conviction.

3. Does the Alleged Misconduct Lead Other Employees to Refuse to Work with the Offender?

Even though the off-duty misconduct has neither affected the employer's reputation nor rendered the employee unable to perform his or her job, the inquiry does not necessarily end. While the off-duty misconduct might have nothing to do with work, a public sector employee can be disciplined when coworkers refuse to work with the employee because of the nature of the misconduct. In the private sector, without the protections of collective bargaining agreements or civil service systems, employers have fewer impediments to discipline.

The issue of coworkers refusing to work with an employee has become increasingly relevant. If a situation arises where the alleged crime is so serious, heinous, or threatening that fellow employees refuse to work with the employee in question, the employer must analyze the off-duty misconduct and the coworkers' refusal. Coworker refusals should be closely scrutinized in order to ensure that they are real and not merely an employer's perception of refusal to work with the employee. Further, that refusal must be related to the off-duty misconduct.

For example, an employee was discharged after pleading guilty to sodomy and corrupting the morals of children while a Boy Scout scoutmaster. The employer claimed that the other employees in the plant refused to work with the employee following the conviction. The discharge was sustained because the off-duty conduct could not be separated from the day-to-day working environment: "A business enterprise by its nature requires collaboration, accord and reasonable harmony among employees. . . . The technical and administrative sides of an enterprise cannot function correctly if the human side of the business is disrupted with conflict."[16] The discharge was upheld with the following caveat:

> [We] are reluctant to sustain discharges based on off-duty conduct of employees unless a direct relationship between off-duty conduct and employment is proved. *Discretion must be exercised, lest Employers become censors of community morals.* However, where socially reprehensible conduct and employment duties and risks are substantially related, conviction for certain types of crimes may justify discharge.[17]

Similarly, in *Lonestar Gas Company*,[18] an employee of a gas company was found guilty of incest. The arbitrator indicated that he could not reinstate the employee where there was credible testimony by the grievant's fellow workers that they could not work with him.

More recently, in *Procter & Gamble Co. and Local 47, PACE,*[19] an employee was discharged for an off-duty threat of violence he made to a member of his work team. The discharge was upheld because the conduct interfered with the effective operation of the work team and resulted in other employees being reluctant to work with the grievant.

However, in *International Paper Company,*[20] an employee was convicted of off-duty battery against his foreman. In the incident, the employee slashed his foreman with a knife in an argument over a woman in a tavern. While the off-duty conduct no doubt involved serious misconduct, the arbitrator reinstated the employee because he believed it would not disrupt the plant operations by creating fear among his coworkers because the confrontation had been between the employee and a supervisor.[21]

As stated above, the refusal to work with the alleged offender must be genuine and not merely perceived. In a humorous but interesting case, *California Air,*[22] an off-duty employee, upon being offered twenty dollars by his coemployees, "streaked" in front of the airport baggage terminal, wearing nothing but a ski mask, T-shirt, and cowboy boots. When news of the incident reached management, the employee was discharged. The company argued that the employee's actions caused other employees to refuse to work with the accused. The arbitrator overturned the discharge. He reasoned:

> [T]he company's witnesses acknowledged that none of them expressed any reluctance to work with the grievant because he had streaked; *and indeed, some had encouraged the grievant to streak.* Concededly, the grievant has not committed a lewd act, and certainly, his continued employment would not threaten the safety of the other employees. Even allowing for perhaps unexpressed opinions of disapproval on the part of some company employees, *there is no basis in the record* for finding that the grievant's conduct created an employee morale problem or in any other way hampered productivity.[23]

In order for an employer to terminate an employee for off-duty misconduct because coworkers refuse to work with the employee in question, there must be an *actual and proven reluctance* on the part of coworkers to work with the other employee. Both positions must be weighed before simply accepting a coworker's statement that he or she cannot work with the employee.

4. Has the Alleged Misconduct Harmed the Relationship between the Employer and Employee to the Extent That It Is No Longer an Acceptable Relationship?

Another factor to consider when determining whether to discipline an employee for off-duty misconduct is what effect the misconduct had on the employment relationship. Off-duty misconduct may damage the "relationship" between the employer and the employee to the point where the relationship simply cannot continue. Another way of describing this factor is whether the off-duty misconduct is incompatible with the employee/employer relationship. This is the test used when the previous three tests do not apply.

For example, in *Fairmont General Hospital*,[24] a maid was discharged for the off-duty conduct of shoplifting. The discharge was upheld. Two factors were: (1) there had been a recent theft problem at the company; and (2) the conviction raised serious doubt about the maid's trustworthiness. However, lest the employer think that this category covers all off-duty conduct situations, a recent case involving the *same* hospital dispels that notion. In that case, the employee, a licensed nurse, pled guilty to shoplifting. The employee's discharge was not upheld, but reduced to a suspension because there was "no proof of actual detrimental harm, or convincing proof from which detriment or harm can be readily or reasonably discerned."[25]

Overall, it is difficult to try to categorize this type of discipline. Therefore, an employer must carefully scrutinize both the off-duty conduct and the nature of the employee's job. The employer must determine whether the individual's action makes it impossible for the employer to "trust" the employee again.

5. Public Safety and Educational Employees: An Exception to the Traditional Nexus Test

The nexus standard for upholding discipline is generally lower in public sector cases involving public safety and educational employees. With public safety and educational employees, arbitrators and courts generally show a greater sensitivity to the reputation and mission of the employer as a government entity. Thus, it is generally easier for a public employer to sustain a dismissal based on off-duty misconduct where the employer establishes that the public trust is a key part of the nexus requirement in the public sector. Traditionally, this applies most frequently to police officers, firefighters, and teachers. In public sector nonsafety employment, the nexus requirement is similar, if not identical, to the private sector.

Public Safety: Police and Firefighters

Perhaps the highest standard for off-duty conduct is reserved for law enforcement. They clearly hold a position of public trust, as they are charged with enforcing the laws and serving and protecting the public. Therefore, almost any infraction with legal ramifications can be argued as establishing a nexus between the officer's position and the mission of the department.

For example, in *City of Fairborn and Fairborn New City Lodge No. 48, FOP*,[26] an officer was discharged for an off-duty DUI. The termination was upheld. It was argued that the conviction would interfere with the officer's ability to perform his duties because "the Grievant's credibility as a police officer in enforcing the laws relating to driving under the influence has been seriously compromised."[27]

In *Department of Correctional Services and NYSCOPBA*,[28] a corrections officer was discharged for off-duty use of marijuana. The arbitrator found that his off-duty conduct was in direct conflict with his duties as a corrections officer, stating that "knowledge of inmates that the grievant does drugs puts him at risk of being compromised in the performance of his duties."[29]

This higher standard has also been applied to auxiliary police officers. In *City of Taylor*,[30] the employee, an auxiliary policeman, was arrested for an off-duty narcotics violation and admitted to drug transactions with a police informant. The termination was upheld because it not only reflected poorly upon the police department's reputation but to hold otherwise would shatter department morale and show contempt for the laws.[31]

Even an officer's financial solvency can become the subject of discipline. In *State of Ohio*,[32] an Ohio state trooper was required to take home a department issued squad car because he was required to be available for emergency recall at all times. The state trooper's phone had been shut off due to financial difficulties, which affected his ability to be contacted for recall. Discipline was upheld because of the nexus between the officer's financial difficulties and the department's recall policy.[33]

False insurance statements can also become a disciplinary issue. In *City of Stamford*,[34] a police officer provided false information in conjunction with an insurance claim he made on his boat. The State Board of Mediation ruled that there was just cause to terminate him because his position as a police officer placed him in the public trust.

While firefighters are not charged with enforcing the law, they are also held in a position of public trust albeit for other reasons. Because of the position of public trust, they are also held to a higher standard for their off-duty conduct. In *City of Flint Michigan*,[35] two firefighters were arrested for off-duty gambling. The city based its disciplinary action on the higher standards for public safety employees:

> Citizens must have confidence in the integrity and honesty of firefighters. Firemen have access to property and in the course of their work. Any acts which try to lower the image of the department can expose firemen to charges of minor thefts from buildings in fire situations. . . . Firemen are expected to be law abiding citizens and their involvement in acts punishable by the law hurts the good name of the department.[36]

Similarly, in *City of Las Vegas Fire Department and IAFF Local 1285*,[37] a firefighter was discharged for shoplifting. The arbitrator used the traditional nexus test to determine that the discharge was appropriate.

While the off-duty conduct of public safety employees is subject to greater scrutiny, there must still be a connection between the conduct and the employer. For example, in *State of Ohio*,[38] a sixteen-year veteran of the state highway patrol was disciplined for failing to make timely cellular phone and car payments. While there was no publicity, creditors contacted the employer. The trooper's suspension was overturned because it was found to have involved off-duty conduct which did not affect his status as a patrol officer or his ability to perform his duties.

In another case, *U.S. Immigration and Naturalization Service & National Border Control Council AFGE Local 2455*,[39] a federal border patrol officer was charged with aggravated assault. The incident was widely publicized, and the agency suspended the officer indefinitely without pay pending the outcome of the criminal matter. He was found not guilty and was reinstated without back pay. The union grieved the loss of pay, and the arbitrator sustained the grievance based on three factors: (1) the officer was not guilty of any crime; (2) there was no showing that the fight underlying the assault charge had any adverse impact on job performance; and (3) there was no showing that the border patrol officer suffered any damage to his reputation or any loss of public confidence.

While the nexus standard may be lowered for public safety employees, there must be an actual connection between the conduct of the employee and the mission of the employer. Accordingly, certain off-duty misconduct committed by public safety employees is still beyond the reach of discipline.

Educational Employees

As discussed above, a public school teacher occupies a special position of public trust in American society. With this special position of public trust comes a level of scrutiny for off-duty misconduct that is similar to the level of scrutiny applied to public safety employees. For example, in *North Haven Board of Education*,[40] an employee lost his job for giving a female student a ride in his car.[41] In upholding the discharge, the arbitrator explained why the educational employees are held to a higher standard than employees in the private sector:

> Due to a sensitive nature of the school-student relationship, its employees must maintain an aura or respect about themselves. They must be above suspicion and guard themselves particularly against being involved in an unfavorable student contact.[42]

Another case that demonstrates the high standards to which teachers are held is *Board of Directors of Lawton-Bronson CSD v. Davies*.[43] The case involved a teacher who was arrested for shoplifting and was later terminated by the school district. In upholding the discharge, the court held that the illegal conduct, together with other incidents of poor role-model behavior in the classroom, provided just cause for termination. The court dismissed the teacher's argument that medication she was taking for a psychiatric condition rendered her manic and unable to resist shoplifting.

Not all off-duty teacher conduct, however, is subject to discipline. In *Erb v. Iowa State Board of Public Instruction*,[44] the court found no nexus between a teacher's position and an off-campus adulterous affair with another teacher. Simply, there were no facts suggesting that the affair was conducted either on school property or during school hours. Without that connection to the school, there could be no discipline.

Like the public safety employee, educational employees are held to a higher standard of conduct while off-duty. While the nexus standard may be lowered for teachers, there must be an actual connection between the conduct of the employee and the mission of the employer. Accordingly, certain off-duty conduct by educational employees will not be subject to discipline.

▌ Conduct While Called to Active Duty

The post–September 11, 2001, military activations have called hundreds of thousands of citizen-soldiers to active duty, many of them public sector employees. The Uniformed Services Employment and Reemployment Rights Act (USERRA) protects their civilian employment. USERRA has two components: (1) prohibiting discrimination in employment based upon military service; and (2) guaranteeing reemployment rights upon return from active duty in the National Guard or Reserve Component of the Armed Forces. Reemployment rights include prompt reinstatement to civilian employment upon return from military duty without loss of seniority, status, or pay rate.

For the protections of USERRA to apply, the service member must meet five eligibility criteria:

1. The employee must have left civilian employment.
2. The employee must have given notice that he or she was leaving to perform military service—with certain exceptions.
3. The cumulative period of service must not have exceeded five years—with certain exceptions.
4. The employee must have been released from military service under honorable or general conditions.
5. The employee must have reported back to work within the statutory time frame.

In the rare instance where an employer would seek to discipline an employee for conduct that took place while the employee was serving in the National Guard or Reserve component of the Armed Forces, the employee would be protected from the employer's discipline provided the employee had been released under a general or honorable discharge from service. Because USERRA is a comprehensive statutory and regulatory scheme and the body of law is still relatively new and evolving, an employer should consult with counsel before disciplining an employee for conduct that occurred while on active duty.[45]

Conclusions and Recommendations

In the public sector, a two-tier approach is applied when reviewing disciplinary cases involving off-duty misconduct of employees who may only be disciplined for cause. For public safety and educational employees, the nexus for upholding discipline is easier for an employer to satisfy. In contrast, in a public nonsafety setting, the standard is nearly identical to that applied in the private sector.

It is difficult, if not impossible, to fashion a blanket "rule" regarding what off-duty misconduct can be subject to discipline. The employer must look at the individual acts and circumstances on a case-by-case basis. As discussed above, what a person does away from work is generally not any business of the employer's, except under a limited range of circumstances. There must be some *connection* between an employee's conduct and his employer in order for the employer to take any action. The general rule is relaxed—but not eliminated—if the off-duty misconduct involves public safety employees. There must still be a relationship between the conduct and the employer.

While there are no hard and fast rules relating to discipline for off-duty conduct, there are some key considerations that should be taken into account. When confronted with an allegation of off-duty misconduct, the employer should consider the following criteria when determining whether to take any action against the employee:

1. Assess the potential for harm the employee poses in the workplace.
2. Assess whether the employee is in a position of public trust.
3. Consult with your counsel to determine if suspension of the employee is appropriate during the pending criminal proceedings and the employer investigation.

4. Do not rely solely on local law enforcement or prosecutors—employers can often conduct their own investigation.
5. Give the employee the opportunity to explain his or her situation before recommending discipline, thereby avoiding a due process violation.
6. Contact the authorities and the prosecutor for copies of charges and police reports, case status, and court dates, and request special conditions of bond or no contact orders if appropriate.
7. Retain any coworker complaints, public complaints, and media reports about the affected employee and the off-duty conduct.
8. Examine the relationship between the off-duty misconduct and the employer, and apply the analysis of the above sections.

Notes

1. Ambach v. Norwick, 441 U.S. 68, 78–79 (1978).

2. For example, the Iowa Supreme Court set forth the following criteria to help determine whether off-duty conduct is just cause for a teacher's discharge in Briggs v. Bd. of Directors of the Hinton CSD, 282 N.W.2d 740, 742-43 (Iowa 1979):

    a. The likelihood that the conduct may have adversely affected students or teacher;

    b. The proximity or remoteness in time of the conduct;

    c. The type of teaching certificate held by the involved;

    d. The extenuating or aggravating circumstances, if any, surrounding the conduct;

    e. The praiseworthiness or blameworthiness of the motives resulting in the conduct;

    f. The likelihood of the recurrence of the questioned conduct; and

    g. The extent to which disciplinary action may inflict adverse impact or chilling effect upon the constitutional rights of the employee involved.

3. Murray Machine Inc., 75 LA 284, 287 (Kerkman, 1980).

4. Inland Container Corp., 28 LA 312, 314 (Ferguson, 1951).

5. 76 LA 961 (Torkus, 1981).

6. 81 LA 712 (Gibson, 1983).

7. Id. at 716.

8. 47 Lab. Arb. (BNA) 62 (Duff, 1966).

9. Id. at 66.

10. 108 LA 7 (Cox, 1996).

11. 72 LA 1262 (Roumell, Jr., 1979).

12. 98 LA 793 (Allen, Jr., 1992).

13. 60 LA 220 (Murphy, 1973).

14. The arbitrator identified several factors for determining if an incarcerated employee should be discharged:

 1. Whether or not confinement of an employee in jail will authorize his employer to take some sort of disciplinary action depends upon all of the circumstances, including, among other things:

  (a) The language of their contract.

  (b) The length of confinement.

  (c) The nature of the cause for the confinement, i.e., whether as the result of an arrest, an inability to post bond, or as the result of a sentence.

  (d) The nature of the conduct resulting in confinement, i.e., its degree of seriousness and impropriety.

  (e) The nature of the disciplinary action to be taken or which results.

  (f) The employee's previous work and disciplinary record.

  (g) The extent to which the absence affected the employee's production, etc.

  (h) The effect upon plant morale.

  (i) Whether or not the conduct occurred on plant property or during working hours.

 2. Generally, the same circumstances are to be considered if the question is only one of denial of leave of absence, but usually less "fault" on the part of the employee is required to justify denial of a leave of absence.

15. 116 LA 462 (Imuundo, 2001).

16. Robertshal Controls, Co., 64-2 Lab. Arb. Awds. (CCH) 8748 (Duff, 1964), quoting Chicago Pneumatic Tool Co., 38 LA 891, 893 (Duff, 1961).

17. Id. (emphasis added).

18. 56 LA 1221 (Johannes, 1971).

19. 114 LA 1185 (Allen, 2000).

20. 52 LA 1266 (Jenkins, 1969).

21. Id. at 1266–1267.

22. 63 LA 351 (Kaufman, 1974).

23. Id. at 353 (emphasis added).

24. 58 LA 1293 (Dybeck, 1972).

25. Fairmont General Hospital, 91 LA 930, 934 (Hunter, Jr., 1988).

26. 119 LA 754 (Cohen, 2003).

27. Id.

28. 116 LA 142 (Babiskin, 2001).

29. Id.

30. 65 LA 147 (Keefe, 1975).

31. Id. at 149.

32. 105 LA 361 (Feldman, 1995).

33. This case also can be viewed as a situation where an employee could not perform his job duties *because* of his off-duty financial difficulties.

34. 97 LA 261 (Pattocco, 1991).

35. 59 LA 370 (Stieber, 1972).

36. Id. at 371.

37. 105 LA 398 (Robinson, 1995).

38. 105 LA 110 (Feldman, 1995).

39. 114 LA 872 (Neas, 2000).

40. 59 LA 99 (Purcell, McDonough, Sirabella, 1972).

41. It is interesting to note that the employee is only identified as a male employee. There is no indication in the case as to whether the employee was a teacher or another school employee.

42. 59 LA at 100.

43. 489 N.W.2d 19 (Iowa 1992).

44. 216 N.W.2d 339 (Iowa 1974).

45. See generally, Brian Clauss, "Called to Duty: Advice for Your Clients," *The Young Lawyer*, American Bar Association, Vol. 11, No. 4 (Jan. 2007).

CHAPTER 6

Employer Liability for Workplace Violence

Mark A. Lies II and James J. Powers

As THE PACE AND EMOTIONAL PRESSURES of everyday life impact employees at home and in the workplace, a distressing and tragic trend is occurring. Employees are unable to control their emotions at work, and violence erupts between coworkers, supervisors and employees, and employees and customers or third parties. The unfortunate statistics show that homicide is the second most frequent cause of death for women in the workplace, and that assaults and violent acts, which include homicides, are the third overall cause for men and women.[1]

Certainly, no employer wants such incidents to occur. Ironically, however, as employers struggle to avoid potential legal liabilities through the creation and enforcement of stringent employment policies, they are met with a host of federal and state laws protecting employee conduct. The legal landscape is particularly daunting for public employers, who must grapple with several additional layers of liability that do not apply to their private sector counterparts. Specifically, constitutional speech, association, and privacy issues may arise in a public employer's attempts at ensuring a safe workplace for its employees.

This chapter provides an overview of the legal liability that a public employer confronts in its efforts to provide a safe workplace. The legal obligation to provide a safe workplace will be examined, along with ancillary issues that frequently arise when a public employer attempts to address the behavior of an employee or customer/client which may be endangering a coworker or third party's safety.

▮ A Public Employer's "General Duty" to Provide a Safe Workplace

Unlike their private sector counterparts, public employers are not directly governed by the federal Occupational Safety and Health Act of 1970. Section 3(5) of the act expressly excludes state and local governmental entities from the act's definition of "employer." Courts have narrowly interpreted this definition to apply only to actual governmental entities, *not* private entities with which public sector workplaces may have contractual relationships.[2] As a result, public employers typically do not have to concern themselves with inspections conducted by the federal Occupational Safety and Health Administration (OSHA).

On the other hand, depending on the state in which the public employer resides, state workplace safety restrictions may apply that essentially parallel the federal OSHA requirements. At the time of this book's publication, at least twenty-three states have passed their own OSHA-approved workplace safety legislation that applies to both private and public employers.[3] Another eight states have passed workplace safety legislation that applies specifically to public employees.[4] Other states have essentially adopted the act's federal regulations as their own.[5] For states that have enacted their own workplace safety requirements, interpretations of the act's federal regulations often serve as the benchmark for understanding the intent and meaning behind parallel state requirements.[6]

In both the private and public sectors, the primary basis for requiring an employer to provide a safe working environment is found in the "general duty" clause of the act. Most states have simply adopted the language found in Section 5(a)(1) of the federal law, which states in pertinent part:

> Each employer—shall furnish to each of his employees employment and a place of employment which are free from recognized hazards that are causing or are likely to cause death or serious physical harm to his employees.

As originally drafted by the U.S. Congress, this provision was intended to address workplace safety issues for which no other specific standard exists. Under both federal and state precedent, violations of this provision occur when an employer has failed to take some action to address a "recognized hazard." For example, a federal appeals court has looked to the "common knowledge of safety experts" within a particular industry or activity in order to determine whether a particular hazard is "recognized."[7] Other sources that provide insight as to whether a particular hazard is "recognized" include industry standards, such as those issued by the National Fire Protection Association, and an employer's personal knowledge that a hazard exists.[8]

In light of these principles, public employers in those states with workplace safety rules may have an obligation to maintain a workplace safe from violence committed by coworkers or third parties. Although the federal law has not yet promulgated specific standards for workplace violence, it has gone on the record as acknowledging that in certain situations, the "general duty" clause is broad enough to encompass the prevention of workplace violence.[9] In addition, OSHA has published a variety of guidelines addressing workplace violence, including, for example, recommendations for workplace safety programs for late-night retail establishments and guidelines for preventing workplace violence against health care and social service workers.[10]

In light of the increasing visibility of workplace violence issues, as recognized by OSHA and other governmental entities,[11] public employers should expect that sooner or later state agencies responsible for workplace safety will hold that workplace violence is a "recognized" hazard necessitating preventive action by an employer. For example, in *Megawest Financial, Inc.*,[12] an administrative law judge for the federal Occupational Safety Health Review Commission declined to find a violation based on an employer's alleged failure to provide a safe working environment for its staff who were being confronted with assault and battery threats. Although the judge found that a hazard indeed existed within the meaning of the "general duty" clause, the hazard was not well "recognized" either by the employer or within the industry that was at issue. However, with more than ten years of additional experience with workplace violence, OSHA and/or state agencies may now be prepared to find that such hazards are indeed "recognized" within the meaning of the "general duty" clause.[13] Based on the guidance published to date, such "general duty" obligations, in the event of violent workplace conflicts, may require employers to address the violent behavior of their employees and/or to adopt an emergency preparedness/evacuation plan.

Several states are beginning to actively target workplace violence deficiencies as a violation of an employer's "general duty" to provide a safe working environment. For example, Indiana and Minnesota are two states that have actually issued citations to employers for violations of the "general duty" clause in the context of workplace violence.[14]

For those public employers who are found to have violated their "general duty" to provide a safe working environment, regulatory agencies typically require the employer to "abate" or "fix" the violation. Depending on the willfulness and seriousness of the violation, monetary penalties may also be imposed.

▌ Common Law Obligations to Prevent Violence by Public Employees

In addition to state workplace safety laws, most states have developed liability doctrines under their "common" (nonstatutory) law. Most of these are based on some type of negligence theory, ranging from negligent hiring and retention to the negligent upkeep of a particular piece of property. In some cases, these common law theories have been applied to public entities in response to claims that the entity "did not do enough" to prevent violent encounters that led to third-party injuries.

Negligent Hiring, Supervision, Training, and Retention

In many states, an employer may be held liable for the violent acts of an employee, if the employer:

- ▪ *Negligently hired* the employee (e.g., failed to investigate the employee's work history to determine if there was prior violent conduct);

- ▪ *Negligently supervised* the employee (failed to warn or discipline an employee who engaged in threatening conduct);

- ▪ *Negligently trained* the employee (failed to provide training to employees regarding prohibited conduct that may give rise to violence and the consequences of engaging in such conduct); or

- ▪ *Negligently retained* the employee (failed to terminate an employee who has engaged in acts or threats of violence).

Public employers often defend themselves against such allegations by relying on state tort "immunity" laws. While many states permit injured parties to sue governmental units, exceptions have been made for those government actions that are based on "discretionary functions."[15] A discretionary function involves the determination of fundamental governmental policy. In these circumstances, the crux of an employer's defense typically involves a claim that a decision to employ, retain, and/or supervise a potentially violent employee is a discretionary function that entails policy evaluation, judgment, and expertise. State courts have differed, however, as to whether such employment-related decisions indeed involve policy making or planning.

For example, in *Doe v. Cedar Rapids Community Sch. Dist.*,[16] the Iowa Supreme Court concluded that the decision of a school district to hire and retain a teacher accused of physical and sexual violence against students was not directly related to the exercise of governmental policy judgments and, thus, was subject to judicial scrutiny. The court first looked to whether the challenged conduct was a matter of choice for the school district, and then whether the district's judgment was of the type intended to be shielded from liability. Here, the court found that the school had made a professional judgment when it hired the teacher, when it retained the teacher after the initial allegations of misconduct, and when it supervised the teacher, so the first prong of the defense was met. However, the court found there were no underlying policy determinations behind the decision to hire, retain, and supervise the teacher, because it did not involve any economic, social, or political policy concerns. Thus, liability was found against the district.[17]

The decision of the Iowa Supreme Court in *Doe* is an anomaly. Most state courts that have decided this question have concluded, like their federal brethren, that negligent hiring claims are barred by the discretionary function exception—keeping the state's sovereign immunity intact. In commenting on the Massachusetts Tort Claims Act, the state law that authorizes lawsuits against a municipality for its negligent or wrongful conduct, the U.S. Court of Appeals for the First Circuit explained that employee hiring and retention decisions often *do* involve important policy-related concerns:

> The federal courts have determined that hiring decisions are susceptible to and involve policy analysis. An entity must

weigh budgetary conditions in determining the number of hires as well as who to hire. In addition, the choice between several potential employees involves the weighing of individual backgrounds, office diversity, experience and employer intuition. These types of decisions are multi-factored and require the balancing of competing objectives.[18]

In light of this standard, the First Circuit concluded that a municipality's decision to hire an officer despite his prior assault conviction was "discretionary," such that an arrestee who was allegedly battered by the officer could not maintain a tort for negligent hiring and retention.

In its decision, the First Circuit explains that a number of other states follow this approach. For example, in *Johnson v. Mers*,[19] the court held that an employer could not be held liable for a decision to hire an off-duty officer who later shot an individual with whom she had a prior relationship. The court explained that the municipality's decision to hire the off-duty officer was a discretionary act, which enjoyed immunity under the Illinois tort immunity act.[20]

Despite this judicial trend toward immunizing a public employer's hiring and retention decisions, a public employer may still lose its potential immunity by failing to perform a background check if such an investigation is required under state or federal law prior to hiring a new employee. For example, in *Mueller v. Community Consolidated Sch. Dist. 54*,[21] the issue of the school district's immunity from negligent hiring and supervision under the state's tort immunity act was not reached. Rather, the court found that a state statute requiring criminal background investigation of school employees vitiated any potential immunity, because the district had failed to undertake a background check of a coach who had allegedly sexually assaulted a student. In recent years, a number of states have passed laws requiring criminal background checks for job applicants who will be working with vulnerable members of the community (e.g., children, the aged, or the disabled), will be working in and around critical infrastructures (e.g., water treatment plants), or will be working with or transporting hazardous materials.

Whether or not a state statute requires employers to conduct background checks of certain job applicants, public employers should still consider using them when making hiring and retention decisions. Assuming that such investigations comply with all other labor and employment laws,[22] background checks can help determine whether a particular applicant poses a potential risk to coworkers and/or third parties. Such background checks can include contacts with prior employers and a review of criminal conviction histories.

Negligent Referral and Defamation

Public employers must also be careful when asked to comment on the work history of employees who have since left public employment. "Overselling" an applicant by providing misleading information to a prospective employer may result in negligence claims. For example, in *Randi W. v. Muroc Joint Unified Sch. Dist.*,[23] a student sued a school administrator who sexually abused her. The student also sued the administrator's former employer for having failed to disclose to the new employer relevant information about the administrator's past sexual misconduct.

The California Supreme Court found that liability could be imposed on a school district based upon its failure to use reasonable care when giving a recommendation for one of its former administrators. The court found that the glowing letters of recommendation, which failed to disclose the fact that the administrator had resigned under pressure due to sexual misconduct charges, constituted an "affirmative representation." The court also found that the prospective employer (which was another school district) relied upon the letters of recommendation in its decision to hire the administrator.

In examining the issue of recommendations, the court determined that a party that gives a letter of recommendation owes a duty to a third person not to lie about the qualifications of the subject employee, especially if the omissions or misrepresentations present a substantial, foreseeable risk of physical injury to third parties. Thus, the court concluded that when the school district elected to provide *some* information about the administrator, it was obligated to disclose *all* other material facts, including the negative information about prior sexual misconduct issues.

In the decade since *Randi W.* was decided, only a few courts in other states have been willing to recognize a third-party claim (by victim, not party requesting the reference) against an employer for making either a knowing or negligent misrepresentation in connection with a job reference of a former employee. Courts in New Mexico and Indiana have recognized such claims.[24] Illinois, on the other hand, has expressly refused to recognize a claim for negligent misrepresentation in the context of a job reference.[25]

Even where the jurisdiction has recognized a claim for knowing or negligent misrepresentation, another hurdle is determining whether, under state law, a public employer may be sued for such a common law tort claim or is immune from liability. In the New Mexico case referenced above, *Davis v. Board of County Commissioners of Dona Ana County*,[26] the defendant county argued that it was immune from liability for a negligent misrepresentation claim. The state appellate court held that the answer to the question was not clear. New Mexico's tort immunity law contained a waiver for personal or bodily injury resulting from actions taken by law enforcement officers while acting within the scope of their duties. The two county employees who provided the misleading job reference were employed by the County Detention Center. The appellate court determined that the individuals met the definition of a law enforcement officer but concluded that a jury should decide whether the employees were acting within the scope of their duties when they provided the written and oral job references. The county had argued that any job reference requests should have been forwarded to the Detention Center's human resources department to be processed.

With only a few courts having addressed the question of whether a claim for a knowing or negligent misrepresentation exists, public employers should be on notice that they *may* have a duty to completely disclose a former employer's past history of violence, especially when they elect to provide a job reference that goes beyond simply providing a former employee's dates of employment and job title. A potential impediment to doing this, however, could be a confidentiality/nondisclosure provision in a separation or settlement agreement. Courts appear to support the disclosure of a former employee's potentially violent conduct, despite the existence of a confidentiality clause in a settlement agreement. For example, an Ohio court of appeals concluded that a nondisclosure agreement between a teacher and a school board that prohibited the disclosure of the teacher's molestation of female students was void and unenforceable as a matter of public policy.[27]

After a number of children reported molestation by the teacher to the school board, and an investigation revealed numerous instances of inappropriate conduct between the teacher and the students, the parties entered into a settlement agreement whereby the teacher agreed to resign and the board agreed not to disclose the incidents except when subject to a court order. Thereafter, a board member learned that the teacher was working for another school district. He contacted the district and informed them why the teacher was fired. The former teacher filed suit, based upon a breach of the nondisclosure agreement. Analyzing the agreement, the court found the nondisclosure clause illegal per se, because it purported to suppress information regarding the commission of felonies, and was void and unenforceable on public policy grounds because it was designed to shield information about the teacher's pedophilia while the teacher sought and obtained other employment in the education field.

Despite cases such as those described above, which encourage employers to fully disclose a former employee's violent acts, a number of legal pitfalls may prohibit and/or limit an employer's ability to do so. For example, a couple of states have passed restrictive personnel record review acts that limit the release of an employee's disciplinary records to a third party absent prior approval from the employee or notice to the employee.[28]

Public employers must also be careful lest their communications about a former employee rise to the level of defamation, which is generally defined as a false statement that is publicized and results in an injury to a third party. Fears about such defamation claims may be alleviated to some extent, however, by a number of laws that insulate *truthful* information provided to a prospective employer. For example, an Illinois law protects both employers who provide truthful, performance-related information to prospective employers, or provide information that they, in good faith, believe to be truthful.[29] Over thirty states have similar "immunity" statutes that, under certain circumstances, can help insulate a public employer when communicating job performance information to a prospective employer.[30]

Premises Liability

Public employers can also face potential liability for the violent behavior of their employees and/or third parties under a common law "premises liability" analysis. Many states recognize that the owner of a business or social establishment owes a duty to a patron to maintain the premises in a reasonably secure and safe condition. This theory has been applied with equal force to public entities who operate structures that are frequented by the general public. State tort immunity laws typically recognize that public entities have a common law duty to maintain their property in a reasonably safe condition. While a public entity is not generally liable for the criminal acts of a third party, liability will be found under one of two circumstances: (1) where the conditions of the premises either prompted or facilitated the criminal act; or (2) where the public entity had unique knowledge regarding the possibility of future criminal acts.[31]

Often these cases turn on whether the public entity had sufficient knowledge to anticipate that a third party would engage in criminal conduct on its premises. For example, in *Sandra T. E. v. Sperlik*,[32] the district court refused to dismiss plaintiffs' premises liability claim against a school district and some of its administrators, finding that plaintiffs had alleged sufficient facts in their complaint to show that defendants, notwithstanding having been previously notified by several female junior high school students that their music teacher had sexually abused them on school grounds, allowed this teacher to use a private room to work one-on-one with his students, thus increasing the likelihood that other students would be abused. The defendants had unsuccessfully argued that plaintiffs' premises liability claim should be dismissed because it was simply a re-allegation of their negligent supervision claims.[33] In *M. W. v. Panama Buena Vista Union School District*,[34] a California school district was hit with a jury verdict in excess of $2 million for its failure to provided a safe environment for a student who was sexually assaulted by another student. There, the court concluded that the school district should have foreseen the risk posed by a fellow student who was the subject of over thirty instances of discipline, some of which involved violent acts directed toward teachers and students.

In contrast, in *Brown v. Ascension Parish*,[35] a Louisiana parish was not held responsible for injuries suffered by the plaintiff while attending a graduation party held at the parish's community center. The injured plaintiff alleged that the parish knew or should have foreseen that a shooting might occur, based on past criminal activity that had occurred at the community center. While acknowledging that such liability might exist if the parish truly "should have known," the court nevertheless concluded that a handful of vandalisms and "break-ins" were insufficient to put the parish on notice that a shooting might someday occur during an organized event.

In practice, most of the aforementioned common law claims will "dovetail" with allegations that a public entity has deprived an individual of his or her federal constitutional rights. Such constitutional claims often concentrate on whether an employer's "policy or custom" actually caused the deprivation of one's constitutional rights.

Section 1983 Liability

Violence committed by public employees can expose public employers to liability under the U.S. Constitution. Sometimes called a "constitutional tort," such lawsuits typically allege that a governmental policy, custom, or practice caused the deprivation of a federal or constitutional right.[36] A plaintiff may also allege that a policy is unconstitutional on its face, and/or unconstitutionally applied due to the public employer's "deliberate indifference" to the rights of the plaintiff.[37]

The primary vehicle by which a public employee can allege a violation of constitutional rights is through 42 U.S.C. § 1983, which prohibits public entities from depriving citizens of any "rights, privileges, or immunities secured by the Constitution and its laws." Section 1983 does not create independent constitutional or statutory rights. Rather, it provides a federal cause of action for claims grounded in the Constitution and other federal laws.[38] Section 1983 is particularly important to public employers and employees alike, because employment decisions involving public employees are often made "under color of" state law. In conducting this liability analysis, most courts assume, without discussing, that the public employee is acting as a representative of the public employer when engaging in violent or unlawful conduct. In addition, a *constitutional* right must actually have been violated; violations of state criminal law are not enough to create liability under "Section 1983" (the procedural vehicle by which a plaintiff can allege a "constitutional tort").[39]

Not surprisingly, most public entities do not have explicit policies that encourage the deprivation of an individual's constitutional rights. Indeed, public employers oftentimes have policies in place that are supposed to help protect an individual's rights, including for example workplace anti-harassment policies. In light of this, plaintiffs often will allege that an unwritten custom or practice is what really caused the constitutional violation. Plaintiffs can attempt to do this in a number of ways, ranging from claims that a superior official explicitly approved a subordinate's actions, or that a superior official "turned a blind eye," i.e., was "deliberately indifferent," to the risk of a constitutional violation. The following cases demonstrate how courts have applied these various legal principles.

In one of the leading cases on the topic, the U.S. Supreme Court addressed the liability of a county for the negligent hiring of a police officer. In *Board of County Commissioners of Bryan County v. Brown*,[40] the Court held that the public employer could not be held liable for the negligent hiring of a police officer, who had a history of physical assaults and arrests. The Supreme Court held that the plaintiffs had to demonstrate that the county was the "moving force" behind the alleged injury, based on deliberate conduct: "[o]nly where adequate scrutiny of the applicant's background would lead a reasonable pol-icymaker to conclude that the plainly obvious consequence of the decision to hire the applicant would be the deprivation of a third party's federally protected right can the official's failure to ade-quately scrutinize the applicant's background constitute 'deliberate indifference.' "[41] Employing this standard, the U.S. Court of Ap-peals for the Eleventh Circuit found that a city was "deliberately in-different" when it hired a city manager "without a resume, interview, background check, or any discussion of his qualifica-tions," who ultimately sexually harassed and raped a subordinate employee.[42] According to the court, the city ignored a known and obvious risk, where the city council was "inundated with articles, faxes, and mail, warning of [the applicant's] problems with sexual harassment and dealings with women" at the time it was debating whether to hire the city manager.

The Eleventh Circuit also found that the public employer had a custom and practice of tacitly approving the behavior of its city manager. The court explicitly found that the workplace was "perme-ated with vulgar, demeaning, and sexually suggestive conversations about women, improper demands for sexual favors and dates, [and] unwelcome sexual advances," but that the city mayor himself took no action to correct this behavior after having been told about it. Such facts helped prove that the city had a "custom and practice" of ignoring or tolerating gross sexual harassment.[43] Although the jury did not find that the city had a custom of condoning the rape of its female employees, the court noted that such a conclusion might be warranted under different circumstances, especially where a rape is found to be a part of a larger pattern of sexual harassment.[44]

Courts will also evaluate whether there is an actual causal "link" between the alleged employer policy and the deprivation of the constitutional right. In other words, a plaintiff must actually prove that the policy *caused* the loss of his or her constitutional rights. In one case, a student filed a lawsuit, claiming that he was subjected to corporal punishment by a teacher as a result of the school's failure to properly train the teacher or through the school's policy of deliberate indifference to students' needs.[45] The court focused on the fact that there was no proof of a causal link between the defendant's alleged failure to train and the student's injuries. In the words of the court, "[a] plaintiff must . . . go beyond a conclusory claim of a need for training and demonstrate how a particular policymaker's specific choice with respect to the training deficiency . . . reflects 'deliberate indifference' to their constitutional rights, and how this indifference caused their injuries."[46]

In other cases, a public employer can avoid liability by proving that it followed a policy designed to avoid injuries to third parties. For example, in *Tilson v. Sch. Dist. of Philadelphia*,[47] the plaintiff claimed that the school's failure to create effective policies regarding employment of personnel, investigation of suspected child abuse, and prevention of child abuse violated the plaintiff's constitutional rights. The plaintiff was a four-year-old student who was allegedly molested by a substitute teacher in the lavatory. The substitute teacher was later convicted of several counts of child rape and child sexual assault and sent to prison. However, at the time that the teacher was hired, a background check revealed that the teacher had only been previously arrested for a drug offense, but never convicted. State law and school board policies prohibited the school from using the arrest as a basis for refusing to hire an applicant. Because of these laws, and the fact that the arrest did not establish that the substitute teacher lacked a good moral character, the court ruled that the plaintiff could not prove a deprivation of constitutional rights based on the hiring of the substitute.

By contrast, the court in *Doe v. Estes*[48] found that the school district's failure to have a policy was fatal. A student was allegedly sexually molested by a teacher. The court framed the issue as to whether the school district maintained a policy or custom that reflected a deliberate indifference to the plaintiff's constitutional rights. The court found that prior to the arrest of the accused teacher, the school district did not have any policy regarding the reporting of suspected incidents of sexual abuse of students, had not trained its employees in recognizing signs of abuse, and had not given its staff guidelines for dealing with suspicions of abuse. Because the danger of students being sexually abused at school was so obvious, the court ruled the absence of such a policy was enough to send the liability question to a jury for final consideration.

The above discussion highlights the importance of implementing policies, procedures, and training for public employees in how to respond to violence in the workplace. Failure to do so can form the basis for common law negligence or constitutional deprivation claims by both coworkers and third parties who might be injured by a violent employee.

▎ First Amendment Speech Restrictions

While public employers have a legal obligation to provide a safe working environment for employees that is free from violence, attempts to do so must be tempered with a realization that certain employee actions are oftentimes protected under federal and state constitutions. Tensions with such federal and state protections typically arise in the context of a public employer disciplining or discharging an employee for having made violent or threatening remarks.

Thus, suits by public employees alleging that they have been denied their constitutional free speech rights by their employer typically are brought pursuant to Section 1983 (discussed earlier in this chapter). Everything an employee says is not subject to First Amendment protection. Rather, only speech involving a matter of public concern may be subject to protection. It is not a given that all speech involving matters of public concern will be protected, however, because in some instances a public employer may be able to show that the speech is so disruptive that it will interfere with the operations of the business. Where the employer's interests in promoting a safe and efficient workplace outweigh the employee's free speech rights, the speech will not be protected.

In *Connick v. Myers*,[49] the U.S. Supreme Court made clear that not all speech uttered by a public employee is protected. Only that speech which addresses matters of public concern will find protection: "[w]hen employee expression cannot fairly be considered as relating to any matter of political, social, or other concern to the community, government officials should enjoy wide latitude in managing their offices, without intrusive oversight by the judiciary in the name of the First Amendment."[50] In order to determine whether an employee statement addresses a matter of public concern, the inquiry should consider the "content, form, and context of the given statement."[51] Examples of speech that involve a matter of public concern include allegations of fraud and waste,[52] corruption,[53] and unsafe working conditions.[54] By the same token, speech relating to political matters has also been found to be a matter of public concern.[55] By contrast, speech addressing purely private "grievances" against a public employer does not involve a matter of public concern.[56]

The U.S. Supreme Court recently clarified the analysis used to determine whether a public employer can discipline an employee for speech that is intimately related to a public employee's job duties. In *Garcetti v. Ceballos*,[57] a supervising attorney, who worked for a district attorney's office, sued his employer, claiming that his First Amendment rights were violated after he was reassigned. As part of his regular job duties, the attorney was responsible for reviewing cases for legal sufficiency, which were pending trial. In one such case, the attorney wrote several memos to his supervisors, recommending that a criminal complaint be dropped because of improprieties connected with how a search warrant had been obtained.

The Supreme Court ruled that the attorney's memos were not protected, because he wrote them as part of his normal job duties. The Court went on to distinguish this case from others where a public employee might complain to the media about the wisdom of spending public funds on certain projects, speech in which any other citizen might engage. By contrast, *Garcetti* involved an attorney whose speech *was* his job. The Court's primary concern appeared to be the prospect of becoming entangled in multiple disputes between public employers and their employees about how a particular job should be performed.[58] As a result, the Court majority concluded that the attorney's "speech" did not enjoy First Amendment protection.

Even when an employee's speech involves a matter of public concern, the speech can still lose its protection due to the form in which it has been uttered. In terms of workplace violence, employers often seek to discipline employees who have used speech laced with profanity, personal insults, or threats. The protected nature of the speech will oftentimes depend on the particular circumstances involved in each case. For example, a lower federal court found that a firefighter's profane reference to his superiors in front of coworkers was not found constitutionally protected.[59] By contrast, an off-duty police officer could not be disciplined for using profanity in referring to the police chief when talking with another officer.[60]

In terms of threats of bodily harm, courts uniformly have ruled that such speech is unprotected. For example, a Louisiana court found that an employer had sufficient cause to discipline a fire captain who challenged his chief to a physical confrontation in order to settle an employment dispute.[61] In another example, a municipality was found to have properly discharged a police officer who invited a city manager to "take a swing" at him so that he could retaliate.[62]

An example in which the interests of the public employer were found *not* to outweigh the free speech interests of an employee is *Rankin v. McPherson.*[63] There, a sharply divided Court held that a sheriff's department clerical employee was protected by the First Amendment when she was terminated for remarking, "if they go for [President Reagan] again, I hope they get him." Rejecting the position of the dissenters "that no law enforcement agency is required by the First Amendment to permit one of its employees to ride with the cops and cheer for the robbers" (Scalia, J, dissenting), Justice Marshall concluded that the comment did not disturb the "effective functioning of the public employer's enterprise." Moreover, unlike the other cases discussed, the employee's remarks did not threaten the safety of anyone in the workplace nor, it could be argued, did they genuinely threaten the safety of the president. In the post 9/11 era, it is entirely possible that the outcome of this case would be different. Nowadays, there is a much lower threshold and tolerance for the kind of speech that was at issue in *Rankin*.

As the above cases demonstrate, determining whether an employee's threatening speech is protected will depend on the particular circumstances of each case. Clearly, the context in which a statement is made will play a critical role in determining whether the employee has, in fact, uttered a "threat." The more flagrant the speech, the more likely it will not be protected by the First Amendment.

If the antibullying proponents begin to make legislative headway, employees may find their First Amendment protections at odds with the efforts of those seeking to ensure that workers are not subjected to an abusive work environment. Since 2003, thirteen states have considered legislation that would outlaw bullying behavior in the workplace. To date, no state has passed antibullying legislation, although similar legislation has been adopted in Europe, Australia, and Quebec. The states that have most recently considered such legislation include: Connecticut (2008 legislative session), New York (2008 legislative session), and Vermont (2008 legislative session). Other states include: California, Hawaii, Kansas, Massachusetts, Missouri, Montana, New Jersey, Oklahoma, Oregon, and Washington. The legislation, which is based on the model "Healthy Workplace

Bill," created by the Workplace Bullying Institute, would make both verbal and nonverbal bullying behaviors unlawful.

▍ Constitutional Association Restrictions

At times, a public employer may have concerns regarding the potential for violence created by an employee's association with various groups or individuals. However, the right of association is another one of the freedoms protected by the First Amendment. When a public employer can demonstrate that the employee's association will likely compromise workplace safety, courts have upheld the dismissal of the employee based on his or her association with a suspect organization or individual.

For example, in *Weicherding v. Riegel*,[64] a state prison guard openly broadcast his affiliation with the Ku Klux Klan (KKK) to coworkers and inmates. After determining that the employee's association with the KKK put workplace safety at risk, due to the racial makeup of the prison inmate population, the correctional facility discharged the employee. The U.S. Court of Appeals for the Seventh Circuit upheld the discharge, finding that the prison's interest in avoiding racial violence outweighed the prison guard's interest in associating with the KKK.[65]

By contrast, the New York Court of Appeals invalidated a state prohibition on prison guards belonging to the KKK. In *Curle v. Ward*,[66] the court affirmed the reinstatement of a correctional officer who had been discharged because of his membership with the KKK, primarily because prison officials had failed to demonstrate any realistic threat of racial violence arising from the officer's interaction with prison inmates. Instead, the prison officials relied only on news articles and commentary about the KKK's social beliefs as a justification for barring correctional officers from belonging to the group.

In an unusual mixed free speech-association case, the U.S. Court of Appeals for the Second Circuit upheld the dismissal of a high school teacher who was an avowed member of the North American Man/Boy Love Association (NAMBLA). In *Melzer v. Bd. of Educ. of City Sch. Dist. of New York*,[67] the plaintiff had been a member of NAMBLA since 1979, but was never accused of engaging in any illegal or inappropriate acts with children. In the early 1990s, the plaintiff's affiliation became publicly known and a widespread debate ensued regarding whether the plaintiff should continue to be employed by the school. Many parents threatened to remove their children from the school where the plaintiff taught. The Second Circuit concluded that even assuming the plaintiff's beliefs were protected by the First Amendment, the school district's interest in avoiding further disruption of the educational process justified his discharge. In particular, the court noted that the plaintiff himself admitted that he might find it difficult reporting an incident of child molestation by another adult if he was called upon to do so.

▌ Constitutional Due Process Requirements

In 1985, the U.S. Supreme Court in *Cleveland Board of Education v. Loudermill*,[68] held that a public employee who may only be dismissed "for cause" is entitled to a hearing *prior* to termination, as well as a *post-termination* hearing. The Court in *Loudermill* held that if a public employee has a "property interest" in his or her position, the employee is entitled to a pretermination hearing in order to help satisfy the basic requirements of the Due Process Clause of the U.S. Constitution. While such a pretermination hearing does not necessarily have to be formal or elaborate, the hearing does need to provide the employee with: (1) proper notice of the charges; and (2) an opportunity to respond. The pretermination hearing is designed as an initial check against mistaken decisions and a method to determine whether there are reasonable grounds to support the employer's action. The Court looked to the requisite *post-termination* hearing to more fully provide the employee an opportunity to be heard, to be represented by counsel, and to examine and cross-examine witnesses.

The Court in *Loudermill* recognized that procedural due process is a flexible concept, and that there is no one set of rules governing the substance of a pretermination hearing. So long as the employer gives the employee some type of information about what the charges against him or her are, and a hearing is held giving the employee an opportunity to respond to the charges where there is a dispute, courts find in most instances that due process is met.[69] However, courts have also held that contemporaneous notice during a pretermination procedure is *not* adequate to satisfy procedural due process.[70]

Since *Loudermill*, courts have confronted the issue of what type of hearing is necessary when the employee is not terminated, but is suspended with or without pay. The majority of courts have found that no constitutionally protected property interest is implicated if a public employee continues to receive full pay and benefits during the time of his or her suspension.[71] However, there is clearly a deprivation of a property interest when a public employee is suspended *without* pay.

In light of the above principles, public employers must be careful when deciding to dismiss, or suspend without pay, a public employee who is suspected of violent behavior or misconduct in the workplace. Assuming the employee enjoys a "property interest" in his or her job, based on a "cause" standard found in some type of statute, handbook, or collective bargaining agreement, the employee is entitled to notice and an opportunity to be heard before the employee's job is terminated. In most nonemergency cases, such notice must be given before the actual "pretermination" hearing.

The Supreme Court somewhat relaxed this requirement in *Gilbert v. Homar*.[72] In *Gilbert*, the Court held that a Pennsylvania state institution did not violate the Constitutional due process rights of a university police officer when it immediately suspended him without pay upon learning he had been charged with a drug felony. Homar was arrested by the state police in a drug raid while off duty.

That same day, the police filed a criminal complaint against him, charging him with felonious activities. The police also notified a university representative, who immediately suspended Homar without pay "effective immediately" pending an investigation into the criminal charges filed against him.

The criminal charges against Homar were dropped within a week of the incident. Seventeen days later, the university met with Homar to give him an opportunity to relay his side of the story. After the hearing, the university demoted Homar to the position of groundskeeper, effective the next day.

Homar filed suit claiming, among other charges, that the university had violated his due process rights by suspending him without pay prior to providing him with notice and an opportunity to be heard. Citing *Loudermill*, Homar contended that the university should have suspended him *with pay* until he was given the opportunity to be heard. Surprisingly, a unanimous Supreme Court disagreed.

The Court stressed that due process is flexible and "calls for such procedural protections as the particular situation demands." Citing its previous decision in *Mathews v. Eldridge*,[73] the Court stated that to determine what process is due a public employee before adverse action is taken, three factors are balanced: (1) the private interests of the employee affected by the official action; (2) the risk of an erroneous deprivation of the employee's interests through the procedures used and the probable value, if any, of additional or substitute procedural safeguard; and (3) the government's interests.

Looking at the first factor, the Court concluded that while the loss of a regular paycheck is a significant interest of the employee, here it was moderated by the *brief length of loss* and the *lack of finality of the deprivation*. Regarding the second factor, the Court stated that the risk of an erroneous decision is minimized where, as in the instant matter, a responsible third party has made the decision to arrest the employee and file formal criminal charges against him. The Court emphasized that the purpose of a *Loudermill* hearing is to ensure reasonable grounds to support the employer's action, and that the unbiased actions of an independent third party to arrest and charge the employee at issue assures such reason.

Addressing the third factor, the Court found that the state has a significant interest in immediately suspending employees who "occupy positions of great public trust and high public visibility, such as police officers, when felony charges are filed against them." The Court did remand the case to determine whether Homar's due process rights were violated by his not receiving a prompt hearing once the charges were dropped.

Granting a prediscipline hearing is generally a simple matter. Therefore, employers should recognize that suspending a "tenured" employee without pay prior to a *Loudermill* hearing has inherent risks, and an employer should rely on *Gilbert* to justify taking action without a prediscipline hearing only in the most extreme circumstances (e.g., where the safety of employees or third parties is at risk). Even then, a short hearing with the "accused," should be held as soon as possible, followed by a more comprehensive due process hearing later on.

▌ Conclusion

As the above discussion demonstrates, public employers must continually balance their legal obligation to provide a safe workplace against the statutory and constitutional rights of public employees. Failure to strike this balance can lead to significant monetary awards, fines, and penalties on both sides of the equation. In terms of an employee's constitutional rights, public employers must be especially careful in light of the potential award of attorneys' fees available under 42 U.S.C. § 1988.[74] And, when one considers the ever increasing awareness of workplace violence by state regulatory agencies, public employers now more than ever need to approach the issue of workplace safety from both a legal and a practical perspective.

Notes

1. See National Census of Fatal Occupational Injuries in 2005, U.S. Bureau of Labor Statistics (Aug. 10, 2006) (available at http://www.bls.gov/news.release/cfoi.nr0.htm).

2. See Brock v. Chicago Zoological Society, 820 F.2d 909 (7th Cir. 1987).

3. According to the federal OSHA, these states include Alaska, Arizona, California, Hawaii, Indiana, Iowa, Kentucky, Maryland, Michigan, Minnesota, Nevada, New Mexico, North Carolina, Oregon, South Carolina, Tennessee, Utah, Vermont, Virginia, Washington, and Wyoming. See 29 C.F.R. Part 1952.

4. These states include Connecticut, New Hampshire, New Jersey, New York, Rhode Island, West Virginia, and Wisconsin.

5. Illinois is one state that has done this, without adopting its own comprehensive workplace safety regulatory scheme.

6. See Fields Corp. v. State Dept. of Labor & Indus., 120 Wash. App. 2064 (Wash. App. Ct. 2004); Midwest Carbide Corp. v. Occupational Safety & Health Review Commission, 353 N.W.2d 399 (Iowa 1984).

7. National Realty & Construction Co. v. OSHRC, 489 F.2d 1257 (D.C. Cir. 1973).

8. Brennan v. OSHRC, 494 F.2d 460 (8th Cir. 1974).

9. In 1992, OSHA's director of enforcement programs wrote a letter to an inquiring employer regarding an employer's obligations to prevent workplace violence. OSHA prominently displays this letter on its Web page. See http://www.osha.gov/SLTC/workplaceviolence/ standards .html.

10. These and other workplace violence-related publications are posted on the OSHA Web site at http://www.osha.gov/SLTC/workplaceviolence/ evaluation.html.

11. See, e.g., Violence on the Job, National Institute for Occupational Safety and Health No. 2004-100d (2004) (discusses measures for identifying risk factors for violence in the workplace and recommends steps to reduce opportunities for such violence).

12. 17 O.S.H. Cases (BNA) 1337 (1995).

13. But see West v. Dept. of Commerce, 601 N.W.2d 307 (Wis. Ct. App. 1999) (potential for violent encounters by campus police officers with criminal perpetrators not enough to qualify as a "recognized hazard" within Wisconsin's "general duty" clause).

14. See http://www.osha.gov/fso/osp/oshspa/grassroots_worker_pro tection99/ index.html#VIII.

15. See Crete v. City of Lowell, 418 F.3d 54, 60 (1st Cir. 2005).

16. 652 N.W.2d 49 (Iowa 2002).

17. Cases cited by the Iowa Supreme Court supporting this conclusion include Doe v. Estes, 926 F. Supp. 979 (D. Nev. 1996) and Willis v. Dade County Sch. Bd., 411 So. 2d 245 (Fla. Dist. Ct. App. 1982).

18. See Crete, supra note 15, at 65 (quotation marks and citations omitted).

19. 664 N.E.2d 668 (Ill. App. Ct. 1996).

20. See also Davis v. DeKalb County Sch. Dist., 996 F. Supp. 1478 (N.D. Ga. 1998); C.B. v. Bobo, 659 So. 2d 98 (Ala. 1995); Willoughby v. Lehrbass, 388 N.W.2d 688 (Mich. Ct. App. 1986); Doe v. Park Ctr. High Sch., 592 N.W.2d 131 (Minn. Ct. App. 1999).

21. 678 N.E.2d 660 (Ill. Ct. App. 1997).

22. Depending on the circumstances, certain provisions of federal and state fair credit reporting acts may impact how a public employer goes about conducting a background and/or credit report on an applicant for employment. See Fair Credit Reporting Act, 15 U.S.C. § 1681 et seq. Also, public employers should consider the relevance, if any, of other state and federal laws that may limit the type of information that may be used in the hiring process. See, e.g., Fla. Stat. Ann. § 112.011; 775 Ill. Comp. Stat. 5/2-103 Minn. Stat. Ann. § 326.336.

23. 929 P.2d 582 (Cal. 1997).

24. See Passmore v. Multi-Management Servs., 810 N.E.2d 1022 (Ind. 2004) (recognizing a claim for making a knowing or conscious misrepresentation); Davis v. Bd. of County Commissioners of Dona Ana County, 987 P.2d 1172 (N.M. App. 1999) (recognizing a claim for a negligent misrepresentation).

25. See Neptuno Treuhand-Und Verwaltungsgesellschaft MBH v. Arbor, 295 Ill. App. 3d 567 (1998) (claim was not brought by a third party but by the employer who relied on the job reference).

26. 987 P.2d 1172 (N.M. App. 1999).

27. See Bowman v. Parma Bd. of Educ., 542 N.E.2d 663 (Ohio Ct. App. 1988).

28. See, e.g., Conn. Gen. Stat. § 31-128f (prior approval required); 820 Ill. Comp. Stat. 40/7 (notice required); Mich. Comp. Laws § 423.506 (notice required).

29. See 745 Ill. Comp. Stat. 46/1 et seq.

30. See, e.g., Alaska Stat. § 09.65.160; Colo. Rev. Stat. §§ 8-2-110 to 8-2-111.5; Fla. Stat. § 768.095; N.M. Stat. § 50-12-1; S.D. Codified Laws Ann. § 60-4-12.

31. Lawson v. City of Chicago, 662 N.E.2d 1277, 1386 (Ill. App. Ct. 1996).

32. 2005 U.S. Dist. LEXIS 31180 (N.D. Ill. Nov. 30, 2005).

33. Id. at *13-14.

34. 110 Cal. App. 4th 508 (Cal. Ct. App. 2003).

35. 887 So. 2d 39 (La. Ct. App. 2004).

36. See Monell v. Dept. of Soc. Servs., 436 U.S. 658 (1978).

37. See City of Canton v. Harris, 489 U.S. 378 (1989).

38. See Harrell v. Cook, 169 F.3d 428 (7th Cir. 1999).

39. See DeShaney v. Winnebago County Dept. of Soc. Servs., 489 U.S. 189 (1989) ("a State's failure to protect an individual against private violence simply does not constitute a violation of the Due Process Clause"); Banks v. Bd. of Educ. of City of Chicago, 1999 WL 1129602 (N.D. Ill. 1999) (complaint dismissed for failure to state a cause of action, where simply alleging a physical assault did not rise to the level of a constitutional violation).

40. 520 U.S. 397 (1997).

41. 520 U.S. at 411.

42. See Griffin v. City of Opa-Locka, 261 F.3d 1295, 1313–14 (11th Cir. 2001).

43. Id. at 1312.

44. Id. at 1312 n.21.

45. Knicrumah v. Albany City Sch. Dist., 241 F. Supp. 2d 199 (N.D.N.Y. 2003).

46. Id. at 208.

47. 1990 WL 98932 (E.D. Pa. 1990), aff'd, 932 F.2d 961 (3d Cir. 1991).

48. 926 F. Supp. 979 (D. Nev. 1996).

49. 461 U.S. 138 (1983).

50. Id. at 146.

51. Id. at 147–48.

52. See, e.g., Johnson v. Multnomah County, 48 F.3d 420 (9th Cir. 1995) (finding allegations of mismanagement and misuse of public funds addressed a matter of public concern).

53. See, e.g., O'Donnell v. Yanchulis, 875 F.2d 1059, 1061 (3d Cir. 1989) (an employee's allegation that the police chief instructed police officers not to issue tickets to certain individuals addressed a matter of public concern).

54. See, e.g., Finch v. City of Mt. Vernon, 877 F.2d 1497 (11th Cir. 1989) (police chief's speech to city officials conveying his conclusion that it would be unsafe to block off a street for a city celebration addressed a matter of public concern).

55. See, e.g., Bieluch v. Sullivan, 999 F.3d 666 (2d Cir. 1993) (speech addressing a public employer's pressure on its employees to work for particular political candidates involved a matter of "utmost public concern").

56. See, e.g., Gaj v. United States Postal Serv., 800 F.2d 64 (3d Cir. 1986) (complaints about noise level were made only to express dissatisfaction with the employee's own working conditions, not to protect the interests of fellow coworkers).

57. 126 S. Ct. 1951 (2006).

58. *Cf.* Piggee v. Carl Sandburg College, 464 F.3d 667 (7th Cir. 2006) (college cosmetology instructor's in-class distribution of pamphlet entitled "Sin City" to a student who was perceived to be gay was not protected by the First Amendment).

59. See Marshall v. City of Atlanta, 614 F. Supp. 581 (N.D. Ga. 1984), *aff'd*, 770 F.2d 174 (11th Cir. 1985).

60. Waters v. Chaffin, 684 F.2d 833 (11th Cir. 1982).

61. See Bouterie v. Dept. of Fire, 410 So. 2d 340 (La. Ct. App. 1982).

62. See McMurphy v. City of Flushing, 802 F.2d 191 (6th Cir. 1986).

63. 483 U.S. 378 (1987).

64. 160 F.3d 1139 (7th Cir. 1998).

65. *Cf.* McMullen v. Carson, 754 F.2d 936 (11th Cir. 1985) (sheriff's department had sufficient justification to discharge clerical employee who openly disclosed to the media that he actively recruited on behalf of organization committed to violent, criminal, and racist conduct).

66. 399 N.Y.S.2d 308 (N.Y. App. Div. 1977). Affirmed by court in Curle v. Ward, 389 N.E.2d 1070 (N.Y. 1979).

67. 336 F.3d 185 (2d Cir. 2003).

68. 470 U.S. 532 (1985).

69. Moore v. Bd. of Educ., 134 F.3d 781 (6th Cir. 1997) (finding that a pretermination hearing satisfied teacher's due process rights with respect to defendant's decision not to renew teacher's contract; teacher was given notice and opportunity to be heard even though superintendent had a dual role as both investigator and presiding officer at the hearing); DeMarco v. Cuyahoga County Dept. of Human Servs., 12 F. Supp. 2d 715 (N.D. Ohio 1998) (holding that employee had no right to knowledge of specific grounds on which adverse action was taken and general notice of prediscipline hearing was enough to satisfy the requirements set forth in Loudermill).

70. Staples v. City of Milwaukee, 142 F.3d 383 (7th Cir. 1988); Morton v. Beyer, 822 F.2d 364 (3d Cir. 1987).

71. Harris v. Bd. of Educ., 105 F.3d 591, 596 (11th Cir. 1997) ("[A] public official has a constitutionally protected property interest only in the economic benefits of his position. . . .").

72. 520 U.S. 924 (1997).

73. 424 U.S. 319 (1976).

74. *Cf.* City of Riverside v. Rivera, 477 U.S. 561 (1986) (plaintiff awarded $245,000 in attorneys' fees based on $33,000 verdict).

CHAPTER 7

Strategies for Preventing Workplace Violence

Gary S. Cohen, Brigitte Duffy, Andrew L. Eisenberg, William R. Heffernan, and Jonathan Moll

WHILE THE PUBLIC SECTOR comprises only 16 percent of the total U.S. workforce, employees of federal, state, and local governments account for 37 percent of the victims of violence.[1] Thus public sector employers face unique challenges in seeking to ensure the health and safety of their employees and avoiding potential liability arising from violence in the workplace.

Can workplace violence be prevented? While workplace violence, like all other forms of violence, is an unfortunate fact of life, there are steps that employers can take to try to mitigate its occurrence. This chapter will discuss a variety of workplace violence mitigation strategies which fall into three general categories: (1) the implementation of policies and practices that can help an employer identify applicants and employees who may be prone to violent behavior and thus present a potential risk of workplace violence; (2) the use of threat assessment teams, security/workplace violence assessment, and employee training to enable an employer to respond more effectively to potentially violent situations; and (3) the establishment of employee assistance programs and conflict/alternative dispute resolution procedures to avoid and defuse violent situations.

▌ Identifying Potentially Violent Employees: Collecting Background Information

One of the most obvious steps employers can take to prevent violence in a workplace is to avoid hiring potentially violent employees by identifying them during the hiring process. In order to do this, an employer must be able to obtain useful information about a job applicant, which can sometimes be done through the application and interview processes by checking job references and conducting pre-hire background checks. Public sector employers, however, must pay close attention to state and federal laws that limit both the type of information employers may obtain about applicants and an employer's use of such information. Improper hiring procedures may trigger violations of laws such as the Americans with Disabilities Act (ADA), Title VII of the Civil Rights Act of 1964 (Title VII), and a myriad of state and local statutes. Therefore, public employers must strike a balance between obtaining and using helpful personal information about job applicants and observing the many federal and state laws that regulate this area.

The Application Process

Through the initial employment application process, employers may be able to obtain important information about potential employees.

A rigorous application process provides an opportune time to eliminate potentially violent individuals from consideration. Thus, employers should carefully review all material submitted by applicants and note any deficiencies or omissions in the employment application.[2]

For example, incomplete work histories (unexplained time gaps) or frequent changes in employment can indicate a problematic applicant.[3] The application form therefore should require potential employees to certify that the information they are providing is complete and accurate. Additionally, applicants should be asked to provide releases so that information can be readily obtained from former employers. For federal employers, job applicants should be asked to complete a Declaration for Federal Employment (OF-306) form, which contains a provision allowing the release of information from employers, schools, law enforcement agencies, and other individuals to the federal government for the purpose of investigating the applicant's ability and fitness for employment.

The Interview Process

The interview process also can provide sometimes crucial insights into a job applicant's propensity for violent behavior. Before interviewing applicants, however, employers should tailor their questions to the actual duties and responsibilities required for the position and ensure that questions comply with all applicable federal and state laws.

During the job interview, employers should observe the applicant's demeanor, emotional state, level of cooperation, truthfulness, physical appearance, body language, and ability to answer questions fully, noting behavioral traits which suggest potential problems.[4] The Equal Employment Opportunity Commission's (EEOC) *ADA Enforcement Guidance: Pre-employment Disability-Related Questions and Medical Examinations* (*ADA Guidance*) is a helpful guide to employers about how to ask questions that comply with ADA requirements.[5]

Checking References

Checking references is one of the most challenging tasks for employers but also can be one of the more effective ways to identify potentially violent employees. Unfortunately, former employers are increasingly hesitant to provide truly substantive information about a former employee for fear of being sued for defamation for having made negative statements. To facilitate this process, employers should ask job applicants to sign a written release in order to encourage employers to be less reticent about providing information on former employees to prospective employers. Nonetheless, it is imperative to try to check applicant references thoroughly as they can provide important information about an applicant's work habits, character, demeanor, and history of violence. Employers should check all references supplied by an applicant and contact former employers. In so doing, employers can show that they exercised due diligence prior to extending any offer of employment. Approaching each reference with specific questions can be helpful.

Some states facilitate reference checks by shielding from lawsuits employers who provide job-related information about their former employees.[6] For instance, Florida permits employers to provide information about former or current employees to prospective employers upon request of the prospective employer and grants former employers civil immunity for disclosing such information as long as the former employer did not knowingly provide information that is false or violates the applicant's civil rights.[7] Nevada requires former employers to provide to the employee one written, truthful statement about an employee's service to the employer and/or the reason for leaving the employer's services. This statement, however, must only be issued after a demand from the employee and after the employee has left the employer's services and is only required for employees who have worked more than sixty days for the employer.[8]

Most states also prohibit "blacklisting" of former employees. Blacklisting statutes typically prevent employers from "preparing, using, or circulating a list of persons designated for special avoidance, antagonism, or enmity."[9] Mississippi and Kentucky are the only states that restrict the blacklisting statutes to specific industries.[10]

Conducting Background Checks

Background checks can be an effective means of identifying potentially problematical or violent applicants, thus avoiding liability for negligent hiring or negligent retention. Most states have enacted legislation requiring background checks for public service workers in certain occupations, such as police officers, firefighters, security guards, teachers, and workers who regularly come in contact with vulnerable populations such as children, the elderly, or the infirm. Public employers, however, must follow permissible procedures for obtaining background information. Inappropriately acquiring or using such information may infringe upon an applicant's privacy rights or violate federal and state fair credit reporting acts and other legislation. Therefore, when performing a background check, all inquiries should be relevant to a job applicant's ability to perform the required job duties.

Criminal Background Checks

Criminal background checks can provide a wealth of information and are invaluable in preventing workplace violence. Criminal background checks are especially important when hiring for supervisory positions, positions requiring the use of weapons, positions with access to valuable assets, or positions requiring contact with children, the elderly, or other vulnerable persons. Some federal and state laws require criminal background checks before applicants may work in certain positions. For instance, most states now have laws requiring child-care administrators, teachers, and school personnel to undergo criminal history checks as a condition of employment.[11] Additionally, the Federal Aviation and Transportation Security Act requires applicants and employees to undergo a criminal history check for most airport and airline jobs.[12]

Although most states provide public access to criminal records, they also tend to restrict the type of information employers may request or use about an applicant's arrest or conviction records. Some state laws allow employers to inquire about prior convictions if they are job-related but prohibit questions about prior arrests that have either been expunged from the record or have not led to a conviction. For instance, California restricts employers from requesting or using conviction records related to a marijuana conviction that is over two years old.[13] Florida and Minnesota do not permit state employers to disqualify applicants solely on the basis of a prior conviction, and Minnesota restricts public employers from requesting records of any arrest that did not lead to the employee's conviction.[14] Hawaii restricts employer inquires about convictions to those that substantially relate, or bear a reasonable relation, to the required job duties.[15] New York and Wisconsin permit inquiries into all convictions but prohibit the use of convictions unless there is a substantial relationship between the conviction and the employee's job.[16] Those few states that do not restrict employment-related use of criminal records prohibit discrimination based on an applicant's criminal history, particularly in public employment.[17]

According to the EEOC, the use of conviction and arrest records may disproportionately discriminate against some races or ethnic groups and may be prohibited under federal law. The EEOC has stated that while requiring an applicant to provide arrest and conviction information does not automatically violate Title VII, a "blanket" policy against hiring individuals with arrest or conviction records will likely violate Title VII because "such policies often disproportionately exclude members of certain racial or ethnic groups."[18] Therefore, the EEOC recommends that employers include a disclaimer on applications which states that disclosing criminal information will not automatically result in disqualification from consideration for a position. Before excluding an applicant from a particular position because of his or her criminal history, employers should consider the nature of the offense, the time since the conviction or completion date of sentence, and the nature of the job sought.[19]

Checking Military Records

Checking a job applicant's military record may provide information about an applicant's current military status, discharge record, or whether he or she had any disciplinary problems while in the military. Military personnel records may contain salient information such as disciplinary actions, administrative remarks, and performance evaluations. They also may reveal whether an applicant has been truthful in answering questions on an application about his or her military experience.

Unfortunately, the military service records of currently enlisted personnel are confidential under the federal Privacy Act of 1974 and are released under limited circumstances.[20] An employer may obtain limited information from military records through the federal Freedom of Information Act. Under this act, the military may release an applicant's name, rank, salary, duty assignments, awards, and duty status without the applicant's consent.[21] In addition, discharged veterans can expressly authorize employers to obtain military personnel records from the National Personnel Records Center, Military Personnel Records (NPRC-MPR) facility in St. Louis, Missouri, by completing the Standard Form SF-180.[22] It may, however, take many months before the NPRC-MPR can provide the requested records.

Credit Checks and Complying with the Fair Credit Reporting Act

When an employer uses a third party to check the references, educational history, driving record, criminal history, or credit history of an applicant or current employee, the employer is generally engaging in conduct governed by the federal Fair Credit Reporting Act (FCRA) and the regulations issued under the act. The requirements of FCRA do not apply when the employer does not engage the services of a third party to conduct the background check.

The FCRA regulates the collection and use of certain background information about individuals when the information is received from a consumer reporting agency. A consumer reporting agency is any individual or business that is paid a fee to collect information about an individual for a third party. While this type of background check is often an important and valuable screening tool, employers must be cognizant of and comply with the legal requirements governing the collection of such information.

Employers must obtain written authorization before requesting a credit report for an applicant or employee.[23] The FCRA defines a consumer report, among other things, as any communication that bears on an individual's credit worthiness, credit standing, credit capacity, character, general reputation, personal characteristics, or mode of living in establishing eligibility for, among other things, employment purposes. Employers must provide the applicant with a document, consisting solely of a written disclosure, which clearly and conspicuously states that the employer may obtain the applicant's consumer report. Employers must certify to the credit reporting agency that the employer will only use the consumer report for permissible employment purposes and will not violate any federal or state equal opportunity laws or regulations. An employer also must certify that it will provide the applicant with a copy of the report and a summary of the applicant's rights if the employer takes any adverse action based in part on information from the report. Furthermore, employers may not obtain consumer reports containing medical information without the applicant's specific prior consent. If an employer wishes to receive any medical information from the report, the applicant must explicitly consent to the release of the medical information in addition to granting permission to the employer to obtain the consumer report.[24]

The credit reporting laws of most states are similar to the restrictions included in the FCRA. While the laws tend to contain similar authorization and disclosure requirements, with some providing time frames for obtaining reports and notifying applicants, employers should always verify that their process complies with *both* federal and state requirements. The FCRA also permits employers to acquire or request that an "investigative consumer credit report" be prepared, even for positions that the individual has not specifically applied for, which can provide important information about an applicant's character and abilities.[25]

Checking Education Background

Many positions require applicants to have certain education degrees. Since applicants can easily fabricate or embellish their educational background and/or qualifications, employers should confirm that they have completed the educational levels and degrees listed on their applications. Employers should verify the schools or colleges attended, establish the dates of attendance, confirm that the applicant graduated and verify the degree received. Employers should not accept unofficial transcripts or copies of documents that purport to be official transcripts. Information that cannot be confirmed or is inaccurate should be grounds for suspicion and closer inquiry.

There are, however, restrictions on the type of information employers can obtain. The Family Educational Right to Privacy Act and the regulations promulgated thereunder generally prohibit schools that receive federal funds from releasing educational records, including transcripts, recommendations, discipline records, and financial information, to any agency or organization without written authorization from the student or parent.[26] However, unless a student has provided written notice to the contrary, schools may release "directory information" such as a person's name, address, date, and place of birth, major field of study, degrees and awards received, dates of attendance, and activities. Employers also should check the accreditation of the institutions attended, as a number of Internet and mail-order colleges allow consumers to purchase degrees without completing any substantive coursework.[27] In addition, numerous "degree mills" issue academic degrees which purport to be degrees issued from legitimate institutions.

Driving Records

Driving records provide comprehensive data about an individual's history of driving violations and suspensions as well as demographic information. This information can be useful since an applicant's history of driving violations may indicate an aggressive personality. However, the Federal Driver's Privacy Protection Act (DPPA) restricts the disclosure and use of certain information contained in driving records for employment purposes.[28]

Employers may only use an applicant or employee's driving record in the normal course of business "to verify the accuracy of personal information submitted by the individual" and "to obtain the correct information, but only for the purposes of preventing fraud by . . . the individual."[29] An employer also may use a driving record to obtain or verify information relating to a holder of a commercial driver's license.[30] Employers may request a driving record that contains nonpersonal information, such as information about an applicant's license class, convictions, accidents, suspensions, and revocations without written authorization from the applicant.[31] Moreover, some state laws, such as the California Vehicle and Public Utility Codes and the Virginia Mandatory and Voluntary Driving Record Monitoring Programs, require certain public employers to check and monitor the driving records of transportation employees.[32]

Searching the Internet

Increasingly both private and public sector employers are conducting Internet searches on potential applicants using the Internet to search sites such as MySpace and Facebook. Conducting such searches can provide valuable information about applicants that they might not list on their application or resume. In particular, employers might uncover information that exposes an applicant's violent tendencies. Public employers, however, should be cautious in accessing and using such information. First, the information obtained from online sources may not be accurate. Second, an applicant's postings, such as Internet blogs, postings, or information posted on social sites may be protected speech under the First Amendment or may be protected under other state or federal statutes. Employers inadvertently may view information that applicants would not disclose during the regular application process, such as disabilities or sexual orientation and could face liability if they consider such information during the employment process.

Identifying Potentially Violent Employees: Using Job Tests

Job tests also can be a useful source of information in identifying potentially violent employees. However, like background checks, the use of testing also is subject to federal and state restrictions.

Medical and Personality Tests

Despite the potential benefits of medical, psychological, and personality tests, there are federal and state laws regulating the use of such tests. Improper use may expose an employer to liability when improperly used.

The ADA prohibits any "medical" testing prior to a conditional offer of employment and prohibits certain preemployment inquiries about an applicant's health or disability. The EEOC defines a medical examination as "a procedure or test that seeks information about an individual's physical or mental impairments or health."[33] While the ADA prohibits preemployment medical testing, a post-offer medical examination can include a complete and detailed medical history.[34] When an employer imposes a post-offer medical examination requirement, it must impose that requirement on all offerees in the same job category. The examination itself need not be limited, but a revocation of a conditional job offer may only be made for a job-related reason and consistent with business necessity. The employer also must demonstrate that there is no reasonable accommodation that would permit the individual to perform the essential functions of the job.

A psychological test may or may not qualify as a medical examination under the ADA.[35] The determination depends upon whether the test is intended to, or actually does, measure medical or biological qualities. Even if a psychological test does not fall within the restrictions of the ADA, an employer should assess whether the test is truly an adequate predictor of potential violence as the factors that lead to violence may be beyond the scope of the examination.[36]

Employers should analyze whether a test disproportionately screens out any population. Tests may violate Title VII by having a disparate impact on a protected group (e.g., a particular race or gender). Under Title VII, an employer risks possible discrimination claims arising from the adverse employment effects of a personality test that does not predict job performance and is not tailored to the requirements of the position. Many courts and states, however, allow personality and psychological testing of public service employees, particularly for police officers and firefighters. For example, the Supreme Court of Iowa upheld the revocation of a conditional offer of employment after a psychological test revealed the applicant was not suited to serve as a police officer.[37] The court found that psychological testing was permissible as part of an employment screening process as long as it tested the applicant's ability to perform the duties of the position.

Except where one can show that the administration of a medical examination is necessary to determine whether an applicant is qualified to perform the duties of the job (i.e., police officer), the ADA does not allow employers to screen applicants for depression and mental instability in order to predict who has a predilection to act out violently. Even if conducted at the correct phase in the hiring process, psychological tests cannot be used to screen out offerees unless the test is conducted for a job-related reason and consistent with business necessity. As with other medical tests, the employer also must demonstrate that there is no reasonable accommodation that would permit the individual to perform the essential functions of the job.

The Seventh Circuit recently held that a test designed to uncover mental health characteristics (e.g., depression, anxiety) is a
medical examination, even if it is not administered to disclose information about one's mental health, provided that the method used for
scoring the test indirectly discloses mental health information that
jeopardizes the applicant's employment prospects.[38] This type of
test will violate the ADA if given before a conditional employment
offer, even if a medical professional does not interpret the test. An
employer, therefore, may not administer a test *before* a conditional
offer of employment if the test *may* reveal any psychological disorders or mental disabilities.

In summary, a medical examination always should be the last
step in the application process. After a conditional job offer has been
extended, all nonmedical components of the application process
must be completed before sending a prospective employee for a
medical examination as a condition of his or her employment.[39]

Drug and Alcohol Testing

The U.S. Department of Health and Human Services Substance
Abuse and Mental Health Services Administration (SAMHSA) estimates that 6.5 percent of full-time workers are current illicit drug
users, with alcohol being the most widely abused drug among adult
employees.[40] Employee substance abuse not only can affect workplace performance and productivity, which can be costly for businesses, but can lead to violent behavior. Therefore, it is essential that
businesses adopt alcohol- and drug-free workplace policies and establish a program for both detecting employees with drug and alcohol
problems and effectively addressing these problems.

Both federal and state laws require certain public employers to
develop alcohol- and drug-free workplace policies. In 1986, President Reagan issued Executive Order 12564, which prohibits drug
use by federal employees and requires federal agencies to develop
drug-free workplace policies and conduct drug screening of employees in sensitive positions.[41] Additionally, the Omnibus Transportation

Employee Testing Act (Omnibus Act) requires pre-employment drug testing of employees in safety-sensitive positions and employees who require a commercial driver's license.[42] The Omnibus Act and Department of Transportation regulations do not require employers to obtain employee authorization to conduct drug testing.[43]

However, federal and state courts have held that drug and alcohol testing by public employers constitutes a search within the meaning of the Fourth Amendment. To pass constitutional muster, such testing must be reasonable. In determining the reasonableness of an employer's drug and alcohol testing program, courts have balanced the degree to which an employee's privacy interests are intruded upon against the employer's legitimate governmental interests. In balancing these conflicting interests, the analysis often turns on the basis upon which the test is being administered. Drug and alcohol testing generally falls into two broad categories: (1) testing of job applicants; and (2) testing of current employees. Among the latter group, testing occurs under the following scenarios: (1) reasonable suspicion, (2) postaccident, and (3) random. Historically, random drug and alcohol testing has generated the most litigation.

Preemployment Drug Testing

Most federal and state courts hold that preemployment drug testing programs by public employers do not violate an applicant's privacy or due process rights, particularly when the job duties implicate public safety concerns. As a result, most courts have upheld preemployment drug testing of public employees, particularly for public safety–related positions, despite an applicant's expectation of privacy. In particular, courts have upheld these tests when the applicants received reasonable notice of a drug testing policy and the testing was part of a medical examination that all applicants were required to undergo for employment, reasoning that the lowered expectation of privacy creates less of an intrusion into the applicants' privacy.

Therefore, when developing a preemployment drug-testing program, public employers should implement the recommendations of the National Academy of Sciences Committee on Drug Use in the Workplace. This publication provides guidelines for instituting procedural safeguards and quality control standards, confirming positive results with better technology and giving applicants the opportunity to challenge the accuracy of positive test results.[44]

Testing Current Employees

As noted above, testing of current employees falls into three categories: reasonable suspicion, postaccident, and random. With respect to the first category, reasonable suspicion, employers encounter few problems conducting such testing provided that their basis for testing the employee is based on a reasonable, individualized suspicion that the employee has used illegal drugs. A reasonable suspicion can be based on information concerning an employee's off-duty activities.[45] A reasonable suspicion is not supported by mere hunches, rumors, or anonymous phone calls.[46] The second category, postaccident, is an extension of the reasonable suspicion standard and generally applies only in the context of serious on-the-job accidents.

The last category, random drug testing, continues to face constitutional challenges in the courts, owing in large part to the significant privacy intrusions employees experience and the absence of a reasonable suspicion basis for conducting the test. While employers have been largely successful in arguing the merits of random drug testing in heavily regulated industries (e.g., prisons, nuclear power plants, U.S. Customs) where genuine public safety concerns are implicated and where employees already have a diminished expectation of privacy due to where they work, other employers have been much less successful in convincing the courts that they should be permitted to randomly test their employees—notably, in the case of police and fire employees.[47] Aside from considering the nature of the work setting, courts look to whether there is evidence of an existing drug problem among an employer's workers and the degree of intrusion caused by the testing procedures (e.g., how the urine sample is collected, percentage frequency an employee would be selected for random testing).[48]

Prohibiting Weapons in the Workplace

According to research performed at the University of North Carolina at Chapel Hill, homicides are five times more likely to occur in workplaces that permit guns than at sites where all weapons are prohibited.[49] Thus, as a general practice employers should enact policies that prohibit firearms in the workplace and notify employees that the employer has the right to and will conduct reasonable searches.

However, over forty states have concealed firearms statutes that permit individuals to obtain a license or permit to carry a concealed firearm. Most states that permit individuals to carry concealed weapons allow employers to ban weapons from the workplace provided they post a notice about the ban. Many state laws also restrict concealed weapon holders from carrying firearms into federal and state government buildings.[50] Public sector employers, therefore, should disseminate workplace policies and conspicuously post notices prohibiting anyone from carrying weapons on the property unless doing so violates state or local legislation.

The specific provisions of firearm laws vary significantly between states. For instance, the Washington Supreme Court held that government entities may establish regulations governing employees' ability to possess firearms.[51] In Utah, state and local governments may not prohibit employees from possessing firearms at work or in their vehicles, except in certain secure facilities, such as mental health facilities and courthouses.[52] Additionally, holders of a "concealed firearms permit" in Nevada may carry a weapon in any public building, except in public airports, public school buildings, and buildings with metal detectors or signs posted at each entrance indicating that firearms are not permitted in the building.[53] However, a total of six states have passed legislation that prohibits employers from enacting policies that restrict a person's ability to store or transport firearms in a locked vehicle in a company parking lot: Alaska, Kansas, Kentucky, Minnesota, Mississippi, and Oklahoma.[54] At the time this book went to press, two other states, Georgia and Florida, were considering adopting such legislation. In 2007, Oklahoma's law was held unenforceable by a federal district court on the grounds that the state law was preempted by the federal Occupational Safety and Health Act (OSHA).[55] Specifically, the court held that the Oklahoma law conflicted with Section 5(a)(1) of OSHA, better known as the "general duty clause." Under the general duty clause, an employer has an obligation to take measures to address known hazards in the workplace. The court found that the Oklahoma law, which criminally prohibits employers from adopting policies barring employees from having weapons in their vehicles, created a "significant obstacle to compliance with the general duty clause" and would impair employers' ability to "comply with their obligation to abate hazards that could lead to death or serious bodily harm in the workplace."[56]

▌ Maintaining a Safe Working Environment: Workplace Searches

The Fourth and Fourteenth Amendments protect public employees from unreasonable searches and seizures from government employers if they have a *reasonable* expectation of privacy. Additionally, state or federal employers may face civil rights claims for violating an employee's Fourth Amendment rights by searching an employee's office, desk, locker, telephone, or personal belongings.[57] Other federal statutes, such as the Privacy Act and the Electronic Communications Privacy Act of 1986 (ECPA), further extend privacy rights to public employees, and some state laws extend privacy protections specifically to public employees.

State and federal courts generally hold that public employees may have a reasonable expectation of privacy in their purses, briefcases, or closed containers brought to work. Individuals also may have an expectation of privacy in an office, desk, locker, or file cabinet. Employers, however, may reduce or eliminate this expectation by posting legitimate workplace policy notices informing employees that the employer retains the right to search such work areas as an employee's desk, locker, file cabinets, and the like. In other words, the reasonableness of a public employee's expectation of privacy will depend on the employer's actual office practices, as well as its written workplace policies and procedures.[58]

In the event a public employer conducts a search of an employee's work area and the employee has a reasonable expectation of privacy, the employer's search must satisfy two requirements in order not to run afoul of the employee's Fourth Amendment rights: (1) the search must be "justified at its inception"; and (2) the search must be reasonably tailored to its purpose.[59] With respect to the first requirement, the employer need only show that it had reasonable grounds to believe that the employee had violated a workplace policy (e.g., prohibition against bringing weapons to the place) or had engaged in unlawful conduct that may or may not have violated workplace rules (e.g., downloading child pornography onto his work computer). With respect to the second requirement, the search conducted by the employer must not exceed the initial justification for the search.[60] Thus, for example, if an employee is believed to be violating the employer's Internet usage policy, the employer's search would be limited to reviewing the employee Internet usage and would not extend to searching the employee's desk or filing cabinets.

▌ Maintaining a Safe Working Environment: Telephone, E-mail, and Computer Usage Policies

Implementing policies that clearly restrict the use of telephones and computer technology for work-related reasons can be important elements of preventing violent or inappropriate conduct in the workplace that is either directed toward coworkers or third parties.

Telephone Use

While it may be unrealistic to bar the use of work telephones for anything but work-related issues, public sector employers should have a policy that reserves the use of the employer's telephone systems primarily for the conduct of business. Employers may restrict an employee's personal use of the employer's telephone system by establishing a telephone usage policy that provides the following:

- Limiting telephone use for nonwork purposes to particular times during the workday, such as breaks and lunchtime;

- Explaining that excessive or unreasonable telephone usage will result in disciplinary action;

- Prohibiting use of the employer's telephones to harass or threaten coworkers, family members, or any other individual(s); and

- Prohibiting employees from using the employer's telephones for illicit purposes.

Additionally, employers should place similar limits on employees' cell phone usage and should limit cell phone use while in the workplace to emergency situations only.

Monitoring telephone calls can provide employers a greater ability to prevent misuse of telephones, but employers must be aware of the restrictions in the ECPA.[61] This act prohibits certain forms of wiretapping and prohibits anyone, including employers, from intercepting and monitoring any person's telephone conversation. The ECPA, however, has several broad exceptions that apply to employers. It allows employers to monitor conversations if one party consents to the monitoring, the telephone call is made in the course of an employer's business, or the employer has an adequate business reason for doing so.[62] Courts have found an implied consent to monitor telephone calls where an employee makes personal calls on a telephone that is to be used exclusively for business calls, and the employer warns the employee not to make personal calls from that telephone.[63] In contrast, merely knowing that a call can be monitored is not sufficient to imply consent.[64] Moreover, courts will determine whether an employer has violated the ECPA based upon the extent of the intrusion, even where an employer has a legitimate business reason for listening to an employee's telephone call, such as investigating theft.[65]

Various states have laws directly related to the monitoring of telephone conversations in the workplace. For instance, Nebraska permits the monitoring of employee telephone communications as long as employers provide reasonable notice of a policy of random monitoring.[66] In Connecticut, employers must provide prior written notice to employees of the potential for and the types of monitoring that might be used before the employer may electronically monitor a telephone conversation.[67] Employers should be familiar with their states' eavesdropping laws before monitoring employee calls because state law requirements may differ from the ECPA. For example, a number of states require the consent of both parties in order to monitor the telephone call.

Computer and E-mail Use

Computers are now an integral part of most workplaces, and employees routinely have access to both the Internet and e-mail on workplace computer systems. Preventing the improper use of e-mail and the Internet is an important component of any employer's efforts to reduce violence in the workplace. While the ECPA does not directly regulate an employer's ability to access employees' files and e-mail messages from an employer-owned computer system, the ECPA generally does protect an individual's privacy interest in e-mail and other electronic information.[68]

That protection, however, seems tenuous as applied to workplaces given the business justification exceptions to the ECPA. Moreover, while Title I of the ECPA prohibits interception of electronic communications, several federal courts of appeal have held that Title I does not apply to e-mail in storage because interception can only occur at the time the e-mail is being transmitted.[69] Additionally, the Third Circuit has held that the ECPA prohibition against searches of electronic communications while in storage excludes all searches conducted by communications service providers, including employers, so that an employer may search employee e-mails stored on the employer's system.[70]

Some states have enacted legislation pertaining to workplace privacy issues and computer-based communications. While both Maryland and Arkansas have legislation criminalizing the use of e-mail or other electronic communications to send obscene, lewd, or profane messages, or to frighten, threaten, or harass others, they also have laws that protect employee privacy in the workplace.[71] Maryland prohibits individuals from accessing a computer without authorization. Arkansas requires employers to notify employees of all e-mail surveillance that might occur.[72] Similarly, the Colorado Public Records Law protects public employees by requiring public employers that maintain e-mail systems to implement a written policy detailing the circumstances under which monitoring of e-mail communications may occur. The policy must include a statement explaining that employee e-mail correspondence may be considered a public record and, therefore, subject to public inspection.[73]

Whether an employee can establish a reasonable expectation of privacy in the contents of his or her office computer often turns on whether the employer has notified its employees that they do not have an expectation of privacy in the contents of their computer files.[74] Other factors include where the computer is located and if other people have access to or use the computer. In a recent court ruling, the Tenth Circuit concluded that an employee who brought his personal computer to work did not have a reasonable expectation of privacy in the material stored on the computer's hard drive, because the employee failed to install a password to keep other employees from using his machine or gaining access to his files and left the computer on at all times.[75]

Despite any privacy rights an employee may enjoy in their electronic communications, an employer may still conduct an investigatory search of an employee's computer for evidence of work-related misconduct as long as the search is reasonable, justified at its inception, and of an appropriate scope given the nature of the investigation.[76] Courts generally have not found that employees have an expectation of privacy in the contents of their computer, including e-mail, where the employer has an established office policy that warns employees that e-mails are subject to periodic or continuous review.[77]

In developing an electronic communications and computer usage policy, employers therefore should include language:

- Declaring that all e-mail and electronic communications sent, received, or stored on the internal, employer-owned computer systems are the employer's property;

- Clarifying that employees should not have any expectation of privacy regarding their e-mail, and posting notices indicating that all electronic communications may be monitored by the employer;

- Prohibiting any transmission of obscene, illegal, or defamatory materials, or any materials intended to harass or defame other people, including family, friends, or other coworkers; and

- Explaining that any misuse of e-mail, electronic communication, or employer-owned computers will result in disciplinary action.

Additionally, employers can provide employees with a daily reminder that they have no reasonable expectation of privacy with respect to their office computer by installing pop-up notices to that effect which appear each time the employee logs into his or her computer system for the day.

Using Threat Assessment Teams

An employer's *threat assessment team* can be one of its most effective defenses in preventing workplace violence. The team's primary functions are preventing, investigating, and responding to incidents and threats of workplace violence and monitoring workplace violence trends. Central to the team's responsibilities is the process of assessing the credibility of threats, responding to those threats, and conducting a post-incident response. As with crisis management committees or emergency response teams, an employer's team should: (1) be established prior to the time it is called upon to act in response to an actual or perceived threat of workplace violence; (2) receive advance training as a group; and (3) assign clearly designated responsibilities to its members. The team's existence and role must be known and understood throughout the organization, and its processes and procedures should be standardized, as appropriate, in all of the employer's locations. The team (or a designated member) should be apprised of each incident or threat—no matter how minor—in order to evaluate the need for (and specific nature of) the employer's response.

Composition of the Team

The recommended membership of a threat assessment team is dependent upon many factors, including the nature of the employer, the makeup of its workforce, the nature and size of its facilities, the location of its facilities, and the employer's prior history of workplace violence or threats of workplace violence. Where an employer has multiple or nationwide locations or units for which a single team would be impractical or ineffective, efforts should be undertaken to ensure that there is consistency and standardization among the practices and makeup of each location's on-site team (even if certain officials from management such as the general counsel or director of security serve on all teams). Doing so is critical in light of litigation that often follows incidents of workplace violence. If one location or unit is fully prepared to address incidents of workplace violence and another location is under-prepared or has failed to follow the organization's workplace violence prevention plan, claims of gross negligence could be substantiated. Where employers have multiple locations, teams from each location should have a forum to share information regularly about workplace violence issues, incidents, and trends.

The prospect of civil litigation is only one reason why employers should adequately address workplace violence concerns. A failure to address workplace violence issues adequately may result in violations of state and federal workplace safety laws. For instance, the federal Occupational Safety and Health Administration has the power to investigate instances of workplace violence and an employer's failure to take appropriate actions to stem such violence.

The Occupational Health and Safety Administration has noted that the threat assessment team should be designated to assess the workplace's vulnerability to violence and reach agreement on preventive actions to take. The team also should be responsible for:

- Recommending/implementing employee training programs about workplace violence;

- Implementing plans for responding to acts of workplace violence; and

- Communicating internally with employees.[78]

The makeup of an employer's threat assessment team varies from employer to employer and industry to industry. In general, the team should include representatives from senior management, human resources, mental health, security/law enforcement, communications or public relations, civil rights/EEO office, union/employee organizations (through a joint safety committee, if one exists), and the general counsel's office. Inclusion of *employee assistance program* (EAP) staff should be considered on a case-by-case basis. Regardless of whether or not the organization has an internal law enforcement capability, representation from, or liaison with, external law enforcement is highly recommended. The team's makeup should be reviewed periodically to address changes in personnel or operations, organizational expansion or contraction, and the number and types of workplace violence incidents and threats that are registered over time.

Responsibilities

Written protocols and "rapid response procedures" should be developed to define the responsibilities of each team member and of the team as a whole. Such protocols and procedures are in addition to the general workplace violence policy that should be circulated to all employees. Employers should develop simplified flowcharts setting forth specific responsibilities of the team as a whole, of specific team members, and of management in the event of a workplace violence incident or threat. Many employers maintain and update their protocols through a Web-based system. It is critical to review all such protocols and manuals at regular intervals. In addition, the effectiveness of an employer's workplace violence protocols should be evaluated in a context in which attorney-client privilege can be maintained following workplace violence incidents.

Security/Workplace Violence Assessment

One of the most critical tasks to be undertaken by the threat assessment team is that of security/workplace violence assessment. This entails an analysis of work environments and units to assess the potential for violence, to review existing security functions and measures, to make recommendations for changes and improvements, and to review policies and procedures in the aftermath of workplace violence incidents.[79] If properly carried out, an assessment can identify gaps that could be exploited by those who may be intent upon entering the workplace for the purpose of carrying out workplace violence, and, in doing so, can enhance safety throughout the workplace.

The assessment process differs significantly from employer to employer, facility to facility, and industry to industry. Assessment is not a one-time function. It is an ongoing process; one which must be renewed regularly and revised in response to internal factors (such as express threats from a former employee) and external factors (such as incidents of violence that are perpetrated against an employer's workforce). A critical shortcoming in many assessments is the failure to evaluate new facilities, changes in facility layout, and changes in organizational operating procedures.

The specific issues that should be addressed in a security/workplace violence assessment include "procedures for securing emergency assistance; access and freedom of movement within the work environment; existing locks, security systems, physical barriers; employees' knowledge of emergency procedures; routine work procedures; escape routes; access to protective and security personnel; cash handling procedures; and signage."[80] In particular, an assessment should focus on the lighting and access to parking areas outside an employer's facility, and special attention should be paid to employees whose work environments are external to a specific facility.

The actual assessment requires, among other things, an analysis of employee practices and procedures, a review of facility floor plans and access points, and an evaluation of security reports, particularly those relating to any prior incidents of workplace violence. Although a high percentage of workplace violence is perpetrated by former employees reentering the workplace, many employers fail to install physical barriers or to adopt specific protocols limiting access to the workplace by nonemployees.

Certain work sites, such as courtrooms, mental health facilities, and hospitals, are particularly susceptible to workplace violence. Studies conducted by governmental agencies and private associations have documented an increased frequency of threats and violence against judges and prosecutors. In response, many newer court buildings separate prisoners from the court employees and judges through use of separate circulation systems, utilize metals detectors and surveillance cameras, and employ video systems for remote prisoner arraignment in appropriate cases.

Statistics show that health care facilities also are highly susceptible to workplace violence. In response, many health care facilities have implemented strategies designed to address their unique populations and layouts. For example, a security screening system in a Detroit hospital included stationary metal detectors supplemented by hand-held units. The system prevented the entry of 33 handguns, 1,324 knives, and 97 mace-type sprays during a six-month period. A violence reporting program in the Portland, Oregon, Veterans Administration Medical Center identified patients with a history of violence in a computerized database. The program helped reduce the number of all violent attacks by 91.6 percent by alerting staff to take additional safety measures when serving these patients. A system restricting movement of visitors in a New York City hospital used identification badges and color-coded passes to limit each visitor to a specific floor. The hospital also enforced the limit of two visitors at a time per patient. Over eighteen months, these actions reduced the number of reported violent crimes by 65 percent.[81]

Following its initial analysis, the threat assessment team should conduct periodic physical evaluations of the work site and be involved in the design process for new or renovated facilities. These physical evaluations should focus on the identification and assessment of workplace security hazards and address changes in employee work practices.[82] The security measures most frequently implemented by employers are: changes in facility design and procedures to limit public access; adding sign-in desks; improving facility lighting, particularly in parking lots; implementing card and other access control systems; issuing ID cards to employees and visitors; and installing closed-circuit or other monitoring equipment.

In short, the threat assessment team is charged with closing so-called security gaps. However, even the most professionally conducted assessment will not be effective unless it is coupled with an ongoing training program for both supervisors and employees.

▌ Training Employees to Prevent Workplace Violence

Violence prevention efforts, including an ongoing workplace violence training program, are essential for all current, reassigned, and new employees, supervisors, and managers. The training should cover topics such as:

- The workplace violence prevention policy;

- Risk factors that cause or contribute to assaults;

- Early recognition of escalating behavior or warning signs/situations that may lead to assaults;

- Ways to prevent or diffuse volatile situations or aggressive behavior;

- A standard response plan for violent situations, including the availability of assistance, response to alarm systems, and communication procedures;

- Ways to deal with hostile people . . . [including visitors].[83]

Supervisors and managers must be trained to recognize and report potentially violent situations and to encourage employees to report them. At a minimum, supervisors need to understand fully the employer's general conduct policies, how to recognize victims of domestic violence, how to detect the warning signs of substance abuse, and how to encourage employees to report threatening or harassing conduct. Nonsupervisory employees must have a clear understanding of the employer's conduct policies and the importance of reporting threatening or harassing conduct by coworkers, other employees, and third parties. Specialized training is required for internal security and law enforcement personnel both to defuse potentially explosive situations and to address individuals who show the potential to perpetrate workplace violence.

Using Employee Assistance Programs to Prevent and Respond to Workplace Violence

An employee assistance program (EAP) is one component of a comprehensive strategy to prevent, mitigate, or respond to workplace violence. EAPs were originally conceived to address the workplace problems associated with the misuse or abuse of, or addiction to, alcohol by employees or their dependents. They have evolved over the last fifty years to respond to a broad range of psychosocial and personal problems experienced by employees that include, but are not limited to, psychological difficulties; addiction to illegal and legal drugs; and financial, family, legal, elder care, and child care problems. In addition to these issues, violence-related cases also are brought to an EAP. Violence in the workplace can take many forms, including worker-on-worker, client/customer-on-worker, domestic violence, random acts during employee commutes, and acts of terrorism, to name a few.

Fundamental to the success of EAPs has been their commitment to confidentiality. Policies should be clear and employees assured that the use of the EAP is confidential and that no other party will know of their program use unless permission is granted. The essential caveat is that employees also must know that the EAP is committed to protecting lives and safety. EAPs are staffed by licensed clinical professionals who are bound by ethical codes and laws that place a premium on patient confidentiality. However, there are exceptions to the confidentiality rules when there is clear evidence of danger to others. In EAP settings where staff have clinical credentials, they must be licensed mental health practitioners (e.g., licensed clinical social workers [LCSW], licensed clinical professional counselors [LCPC], or trained psychologists [Ph.D. or Psy.D.]). Each discipline is bound by state and federal confidentiality laws. Some settings allow nonclinically trained paraprofessionals to conduct EAP assessments. It is questionable whether they are bound by the same confidentiality requirements. Examples requiring a breach of confidentiality can include suicidal/homicidal ideations, child and elder abuse, as well as stalking. Clients should be advised verbally of the exceptions to patient confidentiality practices at the time of their initial contact with the EAP. If they are seen in person, they should receive written notification as well.

Most often, employees seek the services of the EAP of their own volition—usually before their personal concerns cause perceptible problems in the workplace. Occasionally, employees are encouraged to contact the EAP by a coworker, a union representative, or a supervisor who has learned of a personal concern directly or through word of mouth. Employees should be educated about the EAP process, which can include problem assessment followed by brief counseling and referral, when necessary, to external resources.

Coworkers, union representatives, or supervisors also may contact the EAP to "consult" with an EAP representative regarding a coworker's difficulties. Some employees use the EAP as the result of a *job performance referral* (JPR). JPRs typically occur in situations where there has been a substantial violation of company policy (e.g., a positive drug test) or an employee's performance or behavior has declined to a point that disciplinary action, up to and including termination, is being contemplated.

Each route of access represents an opportunity to prevent, intervene, and reduce the potential risk of workplace violence. Employees who access the EAP are always evaluated for the risk of harm they may pose to themselves or to others. On occasion, an employee who comes to the EAP for assistance will acknowledge that she or he has considered self-harm or has a wish to harm coworkers or persons in leadership positions. These thoughts are always taken seriously but, on further assessment, are most often fantasies that the employee has no intention of acting on. There are instances, however, when an assessment of lethality reveals a detailed and fully formed plan, which includes a time line. In these cases, the EAP must respond quickly to secure the safety of the client and to protect those who may be in harm's way. By simply assessing the risk of injury to self or others, the EAP becomes the front line of defense in preventing potential workplace violence situations. It is worth noting that clients "diverted" in this way represent those individuals who are conflicted or ambivalent about their wish to harm. Their ambivalence leads them to seek assistance from a provider who they either knew or suspected would thwart their plan.

In the case of a coworker/union representative/supervisor referral/ or consultation, the process is slightly different but can yield a similar "prevention" effect. These types of referrals or consultations extend the reach of the EAP. Individuals experiencing psychological distress may not appreciate the fact that their difficulties are apparent to others. When the suggestion to seek assistance from the EAP is made by a third party, the employee may be "startled" into attending more seriously to his or her issues. When these individuals call the EAP to "consult" regarding their colleague's distress, another opportunity is created to examine the circumstances that gave rise to their concerns. This window into the situation allows the EAP to assess the risk or threat of harm and provide support and encouragement to the caller. Oftentimes, the troubled employee finally does call the EAP as a result of these consultations. Obviously, a strong message should be communicated to all employees during EAP orientation and during training dedicated to preventing workplace violence, that the EAP is an appropriate resource and point of contact when concerns emerge or fears are aroused.

JPRs are the least common path to the EAP and tend to be emotionally charged for many supervisors. JPRs occur when the supervisor is highly motivated by personal concern, is forced by workplace circumstance (directed to by employee relations), or is disciplined by his or her manager to address the circumstances appropriately. Many people find confrontation uncomfortable and fail to take action until a crisis occurs.

Supervisors wishing to make a JPR contact the EAP directly. The EAP counselor will interview the supervisor regarding the employee she or he intends to refer. The EAP counselor seeks to understand how long the behavior or performance concerns have existed, determines the kind of problems that have occurred in the workplace, and collects any other relevant data. In addition, the counselor will coach the supervisor through the confrontation or corrective action interview with the employee. There are several key points associated with this interview:

1. The goal of the referral is to make every possible effort to connect the employee with the helping resource.
2. The supervisor should assure the employee that the decision to contact or not to contact the EAP will have no bearing on

the outcome of any future performance or behavior issues, and the associated disciplinary action.

3. The supervisor should make clear that the decision to contact the EAP rests solely with the employee. The employer can strongly encourage the use of the program and may even decline to return the employee to work until cleared by the EAP—but ultimately it is the employee's choice.

Formal and informal referrals, consultations, and JPRs are the essential tools and skills used by top-level supervisory staff, labor relations representatives, human resources personnel, and union officials. These interventions, particularly the formal and informal referrals and consultations, also are available to union leadership who have knowledge of a member's personal and family concerns. The services of the EAP, at all levels and of every type, are meant to provide support and necessary assistance. These services are not intended to be punishments or to represent negative judgments. Referral to the EAP should be used as a preventive measure to help thwart potential workplace violence. All personnel in management positions must be reminded that these resources are available and should be recommended whenever a concern emerges.

▌ Diffusing Workplace Violence: Using Conflict and Alternative Dispute Resolution Procedures

Workplace violence and threats of workplace violence are not limited to any one type of employer. They cut across all organizations, public and private, union and nonunion, and national and single location. The causes of workplace violence include workplace pressures, disputes between and among employees and supervisors, "family discord, domestic violence, drug and alcohol abuse and other social ills [that] intrude into the workplace."[84] Since one of the most prevalent causes of workplace violence is conflict between employees and between employees and supervisors, conflict or alternative dispute resolution (ADR) processes can have a marked effect on reducing workplace violence.

ADR "is most effective in resolving disputes when a conflict has been identified early on and one of the following techniques is used: ombudspersons, facilitation, mediation, inter-based problem solving and peer review."[85] Similarly, informal, formal, and negotiated grievance processes can have a significant impact on forestalling workplace violence. While there is no single solution for every employer or every incident or threat of workplace violence, it is clear that ADR and grievance processes can help to stem workplace violence in many instances.

▌ Handling Terminations

One of the most challenging tasks in preventing workplace violence is confronting the risk of violence in connection with employee terminations. While not every termination poses a risk of violence, employers should have basic processes in place to lower the risk that a violent confrontation will occur. In addition, in those instances where the risk of violence appears higher, employers should take additional steps to prevent its occurrence.

Employee terminations can be upsetting and confrontational. Accordingly, the potential for violence associated with an employee's termination should be considered in advance of any termination discussion. Handling the meeting in an organized and controlled manner can be an effective way to avoid unnecessary confrontation and lessen the risk of violence. In addition, treating employees with dignity and respect is critical. It is always a good practice for employers to have a checklist of issues to cover in connection with a termination that address employee questions (such as unemployment or health benefits). Employers should require the return of employer property (telephones, computers, electronic access cards, or keys, etc.). Finally, steps should be taken to reduce the risk of violence and damage to property. For instance, employers should have a procedure in place to immediately cut off access to computer networks, deactivate electronic badges, and collect all keys and access cards to limit the former employee's ability to reenter the workplace.

As a rule of thumb, termination meetings should be staffed by at least two managers. When an employer has an expectation that the employee in question may become volatile during the meeting, the supervising employee should carefully consider who else should attend the meeting—taking into account the relationship that individual has with the employee—and rehearse how the termination will be communicated. While an employer is not required to tell an employee why he or she is being terminated, it is advisable to give an employee all the reasons for its decision in a brief and clear manner. Where there is heightened concern that an employee has the potential to become violent and the means to do so (such as access to or possession of a firearm), an employer should involve internal security, engage an outside security agency, or advise the police of its concern and request assistance. Where the employee in question has exhibited violent behavior or a potential for violent behavior in the past, consideration should be given to seeking guidance from a forensic psychiatrist or psychologist, and the employer should consider holding the meeting in a location near the exit of the offices, have the employee's personal possessions brought to the room, and require his or her immediate departure.

▌ Conclusion

As should be clear from the scope of this chapter, preventing violence in the workplace requires every employer to utilize a multipronged approach. Public employers should audit their applicant screening processes; assess the effectiveness of their policies, procedures, and programs at addressing workplace violence issues; and proactively implement changes.[86]

Notes

1. Jack N. Kondrasuk et al., *Negligent Hiring: The Emerging Contributor to Workplace Violence in the Public Sector*, Pub. Pers. Mgmt., Summer 2001, (quoting Greg Warchol, U.S. Dept. of Justice, *National Crime Victimization Survey: Workplace Violence, 1992–1996* (July 1998)) (available at http://www.findarticles.com/p/articles/mi_qa3779/is_200107/ai_n8965757/pg_1).

2. James N. Madero, *Preemployment Screening and Workplace Violence Prevention*, http://www.irmi.com/irmicom/expert/Articles/2004/Mudero06.aspx.

3. Id.

4. Id.

5. U.S. Equal Employment Opportunity Commission, *Enforcement Guidance: Preemployment Disability-Related Questions and Medical Examinations* (Oct. 10, 1995), available at http://www.eeoc.gov/policy/docs/preemp.html.

6. John F. Buckley & Ronald M. Green, *2007 State by State Guide to Human Resources Law*, 8–62, Table 8-5 (Aspen Publishers, Inc. 2007).

7. Fla. Stat. § 768.095.

8. Nev. Rev. Stat. §§ 613.200, 613.210.

9. Buckley & Green, supra note 6, at 8–61.

10. See Ky. Rev. Stat. Ann. § 352.550 (prohibits blacklisting in the mining industry); Miss. Code Ann. § 77-9-725 (prohibits blacklisting of telephone and railroad employees for union activity).

11. Buckley & Green, supra note 6, at 1–32.

12. See 49 U.S.C. § 44936(a).

13. Cal. Lab. Code §§ 432.7, 432.8.

14. Fla. Stat. § 112.011; Minn. Stat. § 364.04.

15. Haw. Rev. Stat. § 378-2.5.

16. N.Y. Correct. Law § 752; Wis. Stat. § 111.335.

17. See id.; Buckley & Green, supra note 6, at 8–61.

18. Raymond Peeler, EEOC Staff Advisory Letter, Dec. 1, 2005.

19. Id.

20. 5 U.S.C. § 552a(b).

21. See Privacy Rights Clearinghouse, *Employment Background Checks: A Jobseeker's Guide*, available at http://www.privacyrights.org/fs/fs16-bck.htm.

22. The U.S. National Archives & Records Administration, available at http://archives.gov/st-louis/military personnel/index.html.

23. Section 1681b(b) sets forth employers' duties if obtaining credit reports. See 15 U.S.C. 1681b(b).

24. See id. at § 1681b(g).

25. Buckley & Green, supra note 6, at 8–58. An "investigative consumer credit report" "contains information obtained through personal interviews

with neighbors, friends, or associates of the consumer regarding that person's character, general reputation, personal characteristics, or mode of living."

26. See 20 U.S.C. § 1232g(b). See also the U.S. Department of Education, *General Policy Guidance: Family Educational Rights and Privacy Act,* available at http://www.ed.gov/policy/gen/guid/ fpco/ferpa/index.html.

27. The U.S. Department of Education, *General Policy Guidance: Family Educational Rights and Privacy Act,* available at http://www.ed.gov/policy/gen/guid/fpco/ferpa/index.html.

28. 18 U.S.C. § 2721(b)(3).

29. Id. at § 2721(b)(3).

30. Id. at § 2721(b)(9).

31. NYS DMV Internet Office, *Driver's Privacy Protection Act: Frequently Asked Questions,* available at http://www.nydmv.state.ny.us/qaprive.htm.

32. Cal. Veh. Code § 1808.1; Cal. Pub. Util. Code § 1032; Va. Code Ann. § 46.2-340.

33. See supra note 5.

34. In contrast, medical examinations of current employees must be job related and consistent with business necessity.

35. Many people confuse personality and psychological tests. Personality tests seek to assess an individual's motivations in particular fields and, when validated properly, have been shown to adequately predict employment success. These tests normally seek information about an individual's tastes, habits, and propensity to be honest. Some common personality tests are Caliper, Myers Briggs, Chally, Predictive Index, and DISC. Psychological tests, on the other hand, have been developed primarily for use within clinical settings to aid in the identification of personality traits that may be abnormal. Their use as predictors of employee performance is very questionable for occupations other than those which subject employees to extreme stress or duress, such as air traffic control or law enforcement. Some common psychological tests are MMPI, 16PF, NEO Personality Inventory, and Basic Personality Inventory.

36. AFSCME, *Preventing Workplace Violence: A Union Representative's Guidebook,* Chapter 7: The Workplace Violence Prevention Program, available at http://www.afscme.org/publications /2952.cfm.

37. See Bahr v. Council Bluffs Civil Serv. Commission, 542 N.W.2d 255, 257 (Iowa 1996).

38. See Karraker v. Rent-A-Center, Inc., 411 F.3d 831, 837 (7th Cir. 2005).

39. See Leonel v. American Airlines, Inc., 400 F.3d 702, 709 (9th Cir. 2005) (employer violated ADA when it sent prospective employees for medical examinations prior to completing their background checks). See

also Anne G. Scheer, *Pre-hire Testing Prohibited by Americans with Disabilities Act*, New Hampshire Business Review, September 2005, available at http://www.gcglaw.com/resources/employment/ada_testing.html.

40. U.S. Department of Labor, *Working Partners for an Alcohol- and Drug-Free Workplace: General Workplace Impact*, citing U.S. Department of Health and Human Services, *1999 National Household Survey on Drug Abuse* (2000), available at http://www.dol.gov/asp/programs/drugs/workingpartners/stats/wi.asp.

41. Exec. Order No. 12564 (1986).

42. The Omnibus Act and related regulations permit, but do not require, employers to implement preemployment alcohol testing as well. 49 U.S.C. § 5331(b). If the employer decides to conduct preemployment alcohol tests, it must use the procedure stipulated in the regulations. See, e.g., 49 C.F.R. §§ 382.301 (employees using a commercial driver's license), 219.502 (railroad employees), and 655.42 (transit workers).

43. 49 U.S.C. § 5331(b).

44. 96 A.L.R.5th 485 §2b: Validity and Operation of Pre-employment Drug Testing—State Cases.

45. James Baird, David D. Kadue, & Kenneth D. Sulzer, *Public Employee Privacy: A Legal and Practical Guide to Issues Affecting the Workplace* 153 (American Bar Association 1995).

46. Id.

47. See, e.g., International Union v. Winters, 385 F.3d 1003 (6th Cir. 2004) (upheld random testing for certain civil service employees who worked with either former or current prison inmates, included among the affected job categories: probation and parole officers, prison chaplains, counselors, and teachers; this opinion includes a helpful summary of other random test cases); Petersen v. City of Mesa, 83 P.3d 35 (Ariz. 2004) (state supreme court refused to uphold a random drug testing program for firefighters on the grounds that the city only produced evidence of a "generalized, unsubstantiated interest in deterring and detecting a hypothetical drug abuse problem among the City's firefighters"); Anchorage Police Dept. Employees Assoc. v. Municipality of Anchorage, 24 P.3d 547, 558–59 (Ala. 2001) (state supreme court struck down random testing provision applied to police officers and firefighters as being in violation of the state's constitution; as in Petersen, no evidence was presented by the city that there was a substance abuse problem among the affected employees, a factor crucial to the court's ruling).

48. See International Union, 385 F.3d at 1007–1013.

49. Dana Loomis et al., *Employer Policies Toward Guns and the Risk of Homicide in the Workplace*, 95 Amer. J. of Pub. Health 830–32 (2005).

50. See, e.g., Cal. Penal Code § 171b.

51. Jessica Jensen, *Limiting Liability by Maintaining a Gun-Free Workplace*, citing Cherry v. Municipality of Metropolitan Seattle, 808 P.2d 746 (Wash. 1991), available at http://www.omwlaw.com/resources/Limiting LiabilityByMaintainingGunFreeWorkplace.pdf.

52. See Employers Counsel Network, *50 Employment Laws in 50 States: 2006*, 7-3 (M. Lee Smith Publishers, LLC 2006); see also Utah Code Ann. § 63-98-102.

53. Nev. Rev. Stat. § 202.3673.

54. Alaska Stat. § 18.65.800; Kan. Stat. Ann. § 75-7c11; Ky. Rev. Stat. § 237.106; Minn. Stat. § 624.714(18) (2005); Miss. Code Ann. § 45-9-55; Okla. Stat. tit. 21, § 1289.7a(A).

55. ConocoPhillips Co. v. Henry, 520 F. Supp. 2d 1282 (N.D. Okla. 2007) (this matter has been appealed by the state and is pending before the Tenth Circuit).

56. Id. at 1337–1338.

57. 42 U.S.C. § 1983.

58. See O'Connor v. Ortega, 480 U.S. 709, 717 (1987).

59. Baird et al., supra note 45, at 52.

60. Id.

61. 18 U.S.C. §§ 2510–2522.

62. Id. at § 2511(2).

63. *See* Watkins v. L.M. Berry & Co., 704 F.2d 577, 581-82 (11th Cir. 1983) (quoting Simmons v. Sw. Bell Tel. Co., 452 F. Supp. 392, 393–94 (W.D. Okla. 1978), *aff'd*, 611 F.2d 342 (10th Cir. 1979)).

64. Id. at 582.

65. See Deal v. Spears, 980 F.2d 1153, 1158 (8th Cir. 1992).

66. Neb. Rev. Stat. § 86-290(2).

67. Conn. Gen. Stat. § 31-48d(b).

68. Buckley & Green, supra note 6, at 8–79.

69. See Fraser v. Nationwide Mut. Insur., 352 F.3d 107, 113–14 (3d Cir. 2003); United States v. Steiger, 318 F.3d 1039, 1048–9 (11th Cir. 2003); Steve Jackson Games, Inc. v. U.S. Secret Serv., 36 F.3d 457, 461–62 (5th Cir. 1994).

70. Fraser, 352 F.3d at 114–5.

71. See Md. Ann. Code Crim. Law § 3-805(b); Ark. Code Ann. § 5-41-108(a); Buckley & Green, supra note 6, at 8-81–82.

72. See Md. Ann. Code Crim. Law § 3-805(b); Ark. Code Ann. § 5-41-108(a); Buckley & Green, supra note 6, at 8-81–82.

73. Colo. Rev. Stat. § 24-72-204.5.

74. See Leventhal v. Knapek, 266 F.3d 64, 74 (10th Cir. 2001).

75. United States v. Barrows, 481 F.3d 1246 (10th Cir. 2007).

76. Leventhal, 266 F.3d at 75.

77. See United States v. Simons, 206 F.3d 392, 398 (4th Cir. 2000); see also United States v. Angevine, 281 F.3d 1130, 1135 (10th Cir. 2002).

78. Elements of a Workplace Violence Prevention Program, available at http://www.osha.gov/workplace_violence/wrkplaceViolence.PartII.html.

79. Workplace Violence Prevention Guidelines, available at http://www.lacity.org/perEEO/violence.htm.

80. Occupational Hazards in Hospitals DHHS (NIOSH) Publication No. 2002-101, April 2002, available at http://www.cdc.gov/niosh/2002-101.html#safety.

81. Elements of a Successful Workplace Violence Protection Program, available at http://www.osha.gov/workplace_violence/wrkplaceViolence.

82. Guidelines for Preventing Workplace Violence for Health Care & Social Science Workers, OSHA 3148-01R, 2004.

83. Dispute Resolution and Workplace Violence, Dispute Resolution Journal, Jan.–Mar. 1996, available at http://www.wps.org/pubs/dispute-resolution.html.

84. Id.

85. The USDA Handbook on Workplace Violence Prevention and Response, available at http://www.usda.gov/news/pubs/violence/wpv.htm.

86. The authors gratefully acknowledge the assistance with the drafting, cite checking, and proofreading of this chapter provided by Catherine Meek and Karen Thompson (a summer associate at the time), associates at Seyfarth Shaw LLP, and Andrew Day, a law clerk at Seyfarth Shaw LLP.

CHAPTER 8

The Role of Public Employee Unions in Addressing Workplace Violence

Jonathan Rosen

▌ Introduction

Public employee unions have played a significant role in advocating for workplace violence prevention programs to better the lives and working conditions of government workers and the public they serve. Much of the material in this chapter is based on the experience of the New York State Public Employees Federation's Occupational Health and Safety Department in addressing violence in New York State government and in assisting sister unions and organizations nationwide. To better understand the role of public employee unions, it is helpful to look at their history.

Since the 1960s, public sector workers have engaged in a two-pronged struggle to gain collective bargaining rights and join labor unions. It is critical to note that the federal labor relations law does not apply to public employees. Thus, the first task for public employees was to gain passage of collective bargaining laws, which has been accomplished in forty-one states.[1]

Public employee collective bargaining laws establish certain rights. These rights vary from state to state, but typically include:

- Public employees' right to organize and to be represented by employee organizations of their own choice;

- The requirement that public employers negotiate and enter into agreements with public employee organizations regarding terms and conditions of their members' employment;

- Procedures for resolving collective bargaining impasses;

- Definition and prohibition of improper practices by public employers and public employee organizations;

- Prohibition against strikes by public employees; and

- Establishment of a state agency to administer the law.[2]

Once a campaign to pass a public employee collective bargaining law is successful, the focus shifts to organizing members and gaining recognition. In 2007, 35.9 percent of all government workers in the United States were union members. When compared to the 7.5 percent unionization rate among private sector workers, union membership among government workers is significant.[3] The percentage of organized public employees varies from state to state (see Figure 8.1).

Unions collectively bargain the terms and conditions of employment such as wage rates, hours of work, time off, health benefits, and grievance-arbitration procedures to provide due process rights for employee discipline or other disputes. Public employee unions are also very active in civil service matters and in the legislative arena.

Figure 8.1   Public Employee Membership Coverage by State, 2006

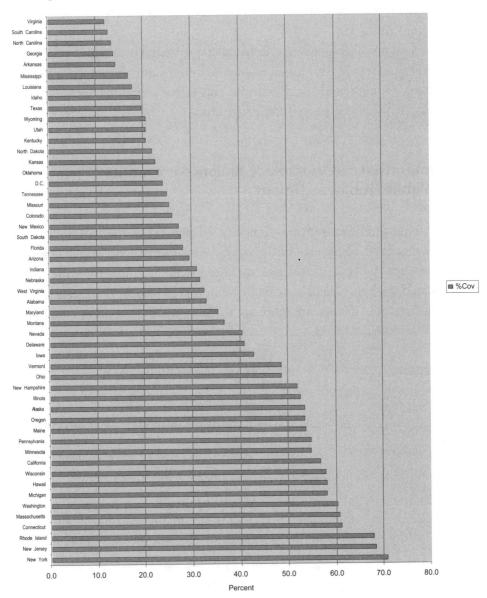

Source: http://www.trinity.edu/bhirsch/unionstats/. Data Sources: Current Population Survey (CPS) Outgoing Rotation Group (ORG) Earnings Files, 2006. Sample includes employed wage and salary workers, ages sixteen and over. %Cov = percent of employed workers who are covered by a collective bargaining agreement. Note: Sample size was very small in some states.

Because so many public employees are prohibited from striking, they tend to channel much of their energy into legislative and public relations initiatives.

Many public employee unions have negotiated health and safety language that calls for initiatives such as joint health and safety committees, training, and specific health and safety programs, including workplace violence prevention programs.

Importance of Workplace Violence Prevention to Public Employee Unions

Although public employees comprise 16 percent of the workforce, they represent 33 percent of the victims of workplace violence.[4] This is principally because of their exposure to violence in certain high-risk occupations (see below). Public employees who work in settings with frequent violence are more apt to demand union action to make their workplaces safer.

Sector	High-Risk Occupations
Criminal Justice	Police, parole, probation, or corrections officer, juvenile justice workers
Social Services	Counselors, social workers, child protective services, case managers
Health Care Services	Mental health, developmentally disabled, public hospital, nursing home, emergency rooms, and home care professionals and service providers
Education	Teachers, aides, bus drivers

Health and safety issues become a priority to union leaders when working conditions become intolerable for their members. Workplace violence in certain public employment positions causes a sense of urgency among the affected workers. Unions and public employers are most likely to take action following a tragic event, such as a severe assault or murder of a coworker. For example, in 1998, Judith Scanlon, a registered nurse, was murdered while conducting a home visit. Scanlon worked as an intensive case manager for mentally ill clients living in the community. This caused her union, the New York State Public Employees Federation, to take action by advocating for the prevention of assaults and homicide among members who conduct home visits. Her employer and the union members at the site responded to the tragedy by establishing a joint health and safety committee and drafting policies and procedures for safety; issuing cell phones for communication in the field; providing training; and enabling case workers to be accompanied by a coworker when conducting home visits in which they felt their safety may be at risk. Tragically, none of these measures were in place prior to Scanlon's death.

Case workers throughout the country have been the victims of similar workplace homicides, including Lisa Putnam, in Michigan (1998); Nancy Fitzgivenns, in Ohio (2001); Nicole Castro, in Maryland (2002); and Marty Smith, in Washington (2005). In each case, affected unions have taken actions such as working with the employer to increase safety measures, filing complaints with the U.S. Occupational Safety and Health Administration (OSHA), or proposing legislation. In the case of Lisa Putnam, the Michigan legislature passed "Lisa's Law" a mere nine months after she was murdered.[5] Lisa's Law requires the Department of Human Services to provide training for its Children's Protective Services workers and to employ a "buddy system" in situations that pose a risk. Training is required to include tactics to defuse threatening behavior, perform a safe visit, and recognize a dangerous situation. If a reasonable risk to safety exists, the worker must be accompanied by another trained worker or law enforcement officer.

The United Auto Workers (UAW) local president and the director of the Michigan Family Independence Agency (FIA) issued a press release that affirmed their commitment to actively prosecute threats, noting that in the year following passage of Lisa's Law:

> Worker Safety classes for FIA staff have been made available statewide. . . . [M]ore than $3 million has been spent on training, cellular phones, vehicle keyless entry/alarm devices and other worker safety tools. . . . [S]everal incidents of worker threats and assaults . . . resulted in prosecutions and jailings in Berrien, Eaton, Houghton, Isabella and other counties.

▌ What Is the Impact of Workplace Violence on Affected Workers and Their Families?

Workplace assaults can result in a range of health effects, from increased stress to career-ending injury. In psychiatric hospitals and emergency rooms, for example, patient assaults on nurses, aides, and other staff often have resulted in permanent disabilities.

In addition to severe physical trauma, many assaulted workers experience some degree of psychological trauma. The psychological impact can lead to sleep disturbance, trouble eating, difficulty concentrating, and paranoia. A common ailment among these workers is posttraumatic stress disorder (PTSD). PTSD is defined as "a psychiatric illness that can occur following a traumatic event in which there was threat of injury or death to you or someone else."[6]

For assaulted workers employed in disciplines such as nursing, social work, and counseling, there is the added stress of shifting suddenly from being a caregiver to being a patient.

Many state workers' compensation programs require injured workers to obtain a physician's referral in order to be seen by a psychologist for care. In many cases, the injured worker must obtain a referral to a psychologist who accepts workers' compensation reimbursement.[7] Furthermore, many state workers' compensation statutes do not allow social workers to provide counseling services to employees experiencing work-related trauma. Of course, injured workers are not generally knowledgeable about these requirements. When they do not have the required referrals, benefits are often cut once the individual's physical injuries are resolved, even though he or she may still be experiencing a great deal of psychological trauma. These problems with the workers' compensation system need to be addressed through legislative reform. It is important that public employers and unions educate employees who have been assaulted about these potential kinks in the system.

Often, public employers and public employee unions have few programs in place to support workplace violence victims who are no longer in the workplace. Disassociation from the workplace harms an injured worker's recovery. Frustration in navigating state workers' compensation systems can add to the trauma experienced by these individuals. When they experience delays in getting approval for medical diagnostic procedures or surgery, it can further delay their return to work and enforce feelings of helplessness, hopelessness, and paranoia. A cut in benefits, a refusal to pay for therapy, or the denial of a workers' compensation claim altogether can further exacerbate symptoms of PTSD. The loss of a sense of safety, the disruption in employment, and the loss of income may further contribute to the psychological trauma experienced by workers who have been assaulted on the job.

Injured workers' families are also often deeply affected by a severe assault. Children may become preoccupied with fear and concern for their parents. In one instance, after a nurse was severely assaulted by a patient in a state institution, her nineteen-year-old daughter was so distraught that she dropped out of college to be with her. Public employee unions have received reports regarding children of assaulted workers who have acted out by engaging in drug and alcohol use or performing poorly in school, among other things.[8]

▌ What Is the Impact of Workplace Violence on the Quality of Work Life and on the Client Populations Served by Public Employees?

Violence is extremely disruptive to a public agency's operations. It causes stress and fear among staff and clients alike, interfering with the delivery of services. For example, an inpatient mental health unit's mission is to help patients recover from their mental illnesses by providing a safe and therapeutic environment in which supportive rehabilitative programs can be implemented. A violent incident in the workplace can severely disrupt a therapeutic milieu. It is especially harmful to patients who have a history of trauma, such as victims of abuse.

On some inpatient mental health units, the rate of violence among patients and between patients and staff is as high as one hundred cases per one hundred workers per year.[9] Negative ramifications may include relapses among patients and loss of experienced staff, in addition to workers' compensation claims and related costs. For New York State government alone, costs are estimated to exceed $50 million per year.[10]

▌ Workplace Violence Typology in Various Public Sector Worksites

One tool for clarifying the focus of workplace violence prevention programs is a workplace violence typology, which categorizes the relationship between the perpetrator and victim. This is useful because the type of intervention employed will depend on the type of violence that is being addressed.

Typology

Criminal intent. The violent person is a stranger who has no legitimate relationship to the work site and is engaged in criminal activity, such as a robbery. An example would be a person entering a department of motor vehicles services office at closing time with the intent to rob the facility and take staff members hostage at gunpoint.

Customer/client/patient. This is the predominant type of violence in health care and social services, and in the public sector generally, and involves patients, inmates, and clients who assault staff.

Coworker. While this may be a significant problem in some cases, it is a myth that this is the predominant form of workplace violence. It comprises only a small percentage of workplace homicides and assaults but gets the most attention from employers and the media.[11] Employers can blame workers rather than examining their own organizational policies and procedures. In workplaces where this type of violence is a problem, unions should be involved in developing organizational systems to prevent, and respond to, conflict.

Personal. This refers to domestic violence situations and is perpetrated by an acquaintance or family member while the employee is at work.

Each type of violence calls for a tailored response. One of the first steps is to become familiar with the frequency and extent of violence in the specific setting of concern. Injury and illness records should be examined; they can provide helpful information on the extent of reported assaults, including what department they are occurring in, and the amount of lost time they are causing. This information can be used to influence management to take the problem seriously. A word of caution: underreporting is common at many work sites. In addition to reviewing these records, other methods may be useful, such as worker surveys, inspections, or interviews with injured staff.[12]

▌ Issues Regarding Key Affected Sectors: Institutional, Field, and Office Settings

The prevalence of workplace violence is not uniform across the public sector. Development of prevention programs requires agency and site specific assessments addressing the predominant type of violence that occurs in a particular setting and that fit with the mission and culture of the agency. To accomplish this, it is useful to consider the characteristics of key public employment sectors.

Institutional Settings

Client, patient, and inmate assaults frequently occur in state and county-run institutions housing the mentally ill, the developmentally disabled, inmates, troubled youth, and the elderly. Enlisting union representatives and direct care staff to evaluate risk factors and develop prevention strategies is key to putting effective programs into place. In these settings, it is the direct care staff who mainly bear the brunt of assaults and who should play a major role in interventions.

One particular problem that has not yet been sufficiently addressed in mental health facilities is identifying effective interventions for a patient who is a repeat and frequent assaulter. The current thinking in mental health is to reduce the use of restraint and seclusion, as these have been associated with numerous patient and staff injuries, as well as having a negative impact on patient rehabilitation. However, in the case of repeat assaulters, the lack of effective intervention means that a handful of very troubled patients can wreak havoc. For example, in one state psychiatric facility, four patients committed 70 percent of all assaults in an adult unit over a recent three-year period.[13] This illustrates why violence prevention strategies must be tailored to the work site and to the type of patient being cared for.

Field Settings

Many civil servants work in the "field" doing home visits, inspections, or audits. These workers are concerned about their safety when they have to go into dangerous neighborhoods. Additionally, home visits can pose an inherent risk of assault or homicide, especially when child custody issues are involved. Public sector occupations that conduct home visits include: social workers engaged in child protective custody, community mental health workers, and juvenile case workers. Home visits raise specific safety concerns: maintaining adequate communication with the home office, being able to staff two-person visits where the need is indicated, and determining how to respond to aggression by family members or visitors. Transporting clients is another task that can pose great dangers to workers.

Office-Based Settings

When dealing with the public in an office setting, the issue of physical security is paramount. What kind of access control is in place in an unemployment office where unemployed workers may get frustrated waiting in line or are angry about the adjudication of their claims for unemployment benefits? Have staff been adequately trained to deal with and defuse aggressive behavior? Lack of proper training could lead to staff escalating a potentially violent situation. What emergency procedures are in place? What measures are taken to prevent a disruptive client from returning to the office and repeating the behavior?

In any public work setting, a certain amount of conflict can be expected among staff or between staff and managers. This type of violence requires programmatic responses such as development of organizational systems for threat assessment, early intervention, dispute resolution, training for staff and supervisors on their roles in preventing and ameliorating conflict, as well as specific policies to address coworker violence. The earlier an organization addresses these issues, the more likely it is that potential problems can be nipped in the bud. All too often a senior manager is assigned to "assess" a threat based on his or her role in the hierarchy, not based on any specific knowledge or training in conflict resolution that he or she may have. Reliance on a traditional investigation/discipline approach can escalate conflict between the parties.

When developing strategies to prevent client/patient/inmate violence, it is key not to "blame the victim" by emphasizing worker behavior as the cause of the violent incident. Although worker training in skills such as de-escalation techniques and the do's and don'ts of responding to an agitated customer are essential, organizational interventions are necessary to prevent violence. These include improvements to the physical environment, such as access control, lighting, and systems to prevent customers from having to wait a long time to be served. Organizational policies, training, and proper staffing also must be considered. Finally, the employer can play a significant role in fostering systems for teamwork and communication among staff.

Key Elements of an Effective Program

OSHA has published guidelines that identify five elements of an effective health and safety program.[14] These components apply as well to the prevention of workplace violence:

- Management commitment and employee involvement;

- Work site analysis;

- Hazard prevention and control;

- Safety and health training; and

- Record keeping and program evaluation.

The OSHA guidelines provide direction for embarking on violence prevention efforts. The pivotal first step is for organizations to initiate a process whereby key workplace stakeholders affected by violence are brought together to interact with those authorities who have the ability to make corrections. Management-dominated committees are problematic in that they do not benefit from the experience of frontline staff. When union representatives are excluded, staff may distrust unilateral conclusions reached by management. Joint problem solving is more likely to identify feasible solutions that all affected workers find trustworthy.

Training is a critical component of a comprehensive program, but it does not, in and of itself, constitute a program. The need for training and educating the workforce is universal, yet the details of any specific guidance or intervention should be site specific. People can usually tell when they are getting generic advice. Canned programs are ineffective in identifying risk factors or potentially effective interventions.

Some employers have issued unilateral policy statements that mandate "zero tolerance" for violence. Rather than encouraging worker involvement in violence prevention efforts, these are often seen as management by decree. Unions tend to be suspicious of these policies, especially when they are not part of a comprehensive plan as outlined above. Often "zero tolerance" policies fail to provide the type of systems approaches that are needed to achieve meaningful organizational change. Also, unions fear the potential violation of due process rights when zero tolerance leads to unqualified disciplinary action, rather than to efforts to prevent or ameliorate conflict.

Organizational culture often plays an important part in violence prevention efforts. If violence is considered "part of the job," as it often is in criminal justice, mental health, and other institutional settings, unions should initiate dialogues to overcome this dangerous mindset. Unions have effectively drawn attention to the human impact of violence through statements and photographs of injured members. This is especially important when workplace policy makers view violence as a low-priority item, or as just another statistical measure to track. The impact of violence on the quality of work is another important topic raised by unionists.

Another key obstacle to instituting violence prevention programs is the hierarchical character of management culture in many workplaces. Top-down management often excludes the involvement of unions and frontline workers, and breeds resentment among the staff. Management control takes priority over organizational improvement. Changing rigid organizational culture is not accomplished easily or quickly, but efforts to establish an inclusive process to address an important problem like workplace violence can help organizations to learn and progress.

▎ What Have Unions Done?

A number of public employee unions have raised the issue of workplace violence during the collective bargaining process and demanded specific measures in health and safety contract language. While the number of such agreements and their specifics have not been documented, examples include agreements to develop a written violence prevention policy, joint study of risk, personal alarm systems, development and delivery of training, minimum staffing levels, and legal support in pressing charges against the perpetrators of such violence, regardless of who they are.

The United Federation of Teachers in New York City, for example, has negotiated language to provide time off from work and legal support for members who are assaulted in schools. The New York State Public Employees Federation has negotiated joint funds to provide small grants to agencies for health and safety projects, and some of the agencies have used the funding to develop violence prevention training and trauma response programs.

Many collective bargaining agreements in the public sector include a provision for joint labor/management health and safety committees. These committees often address the topic of workplace violence. They can provide an effective forum for labor and management to develop preventive programs. For example, the Multi-Union Health and Safety Committee (MUH&SC), of the New York State Office of Mental Health, has developed pilot violence prevention projects, drafted a written policy that was finalized and adopted into formal agency policy on violence prevention and trauma response, obtained funding, and conducted a statewide labor/management conference on the topic, and worked with university researchers on a five-year intervention study.

The experience of MUH&SC was that working with researchers who were respected by both union and management representatives was helpful in reducing traditional labor/management tensions. Furthermore, the significant federal funding that was obtained provided an on-site coordinator. A key to the project's effectiveness was the use of a "participative action research" approach where the researchers and the parties representing the subjects of the research collaborated on the design and delivery of the study and the proposal for intervention. A statewide Project Advisory Committee composed of union and management leaders and staff met periodically with the researchers to provide oversight and guidance throughout the study. The committee collaborated with the researchers in selecting study sites, reviewing research methods, determining staff survey content, planning focus groups, creating an environmental walk-through, and establishing site-based project advisory groups. The local project advisory groups helped plan the delivery of the risk assessment steps and planned implementation of feasible interventions.

Many public employee unions have access to resources to deliver training programs that can raise the awareness of labor and management leaders who are assigned to develop workplace violence prevention programs. Union staff who are assigned to health and safety or education and training may have expertise in these matters. In some cases, the parent organizations (the international unions) can provide this support. Some unions have been awarded grants to develop and deliver health and safety training from state or federal agencies. Jointly negotiated funds also may be used for such purposes.

When cooperative efforts fail, unions revert to traditional union methods such as filing grievances, holding press events, and picketing. For example, after a member was murdered at a youth facility in Virginia, a Service Employees International Union (SEIU) local filed a mass grievance that led to reforms in staffing levels and training.

About half of the states are covered by state OSHA plans that include enforcement of OSHA standards for public employees. The reason only half of the states have OSHA coverage for public employees is that when the federal OSHA law was passed, states were encouraged to administer their own OSHA programs.[15] Currently only half of the states have state plans. They are partially funded by federal OSHA, but this covers only private sector employees, while state OSHA plans cover both private and public sector programs.

While there is no specific federal OSHA violence prevention standard, OSHA's "general duty clause" requires that

> each employer shall furnish to each of his employees employment and a place of employment which are free from recognized hazards that are causing or are likely to cause death or serious physical harm to his employees.[16]

This clause is invoked when there is no applicable OSHA standard. For it to be invoked, however, the following four criteria must be met:

1. *The hazard is serious.* Injury records, testimony, workers' compensation claims, or medical records that show workers have been assaulted or killed on-the-job would establish this element.
2. *The hazard must exist.* Again, there must be a record of injury or risk. The risk cannot be strictly theoretical.
3. *There must be a violation of existing industry standards or practices.* For example, violence prevention training is a routine and accepted practice in psychiatric hospitals. Policies or copies of training curriculum can illustrate this standard practice.
4. *There must be feasible abatement methods.* Increased staffing, changes in procedures, or training would be examples.

In New York State, a number of general duty citations have been issued to public employers regarding the hazard of violence. For example, a state-operated public hospital's psychiatric ward was cited in the aftermath of an attack on a nurse who was attending to a patient in crisis in a secluded wing of the ward. Another case involved a nurse in a state prison, when an inmate tried to rape her in the medical unit. In the latter case, the employer had violated its own key lock procedures and had removed the corrections officer from the post in the medical unit. Violations also were issued in the aftermath of the death of Judith Scanlon, the intensive case manager, who was murdered by a patient while conducting a home visit. The citations issued required training, equipping employees with cell phones or other communication devices, a policy empowering employees to request that a coworker accompany him or her or, in the alternative, refuse to make what he or she believes is an unsafe home visit, and a policy to make sure that staff are accounted for when working in the field. In the Scanlon case, the public employee unions successfully advocated for the state agency to distribute copies of the violations and the model policies developed in response to them to all affected programs statewide. This was done through the efforts of MUH&SC.

Legislative action has been a major arena for activism by public employee unions. In Washington, a coalition that included state and local chapters of SEIU, American Federation of State, County and Municipal Employees (AFSCME), and United Food and Commercial Workers International Union (UFCW), successfully lobbied the legislature to pass laws requiring first studies and later specific standards for violence prevention in private and public hospitals.[17] More recently, Washington State's SEIU 1199NW first submitted draft legislation in that state in 2006, mandating increased staffing levels and other safety precautions following the death of Marty Smith, a mental health case worker, murdered while making a home visit in a case similar to that of Scanlon.[18] Substitute House Bill 1456, referred to as the Marty Smith Act, went into effect on July 22, 2007. Among its provisions, the Marty Smith Act provides for the following additional safeguards for mental health workers who go out into the community:

1. Receive annual safety training;
2. Shall not be required to go out on a high-risk home visit alone;

PREVENTING AND MANAGING WORKPLACE VIOLENCE

3. Shall be provided with a cell phone or comparable device; and

4. Shall have better access to client information relating to a history of dangerousness.

In 2006, then New York governor George Pataki signed into law sweeping violence prevention legislation for public employees[19] (see Appendix for full text of the law). The law was fourteen years in the making. In 1992 four social service workers were murdered in Watkins Glen, New York. The perpetrator, who was disgruntled over the fact that his earnings were being garnished for child support, entered the office where the employees worked and shot them in cold blood. The office had no security features. In the aftermath of the tragedy, the Civil Service Employees Association (CSEA), an AFSCME affiliate, set to work drafting legislation to address the lack of safety and security measures in social service offices, as highlighted by the events in Watkins Glen. The union's efforts culminated, in the summer of 2006, with the passage of the New York State Workplace Violence Prevention Law.[20]

Support for passage of the legislation gained momentum when, earlier that year, CSEA joined forces with the New York State Public Employees Federation (PEF) to build a statewide coalition of public employee unions and public health advocates.[21] For example, PEF conducted a series of one-day trainings to educate and mobilize over three hundred leaders and activists statewide, produced and distributed buttons and flyers, and organized visits to legislators. A seven-minute DVD was produced that allowed injured workers to talk about the devastating impact workplace assaults have had on them, their families, and their patients and clients. The legislative sponsors of the bill were also featured on the DVD, along with the Buffalo district attorney who was responsible for prosecuting the perpetuator in the Scanlon case.

The campaign also included a full-color pamphlet, "Human Faces," with photographs and testimony of ten injured workers. The DVDs and pamphlets were sent to every legislator and district attorney in New York. Further, CSEA and PEF conducted publicity campaigns that included print and radio advertisements. CSEA organized a picket at the governor's mansion in which legislative leaders spoke, and PEF conducted a press conference that featured injured workers, union leaders, legislators, and local district attorneys.

The new law is consistent with OSHA guidelines and requires all public employers to conduct a risk assessment, implement feasible control measures, and provide annual staff training. Employers with more than twenty employees must develop a written violence prevention program.

The law also directed the New York State Department of Labor (NYSDOL) to promulgate regulations detailing requirements and enforcement of the law (see Appendix). These regulations should be finalized in early 2008. A copy of the regulations, as they appeared at the time this book went into production (prior to the regulations being finalized), is included in the Appendix. It was not expected that the final version of the regulations would differ much, if at all, from the version that has been included in the book. The regulations will be enforced by the NYSDOL's Public Employee Safety and Health program, a state OSHA program for public employees. One difference from enforcement of other OSHA standards is that the employee or union must first direct his/her or its complaint to a supervisor and give the public employer an opportunity to correct the alleged hazard before filing a formal complaint with the NYSDOL.

▌ Impact Bargaining

A basic principle in collective bargaining is the right of public employee unions to bargain over the impact of any changes in the terms and conditions of employment on union members. This is true even when the change is prompted by a state or federal agency requirement, such as implementation of an OSHA standard or state safety regulation. Issues relating to the implementation of security measures may also raise "impact bargaining" concerns. For example, if the employer wants to install a swipe card building entry security system or security cameras, it is advisable to involve the union in the selection and installation of such systems.

Generally, union representatives have opposed electronic monitoring of their members. They want assurances that the security systems will not be used to monitor attendance or track employee whereabouts. Engaging the union in all facets of health and safety, and violence prevention, will usually improve results and avoid battles over the unintended impact of such measures. In some cases, unions have advocated for safety systems that included the use of employer-provided cell phones, personal alarms, and procedures for tracking the whereabouts of field employees (e.g., global positioning systems). Collaboration on these matters may also improve labor relations in general.

Trauma Response Programs

Public employee unions have advocated for establishment of critical incident stress management (CISM), or trauma response, programs. These programs play an important role in providing assistance to injured staff, their coworkers, and affected clients during and after a workplace violence incident. These programs use trained staff to provide support through emergency planning, defusing, debriefing, and follow-up. They provide important support to injured workers and to those who have witnessed traumatic events.

It is important for staff to have a forum where they can talk about what happened, how it affected them, and what can be done to prevent similar incidents in the future. Without such a program, organizations are essentially deserting injured and traumatized workers when they are most vulnerable. There are, however, three significant shortcomings with CISM: (1) because some staff are not ready to talk immediately after an incident, CISM interventions may need to be offered more than once, at various intervals, following the incident; (2) some staff have serious enough stress reactions that they may need individual counseling and extended follow-up care; and (3) the important work of learning from the incident, especially, how to prevent future occurrences, is often omitted.

Confidentiality is a cornerstone of any effective CISM program. Depending on the frequency of violent incidents, some organizations choose to train an in-house CISM team while others rely on outside community resources. Both approaches have pros and cons. Training an in-house team should improve access, timeliness of response, and sensitivity of responders to organizational policy, procedures, and culture. However, in organizations that infrequently mobilize the CISM team, team members may have difficulty retaining skills and knowledge learned in CISM team training.

▌ Civil Service and Workers' Compensation Law Reform

From the union perspective, workers should be able to return home from work without broken bones, bruised body parts, and related psychological trauma. Tragically, many workers do not. In the event of workplace injuries, most public employees are covered by state workers' compensation laws. Invariably, this means that assaulted workers will experience wage loss in addition to the insult of being physically attacked at work. Most state workers' compensation laws provide wage replacement that is based on two-thirds of a worker's average annual earnings. However, many states' benefits fall far below that threshold. For example, between 1992 and 2007 workers in New York received a maximum benefit of four hundred dollars per week. In 2007, this rate was equal to only about 40 percent of the statewide average annual wage (SAWW)—a steep decline from the two-thirds average weekly wage rate initially set under the law. Within the first couple of months in 2007, the law was finally reformed to increase the rate to two-thirds of the SAAW, through the efforts of a coalition that included then Governor Elliot Spitzer, leaders of the legislature, the New York State AFL-CIO, and the Business Council.

Some unions have successfully negotiated contract provisions that allow for continuation of employment status, pension, vacation, and, very importantly, health care benefits. Other unions have negotiated provisions that include the use of sick time in controverted cases, light duty return-to-work programs, and joint labor/management workers' compensation committees.

Another problem for injured workers is that in many states an employee can be terminated after being off work for a set time period. In New York, the civil service law permits an employee to remain on job-protected leave (due to an occupational injury) for up to one year. In 2004, the public employee unions successfully lobbied the legislature and governor to amend the rule to allow for up to two years of job-protected leave in cases involving a workplace assault.

▌ Work with Criminal Justice Authorities

Criminal justice authorities often reinforce the mistaken notion that violence is part of the job when injured workers employed in secure institutions seek to press criminal charges against their perpetrators. The mindset is that with limited resources why bother prosecuting an individual who is already locked up. This is an insult to public employees. Civil servants should not have to give up their rights as citizens because they work in a public facility. Unions feel that there should not be a double standard in handling workplace assaults. It should not matter whether the violent act occurred in a bar, a prison, or a hospital. Each case should be prosecuted based on its merits. Additionally, by prosecuting assaulters under existing laws, the legal ramifications of a criminal conviction may serve as a deterrent to future assaults. Conversely, if the assailant "gets away with it," it sends the wrong message to those who would engage in such acts of violence.

In the state of New York, public employee unions have worked with district attorneys to emphasize the importance of prosecuting legally competent patients and clients who physically assault staff.

The unions also have worked hard to convince management officials in state facilities of the importance of prosecuting these cases. All too often injured workers are left on their own to advocate for the prosecution of their perpetuators.

Whether someone is legally competent to stand trial is a major issue in determining whether mentally ill patients who have assaulted facility staff will be held criminally liable for their actions. Although the definition of competency under criminal law varies from state to state, generally it has been defined as being "sufficiently mentally able to stand trial, if he/she understands the proceedings and can rationally deal with his/her lawyer. . . . Capacity is the ability to understand right and wrong and to understand the outcome at the time of the act."[22] It is important for organizations to interact with district attorneys or local prosecuting attorneys to make sure these issues are handled appropriately, and to avoid wholesale dismissal of all assault cases that have taken place in a state or county-run institution.

▌ Conclusion

Workplace violence is a critical issue for public employee unions and their members. The nature of (and the response to) the problem will vary from sector to sector. This makes the development of site and agency-specific interventions very important. Establishment of an ongoing process to assess risk and develop violence prevention programs is the cornerstone of an effective program. When unions and rank-and-file workers are not included in the development of violence prevention programs, distrust and resistance may ensue. The opportunity for collaborative problem solving can make public workplaces safer and improve public services.

Notes

1. AFSCME Laborlinks Web site: Public Sector Collective Bargaining Laws, at http://www.afscme.org/otherlnk/weblnk36.htm.

2. Public Employees Fair Employment Act, the Taylor Law, Civil Service Law Article 14, at http://www.perb.state.ny.us/stat.asp.

3. "Union Members in 2007," Bureau of Labor Statistics News Release, USDL 08-0092, Jan. 25, 2008.

4. "Violence in the Workplace 1993–1999," U.S. Department of Justice, National Crime Victimization Survey, Dec. 2001. This is the most current data collected by the U.S. Department of Justice.

5. FIA and UAW recognize the first anniversary of "Lisa's Law," Release Date: Sept. 3, 2002, at http://www.michigan.gov/printerFriendly/0,1687, 7-124-5458_7691_7752-49834-,00.html.

6. Medline Plus, a service of the U.S. National Library of Medicine and National Institutes of Health, Medical Encyclopedia, at http://www.nlm.nih.gov/medlineplus/ency/article/000925.htm.

7. New York Workers' Compensation Law, § 13-m, Care and treatment of injured employees by duly licensed psychologists.

8. Based on experience of the author in advocating for assaulted members of the New York State Public Employees Federation (PEF).

9. J. Rosen, A Joint Labor/Management Experience in Implementing OSHA's Violence Prevention Guidelines in the New York State Office of Mental Health, Handbook of Modern Hospital Safety, CRC Press, Mar. 1999.

10. This is an estimate based on data provided by the New York State Civil Service Department.

11. According to statistics collected by the federal government, most workplace homicides are committed by persons unknown to the employee/victim or by a customer or client. Most nonfatal assaults occur at the hands of customers or clients, particularly where there is a custodial or client-caregiver relationship between the employee and the attacker. See, e.g., M. Foley & E. Rauser, Violence in Washington Workplaces, 2000–2005, at http://www/Ini.wa.gov/Safety/Research/Files/OccHealth/ViolenceWaWork placesExecSumm.pdf.

12. L.S. Azaroff, C. Levenstein, & D. H. Wegmen, *Occupational Injury and Illness Surveillance: Conceptual Filters Explain Underreporting*, 92 Am. J. Pub. Health 1421 (2002).

13. This statistic is based on the experience of the Mohawk Valley Psychiatric Center, located in Utica, New York. Unpublished data covering the time period 2003–2005 was presented in a written report to a New York Violence Prevention Task Force (made up of facility managers, union leaders, and other staff) in July 2006.

14. "Guidelines for Preventing Workplace Violence for Health Care & Social Service Workers," U.S. Department of Labor, Occupational Safety and Health Administration, OSHA 3148-01R, 2004.

15. 29 U.S.C. § 667, OSHA Act, Section 18, State Jurisdiction and State Plan (c)(6).

16. OSHA Act, Public Law 91-596 84 STAT. 1590, 91st Congress, S.2193, Dec. 29, 1970, Section 5(a)(1).

17. Wash. Rev. Code § 49.19 (Safety: Health Care Settings); Wash. Rev. Code § 72.23.400 (Violence Prevention in State Psychiatric Hospitals).

18. Washington State House of Representatives, Marty Smith Law, SHB 2912 (2006). The final version of the legislation was reintroduced in 2007 under a different number.

19. New York State Workplace Violence Prevention Law, SB6441/AB9691, codified as N.Y. Lab Law § 27-b (2006).

20. Workplace Violence New York Public Employees Campaign, BNA Occupational Safety & Health Reporter, Vol. 36, No. 13.

21. See http://www.pef.org/stopworkplaceviolence.

22. http://www.law.com.

CHAPTER 9

Responding to the Epidemic of Workplace Violence in Public Sector Health Care and Social Service Workplaces

Jane Lipscomb, Matthew London, and Kathleen McPhaul[1]

▌ Introduction and Background

Among the most dangerous workplaces are public sector health care and social service settings.[2] These settings, which often serve society's poorest and most vulnerable individuals, present a substantial risk of workplace violence. This chapter will highlight some of the more serious and prevalent risks and describes violence prevention efforts that are being implemented in an increasing number of agencies and organizations.

The U.S. Department of Justice (DOJ) has estimated that 1.7 million "violent victimizations" (e.g., assaults, verbal threats, harassment) per year occur at work in the United States.[3] Of these, roughly 500 to 600 annually are homicides. The health care sector leads all other industries in the number of nonfatal assaults resulting in lost workdays in the United States; this sector contributes 45 percent of all such assaults. The rate of nonfatal assaults to nursing aides, orderlies, and attendants was 31.8 per 10,000 compared to 2.4 per 10,000 in the private sector as a whole.[4] The DOJ, in their most recent National Crime Victimization Survey (NCVS) report, estimated an overall average annual rate for nonfatal violent crimes at work of 12.5 per 1,000 workers. In the health care field, the average annual rates were higher: 16.2 (physicians), 21.9 (nurses), and 68.4 (professional or custodial mental health workers).[5] Tragically, in some state psychiatric hospitals and schools for the developmentally disabled, the annual rates are even higher—with one hospital reporting 100 assault-related workers' compensation cases per 100 staff.[6]

In 1996, the National Institute for Occupational Safety and Health (NIOSH) issued a bulletin on workplace violence. Based on its review of the published scientific literature, NIOSH listed ten risk factors for workplace violence, two of which included "working with unstable or volatile persons in health care, social service, or criminal justice settings" and "working in community-based settings."[7]

In published guidelines focused on health care and social service workers, the Occupational Safety and Health Administration (OSHA) identified additional risk factors these workers face: the use of hospitals for the care of acutely disturbed and violent individuals; the increased number of mentally ill patients who have been "deinstitutionalized" or released from psychiatric hospitals with inadequate follow-up care; isolated work with clients; lack of staff training; and inadequate staffing during off-shifts and at times of increased activities, such as meal time.[8] (See Figure 9.1.)

Figure 9.1   Risk Factors for Violence in Hospital Settings

- Working directly with volatile people, especially, if they are under the influence of drugs or alcohol or have a history of violence or certain psychotic diagnoses
- Working when understaffed, especially during meal times and visiting hours
- Transporting patients
- Long waits for service
- Overcrowded, uncomfortable waiting rooms
- Working alone
- Poor environmental design
- Inadequate security
- Lack of staff training and policies for preventing and managing crises with potentially volatile patients
- Drug and alcohol abuse
- Access to firearms
- Unrestricted movement of the public
- Poorly lit corridors, rooms, parking lots, and other areas

Source: http://www.cdc.gov/niosh/2002-101.html.

Typically, the perpetrator of violence in these work settings is the patient or client—someone who has a legitimate reason to be present but who commits a violent act nonetheless. In the workplace violence paradigm that was originally developed by the California Division of Occupational Safety and Health (Cal/OSHA) to guide intervention research, this is referred to as Type II violence. Risk mitigation is complicated by contextual factors which underlie the broad risks (e.g., the wide availability of handguns, limits on public funding for social services) and by the rights of those clients being served.[9]

In 2001, a group of experts gathered for a workshop on workplace violence at the invitation of NIOSH and the University of Iowa, at Iowa City. The workshop's findings culminated in the publication of a report titled "Workplace Violence: A Report to the Nation." Among its findings, the report noted the lack of systematic national data collection on workplace assaults, the paucity of data evaluating violence prevention strategies, and the methodological flaws in published intervention research to date.[10]

As background to this report, in 2000, researcher Carol Runyan and her colleagues reviewed the violence prevention intervention literature that was available at the time and found five studies that evaluated violence prevention training interventions, two that examined post-incident psychological debriefing programs, and two that evaluated administrative controls to prevent violence.[11] Findings from the studies were mixed, with six reporting a positive impact and three reporting no or a negative impact. All were quasi-experimental and lacked a formal control group. Runyan and her coauthors criticized the design of the published violence prevention interventions available at the time because they lacked systematic rigor.[12]

In the same year Runyan et al. conducted their review of the existing literature, researchers Judith Arnetz and Bengt Arnetz reported on a randomized control trial of forty-seven health care workplaces. In the intervention facilities, there was "structured feedback" from supervisors following incidents.[13] In the comparison facilities, incidents were reported without structured discussion. This study found that staff in the intervention workplaces reported better awareness of risk situations for violence, of how potentially violent situations could be avoided, and of how to deal with aggressive patients. However, there were significantly more (50 percent) violent incidents reported in the intervention facilities compared with the control group workplaces. The authors attributed this finding to an increased awareness of the workplace violence incidents on the part of staff and improved supervisory support at the intervention facilities.

Between 2000 and 2004, Jane Lipscomb (one of this chapter's authors) and her colleagues conducted an intervention effectiveness study to design and evaluate a comprehensive process for implementing the OSHA Violence Prevention Guidelines and to evaluate its impact in the mental health setting.[14] Program impact was evaluated by a combination of quantitative and qualitative assessments. This work is described in greater detail later in this chapter.

▌ Overview and Context

Patients' rights issues, consumer preferences to live in the community, and the patient safety movement are critical elements of the social service and health care environments. Given reduced public funding for social services, the prevention of workplace violence in these settings involves overcoming many challenges. Among those challenges is that the health care or social service "workplace" may be a street corner, a homeless shelter, or a group home or individual residence. Further complicating the situation is the fact that many social service or health care employers, and often even the workers themselves, accept these dangerous conditions as a part of the job. They may believe that violence in the workplace is inherent and unpredictable, and therefore that nothing can or should be done about it.

The public sector workforce is at extremely high risk for Type II violence, as a large proportion of its workers are employed in high-risk environments. This chapter will focus on the risk of workplace violence in the health care and social service sectors in both institutional and community settings, while recognizing that many of the risks and prevention strategies discussed are applicable to other public service sector work settings.

A number of factors increase the risk of violence toward public sector health care and social service workers, including caring for populations and individuals who: reside in violent communities; have a history of violent behavior; and/or have co-occurring substance abuse disorders, mental illness, or mental retardation. For example, in the fields of mental health and substance abuse services, public institutions are frequently the only facilities in which very high-risk clients, often lacking private health insurance, will be admitted for treatment. It is public sector workers who evaluate child welfare cases, administer public benefit programs, and run medical and psychiatric clinics, often located in violent communities. To date, most of the research on public sector Type II violence risks has focused on health care, with the social service workplace lagging behind, despite the fact that many social service workers care for extremely high-risk clients.

In 2002, the Washington State Department of Labor and Industries issued a report titled "Violence in Washington Workplaces 1995–2000" that presented data from the U.S. Bureau of Labor Statistics' (BLS) Survey of Occupational Injuries and Illnesses and from Washington State's workers' compensation claims related to assaults and violence.[15] For nonfatal violence-related injuries, workers' compensation data ranked social services (142 per 10,000 workers) as the highest risk industry followed by health services (74.6 per 10,000 workers). Residential care was ranked second among *specific* industry codes (301 per 10,000 workers); individual family and social services was ranked tenth (79 per 10,000 workers). Notably, these two specific industry sectors reported the second and third greatest percent increase in assault rates over the period 1995–2000, 46 percent and 33 percent, respectively.

Among Washington State workers across all industry codes, rates of compensable assault cases were substantially higher for state (30.4 per 10,000 workers) and local government workers (8.9 per 10,000 workers), compared with private sector workers (2.3 per 10,000 workers). Differences between public and private workers' risk is due in part to the high concentration of health and social services employment, as well as public safety jobs, within the public sector. While the incidence of workplace assaults has been trending sharply downward for private sector workers, both in Washington State and nationally, the trend has risen significantly for public sector employees.[16]

Workplace violence is one of the most complex and dangerous occupational hazards facing health care and social service workers today. The complexities arise, in part, from a society oblivious to workers' risk of patient-related violence, combined with the attitude that violence for those working with mental health patients "is part of the job." The dangers arise from the exposure to violent individuals in combination with a lack of strong violence prevention programs and protective regulations. These factors, together with organizational realities such as staffing shortages and more acutely ill patients, create substantial barriers to eliminating violence in these work settings.

In addition, government, certifying and/or licensing bodies, managers, and community organizations frequently prioritize patient safety over worker safety, without recognizing that patient and staff safety are inextricably linked. Staff from a state hospital for the mentally retarded and developmentally disabled told the authors that their management's interpretation of federal patient safety and accrediting criteria requires staff to "take the bullet" in the event that a patient is potentially at risk of assault by another patient.

Another significant organizational barrier to violence prevention efforts is the practice of discouraging or refusing to support workers in pressing criminal charges against patients following an assault. Workers are often led to believe that they check their civil rights at the door upon arriving at work. Health care and social services workers are often not given the same rights as other public servants, e.g., police officers, who would never be denied the right to press charges against an individual who has assaulted them while in their custody. In fact, police officers injured in the line of duty are given special protections under the law.

Deinstitutionalization of the mentally ill, the increase in patients with dual addiction and mental health problems, and the overcrowding of U.S. prison systems have resulted in patient and inmate populations across all health care, social services, and criminal justice settings who are more acutely ill and difficult to treat. Staff across these settings consistently report that they do not have the training and resources to adequately care for such individuals.

Insufficient reimbursement for the care of high-risk individuals, many of whom are uninsured or underinsured, leaves public health systems barely functional and exposes the staff caring for them to an unconscionable level of risk of injury from workplace violence. A recent piece of Washington State legislation (the Marty Smith Law), brought about by a broad coalition of advocates for the mentally ill and worker health and safety, can serve as a model for bringing additional financial resources to the table, hopefully improving both patient care and worker safety. The funding provides for an additional person to accompany community mental health workers on high-risk visits.[17]

High Caseloads and Sicker Clients

In 2006, we conducted a field study of Washington State community mental health workers, employers, and advocates for the mentally ill. The following discussion summarizes findings from the focus groups and key informant interviews conducted across the state.[18]

Mental health workers fault the organization and funding of the mental health system as a root cause of violence. Not surprisingly, system deficits that erode patient safety and the quality of care are often the same root deficits that result in unsafe working conditions. Workers, patients, and managers alike all agree that cutbacks and cost shifting in mental health care funding have resulted in higher caseloads and sicker clients. Budget cuts to mental health care mean more clients per worker. Furthermore, staff, consumers, and managers agree that reduced funding forces the system into prioritizing services for the acutely ill, leaving care for the chronically mentally ill and preventive and early intervention care largely unfunded. This means that, in many cases, a person's mental illness has been allowed to progress without care until their condition is acute and life threatening. Thus, patients are sicker by the time they receive care under the current system. Even community care clients are often dangerously ill by the time they are eligible for services. Furthermore, acute hospitalizations, according to staff, are not long enough to return the patient to a baseline functionality or restore their ability to function independently in the community. Community supports are weak, resulting in clients who are not quite ready to be released back into the community but are discharged nonetheless.

According to workers, higher caseloads translate directly into reduced time for case management and therapy for clients. Reduced time for each client means less time to read their history, if there is one, or search databases for information about a history of criminal violence. Higher caseloads mean shorter or less frequent appointments, reducing the likelihood that the client will be able to develop a trusting relationship with the caregiver. Shorter initial appointments are especially problematic. The initial visit is where the case manager and the client develop their relationship and begin therapeutic processes, enabling the case manager to obtain valuable information about the client. Community mental health workers report shortening appointments from one hour to a half hour in the face of radically increased caseloads, up from fifteen to between forty-five and sixty in some instances.

Case workers frequently report that they believe their high caseloads prohibit them from providing the kind of care they were trained to provide. One case worker told the authors that he fears he will be terminated by his supervisor because he neglects paperwork in order to spend more time with his clients. The stress and job dissatisfaction arising from increased caseloads, as well as the related paperwork burdens, have resulted in high turnover and vacancy rates, according to some staff. Qualified workers are changing jobs within the field, and some are leaving the mental health care field altogether. Staff vacancies often result in an inexperienced and highly stressed workforce, continuing the vicious cycle.

That said, mental health workers report that when working conditions permit, the work is highly rewarding. Several focus group participants in Washington State described leaving other occupational fields, including accounting and construction, to work in mental health because they found the personal rewards to be greater. Mental health workers are dedicated to the care of society's most vulnerable and find great personal reward in this work. Unfortunately, when the system cannot support decent, humane, effective mental health care, these workers may be less likely to remain in their jobs.

Incomplete Access to Client History of Violence and Criminal Conduct

In the aftermath of the tragic death of a mental health worker in Washington State, administrators began to investigate the barriers to obtaining relevant information, such as a client's criminal history and evidence of past violent behavior. The problem is that some of this information goes beyond what is generally available in the clinical record, but may be relevant to both client and staff safety. In the Washington State case, relevant information about several past episodes of violent behavior involving law enforcement were not known to the worker when he decided to visit the client alone. This type of information is critical for all psychiatric care workers to have, but is of the utmost importance to community-based mental health workers. Substantive barriers to accessing this information continue to exist. Issues relating to confidentiality, civil liberties, and interagency cooperation (i.e., justice and social services) have been raised and will need to be carefully addressed in order to improve access to information that is critical to both the workers' and the community's safety.

Noncompliant Patients

Mental health workers lament that medication noncompliance is often a reason for decompensation (i.e., medical instability) and acute illness. This may be due to inadequate supervision of the patient, poor access or lack of financial means to purchase medications, the patient entering the criminal justice system, or health care provider unavailability. Suffice it to say, without regular care and adherence to a prescribed medication regimen, many mentally ill patients risk relapsing, potentially resulting in violence toward themselves or others.

▌ Institutional Settings: Risks and Preventive Strategies

Institutional health care settings where workers are especially vulnerable include mental health and acute psychiatric settings, emergency departments, geriatric and gero-psychiatric units, and some intensive care areas such as neurotrauma.

For example, in a Washington State forensic hospital, a facility that treats the criminally mentally ill, staff completed a self-administered survey and reported an incidence rate of 437 assaults per 100 employees per year; on average, each employee suffered more than four assaults per year. Seventy-three percent of staff who completed the survey reported that they had been assaulted by a patient during the previous year and suffered at least a minor injury. Factors such as working in isolation, being a mental health technician, and working on the geriatric-medical hospital unit were associated with more severe employee injuries. Employees suffered less severe injuries if had they received assault management training within the prior year.[19]

Many psychiatric settings now require that all patient care providers receive annual training in the management of aggressive patients. To date, few studies have examined the effectiveness of such training. Those that have done so have generally found improvement in nurses' knowledge, confidence, and sense of safety after being trained in how to manage aggressive behavior. However, in the absence of a comprehensive violence prevention program, training alone is unlikely to significantly improve safety.

The emergency department is another high-risk setting for staff assaults. Individuals carrying weapons in emergency departments create the opportunity for severe or fatal injuries. A National Institute of Justice report estimated that, in 1994, there were enough guns owned in the United States that every adult could have one.[20] Tragically, many of these guns are being brought into the emergency department. A fourteen-year study conducted at a Los Angeles hospital found that between 1979 and 1993, 26 percent of major trauma patients were armed with deadly weapons. The hospital's screening process used either metal detectors or involved the removal and inspection of all clothing. This yielded an average of 5.4 weapons a day, of which 84 percent were guns and most of the remaining weapons were knives.[21] Focus groups conducted by the authors in a number of states have revealed a belief that much of the emergency department violence is gang related, placing both patients and staff at risk.

A recent study of a 770-bed acute care hospital, in Florida, surveyed nurses working in intensive care and the emergency department, and floor nurses. When asked about their experience with workplace violence during the prior year, every nurse in the emergency room reported being verbally assaulted and 82.1 percent reported being physically assaulted. Even among the floor nurses, 80.6 percent reported being verbally assaulted and 63.3 percent reported being physically assaulted.[22]

Staff safety and the quality/safety of client care are inextricably linked. Not surprisingly, many violent patients/clients assault and threaten their peers, not just their caregivers. Researchers have found that violence experienced by health care staff is associated with lower patient ratings of the quality of care.[23] Optimal staffing levels and staff performance are essential in order to provide high-quality care. When significant numbers of staff are injured, the remaining staff may have to work excessive mandatory overtime or there may be short staffing. Additionally, the replacement staff may not be familiar with the patients and may lack crucial information regarding patients' highly individual needs, triggers, and behaviors. In all scenarios, the quality of care suffers.

Although mental health and emergency departments have been the focus of research, and even some legislation, no department within a health care setting is immune from workplace violence. Consequently, violence prevention programs should be developed for all departments and units.

Case Example: Institutional Psychiatric Facility

The OSHA Violence Prevention Guidelines were the basis of a four-year research collaboration (2000–2004) between an academic research team, a state mental health system, and a joint-labor management health and safety committee.* Preliminary work in two state mental health hospitals provided evidence supporting the feasibility of implementing the OSHA Violence Prevention Guidelines by using a participatory approach to develop facility or ward-specific processes.† The project involved three intervention facilities and three comparison or "usual care" facilities. All of the facilities provided inpatient care to the high-risk mentally ill. The agencies and labor unions had already been involved for years in collaborative efforts to reduce workplace violence in their facilities by implementing such programs as training, data collection, and post-assault care. What follows is a brief description of the project's activities.

Each intervention facility formed a facility-level advisory group comprised of direct care staff and management representatives. These labor-management facility advisory committees met regularly and provided input during each stage of the project and directed every aspect of the intervention at their facilities. The project included three hazard analysis activities, staff focus groups, an environmental audit, and staff surveys.

The focus groups provided a confidential forum for staff to discuss the prevalence of violence in their facilities and their perception of the etiology of the violence. Staff were also asked to recommend strategies to prevent or eliminate violence in their facilities.

An architect with experience in security designs conducted the environmental audits in each of the intervention facilities; facility advisory group members participated in these audits. Additionally, other direct care staff who were working at the time were interviewed regarding the physical work environment. This included staff across all shifts. Each facility received a report that included short- and long-term recommendations.

A staff survey, informed by the focus group findings, was developed and administered to all staff during work time. The survey included questions about verbal threats of assaults, as well as physical assaults with mild, moderate, severe, and disabling injuries. Other questions assessed procedures, communication, and work organization, as well as staff perceptions regarding the quality of the OSHA violence prevention elements at their facility and their perceptions of the quality of violence prevention training. This survey was administered early in the project and repeated two years later to evaluate the impact of the program's implementation.

Each intervention facility developed their own hazard control plan based on the findings of their focus groups, their environmental audit, and their staff survey. Control strategies included any engineering, administrative, or behavioral activities designed to protect workers from violence. For example, improved change of work shift communication became a control strategy in one mental health facility, and the installation of a new personal alarm system was a control strategy in a different facility. Midway through the intervention period, direct care staff were brought together for a series of "solutions-mapping" sessions designed to allow direct care staff and management to work collectively on their issues of highest priority. Training and education consisted of their existing 2.5-day initial and one-day annual PMCS (prevention and management of crisis situations) training program. This curriculum was developed by internal experts and had been recently revised; therefore, the emphasis of the project's training component focused on communicating ongoing findings from the risk analysis phase of the project and joint labor-management discussion of solutions to identified problems.

A comparison of pre- and post-intervention survey data indicated an improvement in staff perception of the quality of the facility's violence prevention program as defined by the OSHA elements in both intervention and comparison facilities over the course of the project. The impact on the rates of staff-reported physical assaults was equivocal, however. Qualitative findings included reports from intervention sites of a number of project successes, including a violence prevention training coach at one study site and the adoption of one facility's written violence prevention program into the facility's overall strategic plan. Intervention sites generated a list of violence prevention best practices that were then shared with the directors of their sister facilities within the state system.

* J. Lipscomb et al., *Violence Prevention in the Mental Health Setting: The New York State Experience*, 38 CJNR 96–117 (2006).

† J. Rosen, *A Joint Labor/Management Experience in Implementing OSHA's Violence Prevention Guidelines in the New York State Office of Mental Health*, in Handbook of Modern Hospital Safety, ed. W. Charney (Boca Raton, Fla.: CRC Press, Lewis Publishers, 1999).

Community Settings: Risks and Preventive Strategies

Advocates of the developmentally disabled have successfully pushed for reforms resulting in a transferring of care from restrictive "warehousing" environments to more homelike, less restrictive living environments. While this transformation has been largely positive and beneficial, it poses some problems as well. In general, these facilities are highly regulated for the protection of the clients and subject to frequent audits and inspections by public agencies. Considerably less regulated is the safety of the work environment, despite substantial workers' compensation costs and high staff turnover. Social service workers, particularly those employed by public agencies that provide outpatient and residential services to the severely developmentally disabled or mentally ill, often care for clients whose behavior is not sufficiently stable or safe for these noninstitutional settings.

The risks to visiting social service and health care workers have been documented by a number of researchers.[24] Homicides of visiting social workers and nurses have been reported in Texas, Maryland, Michigan, Kansas, New York, Washington, Ohio, and Kentucky. In response to these deaths, legislation has been introduced in several of these states (Michigan, Kansas, New York, Washington) to strengthen and/or require specific safety measures for these at-risk workers.[25] These measures include community-specific violence prevention training, the use of cell phones or pagers, and visiting high-risk clients accompanied by a coworker.[26]

Important risk factors emerging from these homicides include: (1) the client's perception (regardless of the reality) that the visit would result in removing children from the home (New York, Texas, and Michigan); (2) care provider unknown to the patient (Washington and Maryland); (3) client in mental health crisis requiring possible involuntary commitment (Washington, Kansas); (4) relevant criminal history not known to case worker (Washington, Kansas, New York); and (5) worker visiting alone (all).[27]

Protecting home visiting mental health workers presents substantial and complex challenges. Each home entered by the employee is a unique and unpredictable work environment. Unlike institutional settings, there are no security guards screening for weapons and contraband, no alarm systems or panic buttons, no video monitors, mirrors, special lights, quick release locks, or drop phones, and no additional staff to assist if a patient becomes agitated during the course of the visit.

In addition, home care workers often must conduct a visit relatively ignorant of the patient's history of violence and recent stability and behavior. In community and home-based settings, unlike institutional settings, patient behavior is not typically monitored by qualified clinicians on an around-the-clock basis. Monitoring and documenting patient behavior may not be perfect in institutional settings, but the likelihood of identifying a patient who is becoming unstable is definitely improved. Home visiting pushes the limits of traditional safety programming practice.[28]

Fortunately, the majority of developmentally disabled and/or mentally ill clients who live at home do so because their condition is stable. Home visiting services enable these clients to remain in the community, where they can be close to family and friends. Yet, clients may decompensate (i.e., become upset, agitated, or out of control) and some are "high risk" to a home visiting worker. Home visits which are identified as being "high risk" should always be conducted by pairs of workers. The assessment of risk, while imperfect, should be based on the patient's history, clinical recommendations, and the input of family and friends.

Case Example: Community Setting

Following the murder of a visiting social worker in a northwestern state, the authors of this chapter were invited to conduct a consultative field study. The victim's union arranged for access to multiple administrators, agencies, and groups of community-based field workers caring for the mentally ill. Factors reported to be associated with violence included high caseloads, sicker clients, paperwork burdens, management emphasis on productivity rather than quality or safety, and other concerns such as lack of access to criminal history and patients' inability to obtain needed psychiatric medications.

The frequency of violent encounters varied by mental health setting. By far, community emergency and treatment centers (E and Ts) reported having the most frequent experience with combative and assaultive clients. The very purpose of E and Ts is short-term institutionalization for the acutely and dangerously mentally ill. Staff make the final judgment for involuntary commitment, often in settings like emergency rooms, clinics, and client homes. Generally, outpatient and home visit settings report less overt violence, but more verbal aggression and fear associated with the potential for violence. They also report a lack of safety and security programs, including training.

Unpredictable behavior, a symptom of some mental illnesses, increases the risk of assault to workers. Many outpatient case managers and mental health workers are responsible for transporting clients, frequently without a coworker present. Workers describe instances of unpredictable behavior on the part of their passenger/client, such as changing the gearshift or trying to exit the vehicle while it is in motion.

Staff in the community mental health system reported the full spectrum of violence, from sexual harassment, verbal threats of harm, spitting, profane language, and unwanted touching and physical contact, to major assaults with physical injuries or even death. Generally, physical assaults are the primary cause of concern, as they result in lost work time, medical costs, pain and suffering, and even permanent disability or death. Much of the verbal and sexual aggression and minor assaults are not reported and, thus, not officially recognized. The possible relationships between lower level violence and things like job satisfaction, patient safety, quality of care, absenteeism, and staff retention are not well understood, but merit additional investigation.

Developing a Comprehensive Workplace Violence Prevention Program (WVPP)

There is no federal standard that addresses how to develop a workplace violence prevention program. California and Washington both have adopted legislation addressing workplace violence in health care settings. In 1993, after the murders of three emergency room physicians, Cal/OSHA published the first set of OSHA guidelines (not mandatory standards) describing the components of a comprehensive workplace violence prevention program.[29] These guidelines were followed by a comprehensive health and safety program standard which codified the California guidelines.[30] After several years of pressure from a multiunion task force on workplace violence, federal OSHA followed California's lead and, in 1996, issued a similar set of guidelines, entitled "Guidelines for Preventing Workplace Violence for Healthcare and Social Service Workers."[31]

The 1996 federal OSHA guidelines provide a framework for addressing the problem of workplace violence and include the basic elements of any proactive health and safety program. We have included additional information to buttress and expand the OSHA guidelines.

1. *Management commitment.* Management commitment must be evident in the form of high-level management involvement and support for a written workplace violence prevention policy and its implementation.

2. *Employee involvement.* Meaningful employee involvement in policy development, risk assessment, joint management-worker violence prevention committees, post-assault counseling and debriefing, and follow-up are all critical program components. This should include frontline workers and, where a union exists, union representatives. Without both management commitment and employee involvement, it is unlikely that an effective program will be developed.

3. *Work site analysis.* A work site analysis is the foundation on which an effective program exists. This analysis should utilize all available "data" sources and be repeated, at least in part, on a periodic basis. "Data" sources include: OSHA logs, unusual incident logs, and workers' compensation data. This information can be invaluable in identifying trends and risk factors.[32]

   However, a number of researchers have identified significant barriers and disincentives to reporting workplace incidents and injuries.[33] In the Washington State forensic hospital survey, referenced earlier, staff reported 437 assaults per 100 employees per year. By comparison, the hospital incident reporting system reflected a rate of only 35.3 assaults per 100 employees. Of those reporting a moderate, severe, or disabling injury related to an assault, only 43 percent filed for workers' compensation.[34]

Thus, relying solely on existing data sources may lead to severely underestimating the extent of the problem and failing to take into account significant risk factors that have not been documented. The data sources should be complemented, therefore, by such things as staff surveys, focus groups, and other forms of direct communication with frontline workers.

Finally, regular walk-through surveys of all areas of the facility should be conducted, and should include staff from each area and from all shifts. Special attention should be paid to those areas where assaults have occurred.

NIOSH, in a 2002 report, summarized the risk factors for occupational violence to hospital workers, many of which are applicable to the social service sector, including community and residential settings. Understaffing, especially during times of increased activity such as meal times and visiting hours, is associated with a higher risk of assaults on hospital workers.[35] Staff working alone or in isolation from other staff are vulnerable to assault. Moreover, meal times and times of increased activity on hospital wards appear to result in agitation and violence in some hospitalized individuals. In the social services, as in any setting, the presence of multiple staff is probably a deterrent to assault, but specific studies in this sector are absent.

Transporting patients, long waits for services, inadequate security, poor environmental design, and unrestricted movement of the public are associated with increased risk of assault in hospitals and may be significant factors in social service workplaces as well. Often transportation is provided by social service agencies for clients who are disabled or not competent to drive or get themselves to appointments. This is yet another unexamined aspect of risk among social service workers.

4. *Hazard prevention and control.* Hazard prevention and control measures should be designed based on the risk factors identified above. The classic industrial hygiene hierarchy of controls should be followed: (1) eliminating or reducing the risk through technological or engineering controls (e.g., installation of panic alarms); (2) implementing administrative measures (e.g., policies and procedures, training); and (3) use of personal protective equipment (e.g., protective clothing).

Hazard prevention and control measures to consider include: modifying the layout of admissions areas, nurses' stations, medication rooms, lounges, patient rooms, or offices; limiting access to certain areas; evaluating all furnishings to ensure that they are not used as weapons; installing metal detectors; improving lighting; adding mirrors or cameras, etc. Other options include hiring trained security personnel, adding direct-care staff, or redeploying existing staff more effectively (e.g., adding a second person for overnight duty). Developing and implementing appropriate policies and providing regular training are important administrative controls. Finally, personal protective devices may be warranted, such as issuing cell phones and personal alarm devices to workers.

Staff involvement is just as important in designing effective controls as it is in conducting a thorough risk assessment. Frontline staff and union representatives can help identify unintended consequences of various prevention measures, and can provide feedback as to whether the changes implemented have been effective.

Additionally, programs need to be in place to provide support to assault victims and to their coworkers. These can include easy access to medical and mental health services, assistance with the workers' compensation system, and support in accessing the criminal justice system, when appropriate.

Finally, to the extent possible, exposure to the potential violence should be eliminated. An example would be transferring an unstable, violent patient to a different facility, one that is better equipped to provide care to a high-risk patient.

5. *Training and education.* At the time of hiring and periodically thereafter, worksite- and job-specific training should be provided covering the risk factors, prevention measures, and relevant policies and procedures. This training should not be generic. For direct care staff, training should include skills in aggressive behavior identification and management.

6. *Record keeping and program evaluation.* Record keeping and program evaluation are inextricably linked and should focus on not only incidents of physical and verbal assaults but also on near misses. One is observing only the "tip of the iceberg" if one relies solely on workers' compensation claims or OSHA logs. Reporting should be something that staff are actively encouraged to do. Reports should be followed up and investigated promptly, with the results relayed to the individual who made the report. Obviously, employees should not be retaliated against for filling out an incident report or filing a workers' compensation claim. The reporting and investigation of incidents is a critical means of evaluating the effectiveness of the WVPP and of identifying control measures which need to be modified or implemented.

The OSHA guidelines merely provide a blueprint for developing a violence prevention program. Because these guidelines are "performance-based" rather than prescriptive, the responsibility lies with each employer to develop a specific and effective process for implementing the guidelines along with input from their staff and unions (where present). It should be noted that a number of international professional and governmental agencies have also issued guidance on violence prevention in health care settings.[36]

▌ Recommendations and Conclusions

To curtail the assaults on health care and social service workers, all parties involved must align and define their "safety" goals to include not only consumers/clients and the community but also the workforce. Currently, public safety, patient and consumer safety, and occupational safety pursue parallel and often competing agendas that yield mixed results for various stakeholders and, as is often the case, very unsafe working conditions.

We recommend a regulatory approach that includes mandated comprehensive health and safety programs for all public sector workplaces. These programs should be dynamic; in other words, they should be reviewed and revised periodically, especially following a serious incident. They should include all elements of the OSHA guidelines. These standards should be incorporated into current institutional licensure and accreditation criteria. This has been successfully done with respect to bloodborne pathogen exposure in health care, where both OSHA and the Joint Commission (formerly the Joint Commission on Accreditation of Healthcare Organizations) have provided specific requirements for health care facilities.

Additionally, severe workplace assaults must be evaluated for their possible criminality; and, where appropriate, referrals to the criminal justice system must be made.

Policies to safeguard the rights of the mentally ill and developmentally disabled, while laudable, must be balanced with the right of workers to return home safely to their family at the end of each workday. Ignoring the dangers to the workforce has already contributed to reduced morale, an exodus of experienced staff, and staff shortages—all of which negatively impact the quality of care and increase the likelihood of violence.

Understanding that workplace violence intervention research is only just beginning to identify and test the possible solutions to this problem, we propose a final recommendation. Violence is pervasive both in the United States and globally, and the roots of workplace violence are surely the same as for the violence that pervades our communities. Nevertheless, the principle that employers must provide a safe and healthful workplace for their employees is well established. Given that OSHA has developed a strong framework for workplace violence prevention, we strongly recommend that the existing OSHA Violence Prevention Guidelines in health care and social service workplace settings become the basis for a *mandatory* workplace standard. Any potentially competing standards and regulations should be reviewed to eliminate conflicts and to ensure that the safety and rights of patients/consumers, the community, and workers are all safeguarded.

Unfortunately, Type II workplace violence is endemic in today's health care and social service workplaces. In this chapter we have described the magnitude of the problem, known risk factors, and a feasible program for prevention. An example of an academic, union, and employer partnership that used the OSHA Violence Prevention Guidelines as a blueprint was described. The scientific community, government regulators, health care employers, professional associations, and health care unions should craft regulations acceptable to all parties, with the goal of eliminating workplace violence. Being assaulted at work should never be part of anyone's job.

Notes

1. The authors would like to thank Kelly Flannery, University of Maryland doctoral student, for all of her research and assistance. Most importantly, we would like to thank the thousands of nurses, aides, social workers, and others who provide compassionate care and service to the most vulnerable members of our society. Their wisdom and concern has been communicated to us through surveys, focus groups, and personal conversations. It is to them that we dedicate this chapter.

2. National Occupational Research Agenda Update 2001. Pub. No. 2001-147. Cincinnati, Ohio: U.S. Dept. of Health and Human Services, Centers for Disease Control and Prevention, National Institute for Occupational Safety and Health, 2001; J. Lipscomb & C. Love, *Violence Toward Health Care Workers: An Emerging Occupational Hazard,* 40 American Association of Occupational Health Nurses 219–228 (1992); T.J. Rippon, *Aggression and Violence in Health Care Professions,* 31 Journal of Advanced

Nursing 452–460 (2000); G. Toscano & W. Weber, *Violence in the Workplace*. Washington, D.C.: U.S. Dept. of Labor, Bureau of Labor Statistics, 1995; G. Warchol, *Workplace Violence, 1992–1996*. Washington, D.C.: U.S. Dept. of Justice, Office of Justice Programs, 1998; Occupational Safety and Health Administration (OSHA). 1996. Guidelines for Preventing Workplace Violence for Health Care and Social Service Workers. OSHA Publication 3148. Washington, D.C.: U.S. Department of Labor.

3. D.T. Duhart, *Violence in the Workplace, 1993–99*. Washington, D.C.: U.S. Dept. of Justice, Office of Justice Programs, 2001.

4. Bureau of Labor Statistics, Nonfatal Occupational Injuries and Illnesses Requiring Days Away from Work. Washington, D.C.: U.S. Dept. of Labor, Bureau of Labor Statistics. Pub. No. 07-1741 (2007), available at http://www.bls.gov/news.release/pdf/osh2.pdf.

5. Duhart, *Violence*.

6. S. Manning, *Injury Among Direct Healthcare Staff: An Unheralded Occupational Safety & Health Crisis*, 50 Professional Safety 31–40 (2005).

7. E. Lynn Jenkins. 1996. Current Intelligence Bulletin No. 57: Workplace Violence—Risk Factors and Prevention Strategies. Morgantown, W.Va.: U.S. Department of Health and Human Services, Public Health Service, Centers for Disease Control and Prevention, National Institute for Occupational Safety and Health. DHHS (NIOSH) Publication No. 96-100.

8. OSHA, Guidelines for Preventing Workplace Violence.

9. University of Iowa Injury Prevention Research Center. *Workplace Violence: A Report to the Nation*. Iowa City: University of Iowa (2001).

10. Ibid.

11. C.W. Runyan, R.C. Zakocs & C. Zwerling, *Administrative and Behavioral Interventions for Workplace Violence Prevention*, 18 American Journal of Preventive Medicine 116–127 (2000); H. Carmel & M. Hunter, *Compliance with Training in Managing Assaultive Behavior and Injuries from Inpatient Violence*, 41 Hospital & Community Psychiatry 558–560 (1990); D. Goodridge, P. Johnston & M. Thomson, *Impact of a Nursing Assistant Training Program on Job Performance, Attitudes, and Relationships with Residents*, 23 Educational Gerontology 37 (1997); J.A. Infantino, Jr., & S.Y. Musingo, *Assaults and Injuries Among Staff With and Without Training in Aggression Control Techniques*, 36 Hospital & Community Psychiatry 1312–1314 (1985); L. Lehmann, M. Padilla, S. Clark & S. Loucks, *Training Personnel in the Prevention and Management of Violent Behavior*, 34 Hospital & Community Psychiatry 40–43 (1983); J. Parkes, *Control and Restraint Training: A Study of Its Effectiveness in a Medium Secure Psychiatric Unit*, 7 Journal of Forensic Psychiatry 525–534 (1996); M. Flannery, H. Rosen & K. Turner, *Victims No More: Preventing Home Care Aide Abuse*, 17 Caring 48–50, 52–43 (1998); L.R. Matthews, *Effects of Staff Debriefing on Post-Traumatic*

Stress Symptoms After Assaults by Community Housing Residents, 49 Psychiatric Services 207–212 (1998); J.E. Arnetz & B.B. Arnetz, *Implementation and Evaluation of a Practical Intervention Programme for Dealing with Violence Towards Health Care Workers*, 31 Journal of Advanced Nursing 668–680 (2000); D. Drummond, L.F. Sparr & G.H. Gordon, *Hospital Violence Reduction Among High-Risk Patients*, 261 JAMA 2531–2534 (1989); M.E. Hunter & C.C. Love, *Total Quality Management and the Reduction of Inpatient Violence and Costs in a Forensic Psychiatric Hospital*, 47 Psychiatric Services 751–754 (1996).

12. Runyan, Zakocs & Zwerling, *Administrative and Behavioral Interventions*.

13. Id.; Arnetz & Arnetz, *Implementation and Evaluation*.

14. J. Lipscomb et al., *Violence Prevention in the Mental Health Setting: The New York State Experience*, 38 CJNR 96–117 (2006).

15. M. Foley, *Violence in Washington Workplaces, 1995–2000*. Olympia: Washington State Department of Labor and Industries. Technical Report Number 39-4-2002 (2002).

16. Id.

17. http://www.leg.wa.gov/pub/billinfo/2007-08/Pdf/Bills/House%20Passed%20Legislature/1456-S.PL.pdf.

18. K. McPhaul, J. Lipscomb & M. London, *The Risk of Violence in Mental Health Work: A Report on Workplace Violence in Washington State Community Mental Health Services*, 2006, University of Maryland, Work and Health Resource Center, at http://www.seiu1199nw.org/docUploads/UM%20Safety%Report.pdf.

19. L. Bensley et al., *Injuries Due to Assaults on Psychiatric Hospital Employees in Washington State*, 31 American Journal of Industrial Medicine 92–99 (1997).

20. J. Travis, Guns in America: National Survey on Private Ownership and Use of Firearms. National Institute of Justice, NCJ 165476 (1997).

21. G.J. Ordog, J. Wasserberger, C. Ordog, G. Ackroyd & S. Atluri, *Weapon Carriage among Major Trauma Victims in the Emergency Department*, 2 Academic Emergency Medicine 109–114 (1995).

22. D.D. May & L.M. Grubbs, *The Extent, Nature, and Precipitating Factors of Nursing Assault among Three Groups of Registered Nurses in a Regional Medical Center*, 28 Journal of Emergency Nursing 11–17 (2002).

23. J.E. Arnetz & B.B. Arnetz, *Violence Towards Health Care Staff and Possible Effects on the Quality of Patient Care*, 52 Social Science & Medicine 417–427 (2001).

24. E. Fitzwater & D. Gates, *Violence and Home Care: A Focus Group Study*, 18 Home Health Nurse 596–605 (2000) P. Fazzone, L.F. Barloon, S.J. McConnell & J.A. Chitty, *Personal Safety, Violence, and Home Health*,

17 Public Health Nursing 43–52 (2000); J. Barling, A.G. Rogers & E.K. Kelloway, *Behind Closed Doors: In-Home Workers' Experience of Sexual Harassment and Workplace Violence*, 6 Journal of Occupational Health Psychology 255–269 (2001); A. Bussing & T. Hoge, *Aggression and Violence Against Home Care Workers*, 9 Journal of Occupational Health Psychology 206–219 (2004); S.M. Schulte, B.J. Nolt, R.L. Williams, C.L. Spinks & J.J. Hellsten, *Violence and Threats of Violence Experienced by Public Health Field-Workers*, 5 JAMA 439–442 (1998).

    25. http://www.leg.wa.gov/pub/billinfo/2007-08/Pdf/Bills/House%20 Passed%20Legislature/1456-S.PL.pdf; http://www.pef.org/stopworkplace violence/files/judi_scanlon_bill.pdf; http://www.moore.house.gov/nr.asp?nr_ id=495; http://www.michigan.gov/dhs/0,1607,7-124-5459_7341-15406--,00 .html.

    26. Supra note 17.

    27. Public Employee Safety and Health. Notice of Violation and Order to Comply. General Duty Citation to the New York State Office of Mental (1999); C. Gillespie, *Ohio Children's Service Worker Stabbed to Death*, The Nando Times Nation (2001); P. Ly, *Slaying Raises Mental Care Questions*, 2002, available at http://www.washingtonpost.com.; C.E. Newhill, *Client Violence in Social Work Practice*, The Guilford Press (2003); M. Sedensky, *Kansas: Social Worker Killed August 17 & Her 17-Yr-Old Client Is Charged with Murder*, 2004, at http://www.fightcps.com/2004_08_29_archive .html; L. Austin, *Social Workers Rethink Job Safety: A Texas Slaying Brings New Steps*, 2006, at http://workforce.socialworkers.org/whatsnew/WFC -MediaWatch-Web.pdf; http://www.foxnews.com/story/0,2933,225422 ,00.html; http://www.komw.net/artman/publish/printer_1811.shtml.

    28. Supra note 14; OSHA Fact Sheet: Workplace Violence, U.S. Dept. of Labor, Occupational Safety and Health Administration 2002, available at http://www.osha.gov/OshDoc/data_General-Facts/Factsheet-workplace_ violence.pdf.

    29. Lipscomb & Love, Violence Toward Health Care Workers; J. Simonowitz, *Violence in the Workplace: You're Entitled to Protection*, 57 RN 61–63 (1994).

    30. Occupational Safety and Health Administration. *Guidelines for Preventing Workplace Violence for Healthcare and Social Service Workers.* OSHA # 3148 (1996).

    31. http://lists.cacites.org/pipermail/administrative/2005-August/002470 .html.

    32. Id.

    33. K.D. Rosenman et al., *How Much Work-Related Injury and Illness Is Missing by the Current National Surveillance System?* 48 JOEM, 357–365 (2006); Z.J. Fan, D.K. Bonauto, M.P. Foley & B.A. Silverstein, *Underreporting of Work-Related Injury or Illness to Workers' Compensation:*

Individual and Industry Factors, 9 JOEM 914–922 (2006); L.S. Azaroff, C. Levenstein & D.H. Wegman, *Occupational Injury and Illness Surveillance: Conceptual Filters Explain Underreporting*, 9 American Journal of Public Health 1421–1429 (2002).

34. Supra note 19.
35. http://www.cdc.gov/niosh/2001-201.html.
36. http://www.aacn.org/AACN/pubpolcy.nsf; http://www.nursingworld.org/dlwa/osh/wp6.htm; http://www.cnanurses.ca/CNA/documents/pdf/publications/FS22_Violence_Workplace_e.pdf; http://www.cna-aiic.ca/CNA/documents/pdf/publications/PS57_Violence_March_2002_e.pdf; http://www.ilo.org/public/english/bureau/inf/magazine/26/violence.htm; http://www.who.int/violence_injury_prevention/violence/activites/workplace/en.

CHAPTER 10

What Employers Can Do to Minimize the Impact of Domestic Violence and Stalking in the Workplace

Pam Paziotopoulos
and Robin Runge[1]

▌ Introduction

Domestic violence is an epidemic in U.S. society: one out of nearly every three women will be the victim of domestic violence in her lifetime. Employers are in one of the best positions to make a difference. A little action can have a big positive impact on the survivor's life, on the lives of employees, on the community, and on a workplace's bottom line. Perpetrators of domestic violence regularly stalk, threaten, harass, and physically harm their victims in the workplace. Maintaining steady employment is central to a victim's financial security and ability to be independent from an abuser. Many victims report that keeping their jobs is key not just to their safety but to their self-esteem and well-being.

The epidemic of domestic violence is causing dramatic effects on workplaces in the United States: 98 percent of employed victims of domestic abuse had difficulty concentrating on work tasks because of the abuse; 78 percent reported being late to work as a result of domestic abuse; 47 percent of survivors reported being assaulted before work; 67 percent said the perpetrator came to the workplace; 53 percent reported losing their job due to domestic abuse. In 2005, a national benchmark survey of 1,200 employed adults (age eighteen and older) by the Corporate Alliance to End Partner Violence found that intimate partner violence has a wide and far-reaching effect on the working lives of people:

- 44 percent of employed adults surveyed personally experienced domestic violence's effect in their workplaces;

- 21 percent of respondents (men and women) identified themselves as victims of intimate partner violence; and

- 64 percent of victims of domestic violence indicated that their ability to work was affected by the violence.

Similarly, surveys of perpetrators of domestic violence have shown that they have, and take advantage of, access to their victims' workplaces. A 2004 report, "Impact of Domestic Offenders on Occupational Safety & Health: A Pilot Study from Maine," found that:

- 78 percent of surveyed perpetrators used workplace resources at least once to express remorse or anger, check up on, pressure, or threaten their victim;

- 74 percent had easy access to their intimate partner's workplace;

- 21 percent of offenders reported that they contacted their victim at the workplace in violation of a no contact order; and

- 70 percent of domestic abuse offenders lost 15,221 hours of work, collectively, due to their domestic abuse arrests.

In September 2003, the Council for Women and Domestic Violence Commission, in North Carolina, released results from a survey about the costs of employing batterers. The findings showed that 81 percent of abusers were employed while abusive toward their partners, and 28 percent of the perpetrators stated that they worked for the same employer as their victim.

Moreover, domestic violence imposes a huge financial burden on employers. According to a 2003 report by the Centers for Disease Control and Prevention (CDC), employers experience $1.8 billion per year in lost productivity. The U.S. Department of Health and Human Services (HHS) found that "intimate partner violence," particularly against women, exacts an enormous and adverse impact on the corporate sector in terms of lost worker productivity and increased costs of health care. The estimated total value of days lost from employment and household chores exceeds $850 million, while the total health care costs, including medical and mental health care services, are nearly $4.1 billion.

Development and Implementation of a Domestic Violence Policy

The most effective way to address domestic violence and stalking in the workplace is to develop and implement a workplace policy on domestic violence and stalking. Such a policy should address scenarios where employees may be victims or abusers, and where all employees work to create and foster a safe workplace. By developing policies and procedures, and conducting trainings with minimal effort and cost, employers can address safety concerns and support their employees, thereby increasing productivity, minimizing costs, and avoiding liability.

Some points to consider when developing such a policy include the following:

- *Define domestic violence.* There are many ways to define domestic violence, and how it is defined will determine the scope and implementation of the policy. Employers should develop a definition that is enforceable and that fits their workplaces. For example, the clothing manufacturer Liz Claiborne, Inc. defines domestic violence as, "a pattern of coercive behavior that is used by one person in an intimate relationship to gain power and control over another. Domestic violence includes physical, sexual, emotional, psychological, and financial abuse. Some examples of coercive behavior are the following: hitting, punching, shoving, stabbing, shooting, slapping, threatening behavior, name calling, humiliating in front of others, controlling what one wears, says, and does, controlling the financial decisions, stalking, destroying or attempting to destroy property, and using children to control. Domestic violence occurs between people of all racial, economic, educational, and religious backgrounds, in heterosexual and same sex relationships, living together or separately, married or unmarried, in short-term and long-term relationships."[2]

- *Review existing policies and guidelines.* Determine whether these policies and guidelines can be modified to address partner violence.

- *Determine what new policies must be developed.* When determining whether any new policies are necessary and, if so, what they should address, take into consideration the need to identify employees as perpetrators of domestic violence, as well as those who seek assistance as victims of domestic violence.

- *Include provisions that allow employees time off.* Employees may need time off to seek protection, go to court, look for new housing, or enter counseling for abuse (for victims and abusers), or for other reasons related to partner violence. Such provisions could include flexible work hours, short-term leaves of absence, and extended leaves of absence.

- *Accommodate the victim.* Consider which changes you may be willing or able to make in the workplace for victims of partner violence (e.g., relocation help, escorting an employee to her car, changing an employee's work phone number), while maintaining the integrity of the workplace and safety of all employees.

- *Provide specific procedures informing supervisors and/or employees how to respond to a violent situation in the workplace.* These procedures should address a variety of roles: employee/victim, coworker, manager or supervisor, human resources, and security personnel.

- *Communicate policy clearly to all employees.* Disseminate the policy to all employees and provide any needed training. Establish a specific reporting protocol so that employees at every level know who to report to and under what circumstances information is to be reported.

- *Assure victims that they will not be subjected to retaliatory treatment.* Job programs and benefits available to other employees should not be denied to employees based solely on violence-related problems. By the same token, these employees should have set performance expectations, just as all employees do.

- *Include procedures and protocols for assisting victims, as well as employee perpetrators.* Policy should include references to existing employment benefits that a victim or perpetrator can avail her/himself of such as paid or unpaid leave, counseling, etc. It should include emergency protocols as well as ongoing preventive measures.[3]

Implementation

A workplace domestic violence policy is only as effective as its implementation. Buy-in—from the head of the agency or department to frontline management to the custodial service and security staff—is critical. Without commitment at every level, an effective domestic violence policy cannot be achieved. Employees who are survivors will not feel safe and thus will not disclose their physical safety concerns in the workplace. This makes it nearly impossible to prevent workplace incidents related to domestic violence.

A key part of implementation of a domestic violence policy is training. On a regular basis, employees at all levels must receive information and training on the policy. Clearly, the training should depend upon the employee's position at work. Company representatives should not give personal advice or counseling. This should always be provided by trained counselors from community-based organizations that offer services to survivors of domestic violence. Training should address what actions are appropriate and what referrals are available. It is important to be mindful that policies and protocols are simply guidelines; there are rarely, if ever, black-and-white "right answers." Most issues should be handled on a case-by-case basis. Be clear about how to address performance issues with employees who may be victims of domestic violence.

By identifying survivors of domestic violence in the workplace, an employer may be able to reach out to them, offer support, and prevent possible incidents at work. Without an environment in which a survivor feels comfortable disclosing his or her status as a victim, a workplace policy cannot be effective. Although there is no "typical" victim of domestic violence, an employee may exhibit characteristics that may indicate fear for his or her safety, such as:

- Changes in behavior (for example, a previously punctual employee who develops an attendance problem, becoming frequently absent or late for work, or unable to meet deadlines);

■ An employee who wears long sleeves during the summer months, has bruises or unexplained injuries, or can be observed arguing or crying during increasingly frequent personal calls.

Employers should watch for a pattern of warning signs and make emergency information available, such as the National Domestic Violence Hotline (800-799-SAFE). It is crucial that an employee understands that s/he is not being "singled out" or "picked on" because an employer suspects s/he is a victim of domestic violence.

It is equally critical to identify perpetrators of domestic violence in the workplace. As indicated by the surveys noted earlier, perpetrators often use workplace resources, such as e-mail, phone, and fax, to harass, stalk, or assault their victims either from the same workplace as the victim or a different one. They may also miss work for court dates or after arrests related to domestic violence incidents. A nonemployee may also threaten or harass coworkers at the victim's workplace. It is important to keep in mind that there are no classic traits or profiles that indicate whether someone is a victim or abuser.

▌ Liability Issues

In addition to design, development, and implementation of a workplace policy on domestic violence, existing state and federal employment laws may raise liability issues if workplace violence related to domestic violence is not prevented or appropriately addressed.

Antidiscrimination Statutes

Although domestic violence victims are not specifically mentioned in most federal and state antidiscrimination in employment laws, these laws may provide protections to employees who are victims of domestic violence. Title VII of the Civil Rights Act of 1964 (Title

VII), as amended, prohibits discrimination against an employee in hiring, terms and conditions of employment, and firing based on sex (including pregnancy), race, national origin, religion, and color.[4] Courts have also recognized that sexual harassment is a prohibited form of sex discrimination.[5] The Age Discrimination in Employment Act prohibits discrimination against an employee age 40 and over. Each state also has antidiscrimination provisions that prohibit discrimination on some or all of these bases as well, some of which provide more protections, such as covering smaller employers or providing protection for a characteristic not recognized under federal law. Although not initially obvious, each of these laws may provide protections to an employee who is a victim of domestic violence. For example, a victim may be sexually harassed or assaulted at work by her batterer who is also a coworker or supervisor, exposing an employer to liability. (See Discrimination Against Domestic Violence Victims in this chapter.)

Antidiscrimination Against Domestic Violence Victims Laws

All federal and most state antidiscrimination in employment laws do not expressly prohibit discrimination against victims of domestic violence victims. In recent years, however, some states have begun to pass legislation specifically prohibiting discrimination against victims of domestic violence and sexual assault. As of this writing, Illinois and New York City both specifically prohibit employers from discriminating against employees because they are victims of domestic or sexual violence.[6] Another eight states—California, Colorada, Florida, Hawaii, Kansas Maine, North Carolina, and Oregon—prohibit employers from discriminating against domestic violence victims who take leave provided for them under state law.[7] Under these provisions, discrimination is defined to include firing or penalizing a victim because of actions of her abuser. Similar legislation has been considered by the U.S. Congress in recent years but none has become law.

Family and Medical Leave Laws and Domestic Violence

The federal Family and Medical Leave Act (FMLA) provides job-guaranteed leave from work for employees. Although this law does not expressly mention domestic violence, it can offer job-protected leave to victims of domestic violence to heal from mental or physical injuries caused by the violence, or to care for a child who is healing from injuries, if s/he is eligible and if the injuries rise to the level of a "serious health condition."[8]

The FMLA provides up to twelve weeks of unpaid, job-guaranteed leave every twelve months to employees who: have worked for their employer for at least twelve months and 1,250 hours in the last twelve months; work at a site with fifty employees or for an employer who has fifty or more employees within seventy-five surface miles of that work site; require leave to heal from a "serious health condition" or that of a child, spouse, or parent; or require leave for the birth of the employee's child or placement of a child with the employee for adoption or foster care.[9] At the beginning of 2008, the FMLA was amended to provide two new types of leave, affecting servicemembers and their families. The new leave provisions consist of the following: (1) provides up to twenty-six weeks of leave in a single twelve-month period to care for an injured servicemember; and (2) provides up to twelve weeks of leave in a twelve-month period due to any "qualifying exigency" (to be defined in regulation drafted by the U.S. Department of Labor) arising out of the fact that an employee's family member has been notified of an impending call or order to active duty or is already on active duty. Only employees taking leave to care for an injured servicemember are entitled to the *additional* fourteen weeks of leave. An employee qualifies for this additional leave if any portion of his or her leave is taken to care for an injured servicemember.

Federal regulations define a "serious health condition" as an illness, injury, impairment, or physical or mental condition that causes incapacity and requires either or both an overnight stay in a hospital or similar facility or continuing treatment by a health care provider.[10]

"Continuing treatment" by a health care provider is defined as: (1) a condition causing incapacity and an inability to work for three or more days that requires two or more visits to a health care provider, or one visit and a regimen of treatment; or (2) a chronic condition continuing over an extended period of time requiring periodic doctor's visits and which may cause episodic incapacity; or (3) absences to receive multiple treatments for an illness or injury which would cause a period of incapacity of more than three days if not treated; or (4) pregnancy.[11] An employee who qualifies for FMLA leave receives:

- Unpaid leave, though she may be able to use vacation, sick, or other accrued paid leave;[12]

- Continuation of health care benefits if she received them previously;[13]

- Job protection—she cannot be fired for exercising her right to take the leave;[14] and

- Job restoration rights to the same or an equivalent position at the end of the leave.[15]

An employee who requests leave under the FMLA may be required by her employer to provide certification of the need for leave.[16] If you have an employee who has experienced an injury caused by domestic violence and she has missed work because she is incapacitated due to the injury, she may qualify for job-guaranteed leave under the FMLA. This statute is enforced by the U.S. Department of Labor. An employee who believes her rights under the FMLA have been violated may either file a complaint with the U.S. Department of Labor or file a complaint in federal court within two years of the violation.[17]

State Leave Laws and Domestic Violence

A majority of the states have family or medical leave laws that provide unpaid job-guaranteed time off for a variety of reasons related to family or illness including to attend a child's school event or to heal from the employee's serious health condition.[18] In 2004, California implemented the first paid leave legislation in the country.[19]

In the 1990s, victim advocates began working with workers' rights advocates, welfare advocates, and women's right groups to pass state laws providing targeted leave for victims of domestic violence. As of this writing, nine states plus New York City have statutes and/or ordinances providing unpaid, job-guaranteed leave (or leave as a reasonable accommodation) specifically for victims of domestic violence.[20] These laws are similar in many ways to the FMLA in terms of enforcement, but provide leave for victims to:

- Go to court to obtain protection for themselves and their family

- Seek medical attention

- Obtain services from a domestic violence or rape crisis program

- Obtain legal assistance

Like the FMLA, these laws prohibit an employer from discriminating against an employee for exercising their right to the leave, and the employer may require the employee to provide certification of their qualifying need for leave. If it is found that an employer failed to provide leave under these laws, and thus illegally fired a victim, s/he may be entitled to reinstatement and back pay.

Additionally, about half of the states have "crime victim leave laws" that give victims of crimes, including domestic violence, sexual assault, or stalking, time off to go to criminal court if subpoenaed to appear as a witness or victim of a crime.

Wrongful Discharge in Violation of Public Policy

Almost every state recognizes "wrongful discharge in violation of public policy" as an exception to the general rule of at-will employment. As a result, employees who are fired for a reason deemed to violate a state's public policy (e.g., firing a whistle-blower), may have an avenue of recourse. Public policy generally must be based in the state's laws and policies, in this case, the statutes and regulations addressing domestic violence. Virtually every state has enacted statutory and regulatory schemes that could be argued as creating a strong public policy against terminating victims and survivors. A Massachusetts court found that firing an employee after she took one day off from work to get a protective order could state a claim under this theory.[21] Moreover, employees have challenged a firing because of their involvement in a domestic violence incident that "reflected badly" on the employer.[22] Whether such public policy claims achieve greater recognition, however, remains to be seen.

Workers' Compensation and Tort Actions

When employees are injured in the workplace or while on the job, they may be entitled to compensation either through the workers' compensation system or under a tort claim theory. Both possibilities may apply to victims of domestic violence or stalking who are assaulted at work. Generally, state laws permit employees to pursue one or the other when seeking a remedy, but not both.[23]

Workers' compensation is a state-run system of workplace insurance that employers are required to carry to cover medical care and partial lost wages for an injury occurring in the course of employment. While the actual mechanisms vary, in all states workers' compensation is the presumptive remedy for employees who sustain injuries while on the job. It is the exclusive remedy in many jurisdictions, which means that once a victim files a claim within the workers' compensation system, the employee can lose the right to pursue alternative actions against the perpetrator, such as filing a tort claim.[24] The workers' compensation scheme, while providing certain job and benefits protections (e.g., leave or a reduced work schedule, protection from retaliation), does not require that an employer leave a job open indefinitely in the case where an employee faces a lengthy convalescence. Moreover, intentional torts committed by employees against other employees are generally excluded from the workers' compensation system. When addressing workers' compensation issues, it is important to check the applicable state case law and/or consult a workers' compensation attorney.

To be eligible for workers' compensation benefits, the assault must have occurred within the scope of employment. For example, the Georgia Court of Appeals has specifically found that where the circumstances of employment involve an increased risk of sexual assault and the assault was not personal, then such an assault is compensable under the Georgia Workers' Compensation Act.[25] Workers' compensation is normally not available where an employee was equally exposed to the hazards of sexual assault outside of her employment, and the risk of sexual assault was unconnected with the responsibilities of the employment.[26]

In situations in which workers' compensation laws do not apply, the employee may be able to successfully pursue a tort action against her employer.[27] Tort actions are generally used to hold the employer vicariously liable for the act of violence committed in the workplace using negligence theories. For example, if the employee was sexually assaulted in the parking lot of her office by a coworker, she could seek damages from her employer by filing a claim for negligent hiring and/or retention of the coworker/perpetrator, if the employer knew or should have known that the coworker/perpetrator posed a risk of violence and failed to take preventive or remedial action.

Another theory of tort liability that an assault victim might be able to pursue is intentional infliction of emotional distress, if the victim can demonstrate a causal connection between the employer's intentional or reckless behavior and her emotional distress.[28] A Fourth Circuit case exemplifies this principle. In *Gantt v. Security, U.S.A., Inc.*,[29] the court reversed summary judgment for the employer in a case where a supervisor's actions led directly to the kidnapping and rape of an employee by her former boyfriend. The supervisor had ample knowledge of the boyfriend/perpetrator's history of violence and of the victim's fear that he would come to the workplace to harm her but, nonetheless, insisted on assigning the plaintiff to work in an unsecured outdoor post. The plaintiff was abducted from that location after the boyfriend arrived at the job site seeking to talk with her (the supervisor having told the boyfriend where he could find the plaintiff).[30] The court found that the supervisor's behavior could provide the necessary intention and causal connection for a jury to conclude that the employer (through the actions of its supervisor) placed the victim in harm's way and was responsible for her emotional distress claim.[31]

Occupational Safety and Health Laws

Under the Occupational Safety and Health Act (OSHA), employers may face liability for sexual assaults that occur in the workplace due to the failure to implement adequate safety measures.[32] OHSA standards contain a general duty clause applicable to employers which requires them to "furnish to each of his employees employment and a place of employment which are free from recognized hazards that are causing or are likely to cause death or serious physical harm to his employees."[33] This clause provides a viable means of holding an employer liable under OSHA for penalties for failing to have a workplace violence policy. While there are no federal OSHA regulations that specifically govern violence in the workplace, each state's laws, regulations, and executive orders should be consulted to determine whether there is legal requirement that an employer have a workplace violence policy in place.

The National Institute for Occupational Safety and Health (NIOSH), at CDC, has recognized that violence against women in the workplace, and particularly intimate partner violence, is one of the most pressing concerns related to workplace injury today.[34] A typology of workplace violence has identified four main types of violence, one of which addresses violence that occurs between a perpetrator and victim with a personal relationship.[35] Because women are most likely to be sexually assaulted by someone they know, employers must exercise their general duty of care to address this potential for sexual violence in their workplaces. If, for example, an employee has regularly complained about the fact that she must walk through a dark, narrow alley to reach the employee parking lot and is sexually assaulted in that alley one night, her employer might be held liable for refusing to respond to her complaints by installing lighting in the alley, hiring security, or allowing her to park closer to the front door.

Unemployment Insurance Benefits

Unemployment insurance is a state-run social insurance program that provides temporary income to workers who lose their jobs through no fault of their own. Unemployment insurance is primarily funded through employers' payroll tax deductions. A claimant is typically disqualified from benefits for leaving work voluntarily without good cause, having been fired for reasons amounting to misconduct, or refusing to work without good cause. Benefits amounts are calculated using a "base period" which reflects the applicant's income from employment in the last twelve months preceding the application. In most jurisdictions an applicant must have made a certain amount in the "base period" to qualify for benefits.

Until recently, it was unclear whether victims of domestic violence were eligible for unemployment insurance if they were fired or forced to quit their jobs because of the violence. As of this writing, twenty-eight states, along with the District of Columbia, have amended their unemployment insurance codes to clarify that victims of domestic violence are eligible for benefits.[36] Even if a victim is in a state without one of these laws, survivors of domestic violence who lose their job may still qualify for benefits. Alaska, Hawaii, Nevada, Ohio, Pennsylvania, South Carolina, Utah, and Virginia, for example, permit claimants to qualify for benefits if they are forced to leave their jobs for "personal" reasons, as a qualification for good cause.[37]

▌ Orders of Protection

Victims of domestic violence may avail themselves of a court order to help protect themselves and their family from an abuser. These court orders are frequently referred to as "orders of protection" but also may be called protective or restraining orders. Every jurisdiction in the United States provides a way for a domestic violence victim to obtain an order of protection. However, each jurisdiction has its own requirements as to who may qualify for an order of protection.

A person requesting an order of protection is often called the "petitioner," and the person whom the order is against is often called the "respondent." Employers should educate themselves on their jurisdiction's laws governing orders of protection in order to take full advantage of this legal protection. The petitioner may request various terms and conditions as part of the order that imposes certain requirements and restrictions on the respondent. Once the order has been served upon the respondent, the respondent may be charged civilly and/or criminally for violating the conditions of the order.

Workplace Protection Orders

In the 1990s, led by California and Georgia, states began passing laws enabling employers to petition to obtain workplace protection orders on behalf of employees who were threatened at the workplace. The purpose of these laws is to enable employers to protect their employees from violence, harassment, and stalking, as well as protect employers from liability for such conduct. Today, ten states permit employers to obtain workplace restraining or protection orders.[38] Some of the newer laws specifically reference domestic violence victims.[39] Obtaining a workplace protection order may be an effective way for an employer to improve the safety of the workplace and meet its responsibilities under state and federal occupational safety and health laws. Employees should always be consulted, however, before such an order is obtained. Sometimes, obtaining a protective order may place a potential victim at greater risk by angering the perpetrator.

Qualifications to Obtain an Order

To qualify for an order of protection, a petitioner typically has to satisfy three conditions: (1) that s/he stands in relation to the respondent as a family or household member (defined differently depending on the jurisdiction); (2) that there is ongoing abuse between the petitioner and the respondent; and (3) that the petitioner fears abuse in the future if the order is not granted. Each jurisdiction has a different definition of who qualifies as a family/household member in relation to the respondent. In all jurisdictions, spouses or former spouses, and dating partners or former dating partners, qualify. In some jurisdictions one can petition for an order against one's sibling, parent, stepparent, or other family relations through marriage. Check local statutes for a complete list of qualifying relationships.

A petitioner may also seek an order on behalf of others, such as a minor, disabled, or elderly individual. A petitioner also may request of the court that other parties be added to the order to obtain protection from the respondent. For instance, a petitioner may request that her children be listed on the order as additional parties to be protected.

How to Obtain an Order

Depending on the jurisdiction, orders of protection may be issued by a civil or criminal court.[40] In jurisdictions that utilize the criminal court system to issue such orders, an order of protection is often issued in conjunction with a pending criminal matter against the respondent.

Terms and Conditions of the Order

Available Remedies

Available remedies vary from state to state. One useful Web site, http://www.WomensLaw.org, provides information not only on remedies that are available in each state but also on how to obtain an order of protection.

Prohibition Against Possession of Firearms

State law varies with respect to whether a respondent who is subject to an order of protection is lawfully entitled to possess a firearm. Most orders include some provision restricting firearms possession. Federal law prohibits a respondent on valid order of protection from possessing firearms and ammunition.[41]

Duration of the Order

The duration of an order of protection varies depending on the circumstances in which the order was obtained. For example, orders that are obtained on an emergency basis typically are of a short duration because they are issued on an ex parte basis—meaning that only the petitioner would have been present in court when the order was issued. In this instance, the order may be good for only a few weeks. This "temporary" or "emergency" order would then be served upon the respondent by law enforcement personnel or other process server. This would be the respondent's first notice of the order. Once given notice of the contents of the order, the respondent can be charged with violating the order. Service of the order also constitutes notice of the hearing date—usually the same date that the emergency or temporary order expires. At the hearing, the respondent may contest the order and demand a hearing on the merits of the order, agree to an extension of the order, or ask for a continuance of the hearing to a later date. Conversely, if a final order is issued by the court—also referred to as a permanent or plenary order—the duration of the order could last for a period of several years.

Enforcing the Order

Depending on what kind of court issued the order, a "violation" of a valid order of protection could be criminal or civil in nature. If a petitioner (or other listed protected party on the order) believes that a violation of that order has occurred and/or that a crime has occurred, the police should be notified. Responding law enforcement will first check to see that the order was validly served on the respondent and that its terms have not expired before it will move to enforce the conditions of the order. If the respondent commits a criminal act in the process of violating the order, the responding officer should arrest the respondent pursuant to the enforcing jurisdiction's law. Thus, the alleged conduct may constitute a crime in and of itself, as well as a criminal violation of an order of protection.

If the protected party believes that the violation of the order did not result in a separate criminal offense, they should return to the court that issued the order and request relief from the court, such as holding the respondent in contempt of court. Civil contempt penalties may include a fine, jail time, or other restrictions.

Full Faith and Credit

Congress enacted the Violence Against Women Act in 1994. The law was amended in 2000.[42] This act contains a provision directing all states—as well as the District of Columbia, Indian tribes, and all territories of the United States—to give full faith and credit to valid civil or criminal orders of protection issued by other foreign states or tribal courts. In other words, a valid order of protection will be enforced wherever a violation of that order occurs, even if the violation occurs in a state other than where the order was issued. The abuser is bound by the terms of the order regardless of where he or she is when the order is violated. Law enforcement is only required to ensure that the order appears valid on its face, meaning that it contains: the names of the parties, an expiration date, specific terms and conditions directed toward the respondent, and a signature of a judicial officer. There is no federal requirement that the victim register the order in the enforcing jurisdiction or that the issuing state affix or seal or stamp the order before it may be enforceable. In fact, in a majority of states, the petitioner or a protected party need only present a paper copy of the "foreign" order of protection to law enforcement.

The end result is that a valid order of protection granted by a court of any jurisdiction shall be recognized and enforced as if it were issued by the court where the violation occurred. Thus, an abuser can be arrested for violating the order of protection as long as there is probable cause to believe that a violation of the order occurred in the enforcing jurisdiction. Moreover, the full faith and credit provision requires that law enforcement enforce the conditions of the order as contained therein, even if the protections afforded to the victim are more broad than those available in the jurisdiction where the violation occurred. This provision also enables law enforcement to apprehend stalkers who cross state lines to abuse victims. Additionally, the order may be enforced in several states simultaneously.[43]

Employer as Petitioner on an Order of Protection

There are many reasons why an employer may wish to petition on behalf of an employee for an order of protection. When an employer petitions for an order of protection, it designs the terms of the order to suit its particular needs. The employer is in control as to the duration of the order as well as to what remedies are sought to be included in the order. If the order has been violated then the employer can enforce the order regardless of the employee's wishes. However, the employer needs to ensure that any enforcement of the order will not jeopardize the employee's safety.

Employer/Employee Working Together

An employee who has obtained a valid order of protection should ensure that her employer has a copy of the order along with a photograph of the offender/respondent if one is available. That way, the employer, through its frontline personnel, can assist with the enforcement of the order. If an order of protection prohibits the offender/respondent from coming to an employee's job site or coming in contact with the employee, the employer should immediately contact law enforcement if the respondent/offender is seen at the job site. Having a copy of the order of protection on hand when law enforcement arrives greatly aids in the investigation of such an incident.

▌ Risk Assessment

Domestic violence cases are complicated. These cases often appear innocuous, especially where no physical evidence or additional witnesses are available to corroborate the abuse. For example, in some cases a batterer is charged with phone harassment, or an abuser may violate a protective order by appearing at the victim's home. Initially, it may not be apparent that the situation has reached a serious stage and could result in a homicide. In such cases, employers should search for ways to gain insight on how far along the path an offender is in attacking his or her victim. The first requirement for protecting employees from domestic violence/stalking behavior is to identify the threat, assess the likelihood of future violence, and determine the best means of intervention. Both during and after the assessment someone from security, human resources, or a supervisor should monitor the victim. If the violence appears to be escalating, the victim could be at great danger.

When a serious incident of workplace violence occurs, people are often apt to say that the individual just "snapped." It is well recognized among threat assessment professionals that people don't just "snap"; rather, there were pre-incident indicators suggesting the potential for violence. The goal for security personnel or anyone conducting a threat assessment is to identify the potential problem early enough in order to be in a position to prevent or defuse the situation. Assessments can take a number of forms—including the detailed and psychologically sophisticated assessments commonly referred to as "threat assessments," "fitness for duty evaluations," and/or "lethality assessments." These assessments should be performed by trained professionals. However, nonexpert managers and coworkers can and should be able to start the assessment process and refer a situation to the experts when appropriate.[44]

If the victim is prepared to discuss the abusive situation, a nonexpert, coworker, or supervisor can assess it. However, it is highly recommended that the responses of the victim be documented in writing to determine whether the indicators listed below are present. Moreover, when interviews are being conducted, it is imperative for the interviewers not to limit their questions to the incident at the workplace. As an example, if the abuser had phoned the victim, the interviewer may simply restrict his questions to the call: "When did it occur? What was said?" Just asking the who, what, when, how, and why questions may achieve quick results for documentation, but it fails to touch the underlying issues. It is imperative for victims of domestic violence that their abusive incident be met with prompt and supportive attention by the employer. This reaction will both validate the victim's concerns about safety and communicate the employer's concern and interest in the matter.

The initial byproducts of domestic violence that seep into the workplace are usually smaller bits of larger, more complicated, problems. Unpleasant or threatening phone calls at work provide little insight into the severity of the situation being encountered by an abused employee. It is important, therefore, to keep in mind that a phone call may be just the tip of the iceberg, and that what may seem like a harmless situation can quickly escalate into something more. The following list of pre-incident indicators, or "red flags," may be incorporated into an interview to help obtain information about the employee and the severity of the abuse. This information may be extremely helpful to law enforcement personnel if they become involved and if charges are brought against the abuser. In some states, risk assessment information is used during the bail hearings. In those situations, the victim is not present for the bail hearing, nor has the prosecutor had an opportunity to review possible red flags with the victim. Thus, if an employer has the opportunity to interview the victim and determine which of the following factors are present, it is useful to share this information with the police officers and, ultimately, the prosecutors. In any event, this information will provide tremendous insight into the nature and level of violence existing within a particular situation.

Pre-Incident Indicators

- *Status of relationship.* The first question that should be asked, and the factor that will yield one of the most important indicators of escalation of violence, is, "Have you told the abuser that you intend to leave this relationship or have you already curtailed it?" There is wide agreement that in most domestic violence homicides the victim *recently* had either terminated the relationship or communicated to the perpetrator that the relationship should end. If the answer to this question is "yes," the employer will know that the victim is entering a potentially highly dangerous situation. It is imperative that the employer work with the victim to devise a safety plan for work, while looking for ways to adjust the victim's work schedule and/or workload to ensure that she or he is protected while arriving at and departing from work, as well as during work hours. During this time, the employer will most likely see a pattern of behavior generally referred to as "stalking."[45] When the abuser no longer has immediate access to the victim (that is, they are no longer living together), the controlling behavior of the abuser reveals itself in public rather than in private. This behavior can manifest in phone harassment, violating an order of protection, and showing up at the victim's workplace.

- *The abuser's reaction to breakup.* How did the abuser handle the breakup? Did the abuser try to prevent the victim from leaving home? Rip out the telephone? Follow the victim to a friend's house? Become obsessed with finding the victim? Experts characterize this reaction as "interfering with the victim's 'help-seeking

behavior.'" Violence can escalate during this period because the
perpetrator fears losing control over the victim and will generally
increase the level of violence to increase the victim's fear.

- *Order of protection.* Determine whether the victim has sought an
order of protection (or restraining order) in the present situation
or ever applied for one in the past. If the answer is "yes" to either
question, the situation has probably escalated.[46] The next vital
question is how has the abuser reacted to the order? If the order
has been violated, the employer can assume that the criminal justice system will not be a deterrent for this individual.

- *Abusers who resist arrest.* If the abuser has ever been arrested for a
domestic violence offense or any other criminal offense, there is a
chance that the person may have fought with the police officers
or attempted to resist arrest. If this is the case, then again the employer can assume that the criminal justice system may not be a
deterrent for this individual.

- *Using alcohol or drugs.* A misconception widely held is that
abusers physically or mentally abuse others because they are under the influence of drugs or alcohol. This is not supported by
fact. There are abusers who have never used drugs or alcohol,
and there are alcoholics or drug addicts who have never abused
their partners. The only link between substance abuse and domestic violence seems to be that domestic violence may be exac-
erbated by an abuser's recently increased intake of drugs or
alcohol.

- *Fear.* Employers often forget to ask the victim some very obvious
questions. Do not forget to ask the simplest of questions:

  - "Are you afraid of the abuser?"

  - "Have you ever gone to a domestic violence shelter?"

  - "Has the abuser ever physically abused you to the point that
  you had to seek medical attention?"

■ *Guns.* It is important to know whether the abuser possesses a weapon. The recent acquisition of a gun can suggest a greater potential of danger than if the individual has kept a gun in the house for twenty years. Recent gun acquisition in this situation may be a warning sign of an impending act of violence.

■ *Suicide.* Obviously, thoughts of suicide, severe depression, and other mental illnesses can contribute to an abuser acting out violently. Many times, abusers who have been prescribed medications by their doctors fail to comply. This decision can result in dangerous consequences for the victim. Additionally, many abusers express a desire to commit suicide. If these factors are present, it is important to find out: What medication is the abuser taking? For what illness? If statements regarding suicide have been made, how specific was the abuser in articulating a suicide plan. Did the plan include murdering the victim too? Did it include harming the children? The more specific the plan, the more dangerous the situation.

■ *Children.* Does the violence occur in front of the children? Committing violence in front of children generally escalates the potential harm to the mother. If the abuser becomes violent irrespective of audience, it often indicates violence that is out of control and could be expected to escalate. Teenagers often try to intervene to stop the abuse and are injured in the process.

■ *Symbolic violence.* Abusers often destroy property that is special to the victim. It may be an award received at work or favorite photographs. A similar tactic is sending the victim dead roses. This suggests the destruction that the abuser wishes upon the victim.

■ *Threats.* If the abuser has been threatening the victim, it is important to evaluate those threats. How does the abuser communicate the threats? How specific are they? Even a love note, flowers, or a card can be construed as a threat if the victim has dissolved the relationship.

- *Attempting to maintain access.* When a victim terminates the relationship and moves out of a shared residence, the abuser loses access and may begin stalking. The abuser is now trying to exert power and control over the victim and in the process escalates the risk of arrest. If the abuser physically assaults, follows, or displays threatening behavior toward the victim in public places, violence toward the victim may be escalating.

- *Abuser experiencing a downward turn in life.* What is going on in the abuser's personal and professional life? Is the abuser employed? Recently demoted or fired? Has the abuser experienced any personal losses, such as death of a loved one, or a recent divorce? If the abuser's personal or professional life has taken a turn for the worse, the abuser may be spiraling downward quickly and could decide to take the victim down too.

- *Assessing past physical violence.* It is important to determine if there is a past history of physical violence. All physical violence should be documented and noted, including what the victim may characterize as only a "push" or "shove." Some victims may not characterize a push or a shove as physical violence, so it is essential to probe the victim who replies that there has been no physical violence. *At the other extreme, if the abuser has ever put hands around the victim's neck and attempted strangulation, the employer should consider it a very high indicator of future violence.* To determine the severity of the violence, an inquiry should be made if the violence has been increasing in frequency and severity.

- *Past relationship history.* More often than not, if the abuser had a past relationship, there was abuse in that relationship. In many situations, the victim will be aware of how that past relationship ended, and whether or not that individual had to seek a protective or restraining order against the abuser to end the earlier relationship. Be sure to note the history of the abuse.[47]

It is difficult to state which of the following indicators are more likely to point to a future homicide. However, the U.S. Department of Justice refers to the following list as the top five risk factors. The numbers in parentheses indicate the degree of homicidal risk for women faced with this plight in contrast to women who have not encountered this situation.[48]

■ Has the abuser ever used, or threatened to use, a gun, knife, or other weapon against the victim? (20.2 times more likely)

■ Has the abuser ever threatened to kill or injure the victim? (14.9 times more likely)

■ Has the abuser ever tried to strangle (choke) the victim? (9.9 times more likely)

■ Is the abuser violently or constantly jealous? (9.2 times more likely)

■ Has the abuser ever forced the victim to have sex? (7.6 times more likely)

Although there is no way to determine with certainty how lethal a situation may be, these factors, in the context of the totality of the circumstances, should be carefully evaluated.

Partnering with Domestic Abuse Prevention Organizations

Partnerships can be formed between an employer and an organization committed to preventing domestic abuse. These partnerships help to provide agencies that service the domestic violence community with additional funding for their programs. By launching campaigns to aid these agencies, both public and private employers enhance their public image within the domestic violence communities whose populace includes many of their customers or constituents.[49] Typical activities at a workplace might include:

- providing domestic violence awareness training for managers;

- coordinating a citywide conference on domestic violence in the workplace;

- implementing domestic violence awareness poster and billboard campaigns;

- running articles about abuse in employer newsletters;

- hosting community speakers on domestic violence-related topics;

- encouraging community volunteer efforts;

- collecting toiletries and secondhand cell phones to provide to domestic violence shelters;

- holding brown bag lunches where domestic violence is discussed; and

- hosting news conferences with law enforcement and other government officials on state, county, or local efforts to address domestic violence in the workplace.

Materials can be prepared to inform victims about assistance that is available. For instance, many victims may not realize that they can apply for an order of protection and designate their workplace address as a protected location, thereby preserving the confidentiality of their home address from their abuser. This information helps those who may be suffering in silence because they do not feel their employer can assist them in protecting them from the abuse.[50]

One of the most successful of these efforts to date has been the sponsorship and coordination by the Family Violence Prevention Fund (FVPF) of the National Work to End Domestic Violence Day, held in October, which has been declared Domestic Violence Awareness Month. Started in 1996, this initiative provides a designated day when public agencies, private companies, and unions sponsor programs and disseminate information to alert workers to the prevalence and severity of domestic violence.

Many businesses have collaborated with governmental prosecuting offices, domestic violence task forces, and other organizations committed to preventing domestic abuse. These partnerships have improved services to victims; promoted consciousness raising in the community regarding the prevalence and dynamics of domestic violence; and enhanced the public image of the employer sponsor.

Employers can collaborate with these organizations to create safety plans for victims; provide a larger audience for the prosecutor's message about the consequences of reporting domestic violence; educate the public about domestic violence; and disseminate resources and referral information to victims. For instance, when banks or grocery stores disseminate information about local battered women's shelters, they provide helpful information to potential victims without raising the abuser's suspicion or escalating the threat of violence.

Employers, large or small, are vulnerable to the spillover of domestic violence and stalking in the workplace. This makes it essential for businesses to prioritize the process of creating internal programs and policies to address these issues. Responsible officials should be consulted about the possibilities of instituting a formal program. Commitment is necessary to change or improve current response preparedness, create awareness around the topic, and take the steps necessary to secure and safeguard the workplace. Employers have the power to save lives.

Notes

1. The authors would also like to acknowledge the contributions of their research assistant, Andrea Kovach, to this chapter.
2. See Liz Claiborne, Inc. Policy on Domestic Violence, available at http://www.loveisnotabuse.com/pdf/domestic_policy.pdf (last visited Nov. 21, 2006).
3. This information was drawn from materials produced by the Corporate Alliance to End Partner Violence, at http://www.caepv.org.
4. 42 U.S.C. § 2000e (2004).
5. Burlington Indus., Inc. v. Ellerth, 524 U.S. 742 (1998); Faragher v. City of Boca Raton, 524 U.S. 775 (1998).

6. 820 ILCS 180/1-45 (West 2004); N.Y.C. Admin. Code § 8-107 (2004).

7. See Cal. Lab. Code §§ 230 & 230.1 (West 2004); Colo. Rev. Stat. § 24-34-402.7 (2004); Fla. Stat. § 741.313 (2007); Haw. Rev. Stat. § 378-72 (2004); Kan. Stat. Ann. §§ 44-1131 & 44-1132 (2007); Me. Rev. Stat. Ann. tit. 26, § 850 (2004); N.C. Gen. Stat. § 95-270(a) (2004); Or. Rev. Stat. § 659A (2007).

8. See, e.g., City of Anchorage v. Gregg, 101 P.3d 181 (Alaska 2004).

9. 29 U.S.C. §§ 2601 *et seq.* (2004); 29 C.F.R. §§ 825.100 *et seq.* (1995).

10. 29 C.F.R. § 825.114 (1995).

11. 29 C.F.R. § 825.114.

12. 29 U.S.C. § 2612 (a-d).

13. 29 U.S.C. § 2614 (c).

14. 29 U.S.C. § 2615.

15. 29 U.S.C. § 2614 (a).

16. 29 U.S.C. § 2613.

17. 29 U.S.C. § 2617.

18. See http://www.nationalpartnership.org for additional information about state leave laws (last visited Nov. 21, 2006).

19. Cal. Unemp. Ins. Code § 3300 (West 2004).

20. Cal. Lab. Code §§ 230 & 230.1 (West 2004); Colo. Rev. Stat. § 24-34-402.7 (2004); Fla. Stat. § 741.313 (2007); Haw. Rev. Stat. § 378-72 (2004); 820 ILCS 180/1-180/45 (2004); Kan. Stat. Ann. §§ 44-1131 & 44-1132 (2007); Me. Rev. Stat. Ann. tit. 26, § 850 (2004); N.C. Gen. Stat. § 95-270(a) (2004); Or. Rev. Stat. § 659A (2007); N.Y.C. Admin. Code § 8-107.1 (2004).

21. Apessos v. Memorial Press Group, 2002 Mass. Super. LEXIS 404, at *10 (Super. Ct. Mass. Sept. 30, 2002).

22. Imes v. City of Asheville, 594 S.E.2d 397 (N.C. Ct. App. 2004); see also M.W. v. California Co. No. BC314320 (Cal. Sup. Ct., L.A. County filed April 23, 2004).

23. For example, the Maryland Worker's Compensation Act provides the exclusive remedy for workplace injury *unless* the employee can prove that she was injured "as a result of the deliberate intent of [her] employer [to] injure" her, in which case she could pursue a tort claim. Md. Code Ann., Lab. & Empl. § 9059(A)-(D).

24. Id.

25. Insurance Co. of Alabama v. Wright, 133 S.E.2d 39 (Ga. App. 1963).

26. See, e.g., Williams v. City of Norfolk, Dept. of Soc. Servs., 1995 Va. App. LEXIS 73 (Va. Ct. App. 1995) (holding that an employee who was raped in the stairwell of her office building did not qualify for workers'

compensation benefits because she failed to prove that the nature of her employment was related to the attack).

27. See Kennedy v. Pine Land State Bank, 439 S.E.2d 106 (Ga. Ct. App. 1993).

28. Restatement (Second) of Torts § 312 (1965); 870 (1979).

29. 356 F.3d 547 (4th Cir. 2004).

30. Id. at 549–51.

31. Id. at 557.

32. 29 U.S.C. § 651 (2004). For more information, see the Department of Labor's Web site detailing the full scope of OSHA, at http://www.osha.gov.

33. 29 U.S.C. § 654(a)(1).

34. Leslie Loveless, ed., *Violence in the Workplace: A Report to the Nation* (2001), available at http://www.public-health.uiowa.edu/iprc/NATION.PDF.

35. Id.

36. A.R.S. § 23-771; Ca. U.I. Code §§ 1030, 1032, 1256; Colo. Rev. Stat. Ann. §§ 8-73-107(1)(G), 8-73-108(4)(R); Conn. Gen. Stat. § 31-236(A)(2)(A); Del. Code Ann. tit. 19 § 3314(1); D.C. Code § 21-131; 820 ILCS 405/601; Ind. Code § 22-4-15-1(1)(C)(8); Kan. Stat. Ann. § 44-706(A)(12); Me. Rev. Stat. Ann. tit. 26, §§ 1193(A)(4), 1043(23)(B)(3); Mass. Gen. L. Ann. Ch. 151A, §§ 1, 14, 25, 30; Minn. Stat. §§ 268.095(1)(8), 268.095(6)(A)(C); Mont. Code Ann. § 39-51-2111; Neb. Rev. Stat. Ann. § 48-628(1)(A); N.H. Rev. Stat. Ann. tit. 23 § 282-A:32(I)(A)(3); N.J. Rev. Stat. § 43:21-5(J); N.M. Stat. Ann. § 51-1-7(A); N.Y. Lab. Law § 593(1)(A); N.C. Gen. Stat. § 96-14(1F); Okla. Stat. tit. 40 §§ 40-2-405(5), 40-3-106(G)(8); Or. Rev. Stat. § 657.176(12), as amended by 2005 Or. Laws 278; R.I. Gen. Laws § 28-44-17.1; S.C. Code Ann. § 41-35-125, 41-35-130; S.D. Codified Laws § 61-6-13.1; Texas Lab. Code Ann. §§ 207.045, 207.046; Vt. Stat. Ann. tit. 21, § 1251 *et seq.*; Wash. Rev. Code §§ 50.20.050, 50.20.100, 50.29.020; Wis. Stat. § 108.04(7)(S); Wyo. Stat. § 27-3-311.

37. See, e.g., Rivers v. Stiles, 697 S.W.2d 938 (Ark. Ct. App. 1985).

38. Ariz. Rev. Stat. § 12-1810, Ark. Code § 11-5-115, Cal. Civ. Code § 527.8, Colo. Rev. Stat. 13-14-102(4)(B), Ga. Code Ann. § 34-1-7, Ind. Code § 34-26-6, Nev. Rev. Stat. § 33.200-.360, N.C. Gen. Stat. 95-261, R.I. Gen. Laws § 28-52-2, 20; Tenn. Code §§ 20-14-101-109. See *Workplace Restraining Orders: State Law Guide,* Legal Momentum, publication, available at http://www.legalmomentum.org/site/DocServer/restraining.pdf?docID-534.

39. See, e.g., Ark. Code Ann. § 11-5-115.

40. Some jurisdictions mandate that victims have access to obtaining an order of protection twenty-four hours per day, seven days per week. In those jurisdictions, judges may be on call and once alerted, may grant an

order of protection over the phone. *"Beeper Judge" Program Successful Helping Domestic Violence Victims,* Brian Hamlin, Times-Herald, Mar. 6, 2005.

41. 8 U.S.C. § 922 (g)(8).

42. 8 U.S.C. § 2265.

43. Technical assistance on full faith and credit issues is available at the Full Faith and Credit Project, (800) 256-5883; and the International Association of Chiefs of Police, (800) The-IACP.

44. *Workplace Violence Prevention Book,* STP Publishers, "Domestic Violence and the Workplace." Pam Paziotopoulos, Oct. 2002, Tab F, Ch. 1. A number of instruments are used to help identify high-risk cases. For a more detailed analysis of the accuracy of these different approaches (used to predict risk of future harm or lethality in domestic violence cases), see "Intimate Partner Violence Risk Assessment Validation Study: The RAVE Study." This document was a research report submitted to the U.S. Department of Justice and conducted with the help of a National Institute of Justice grant. This particular study tested four methods: Danger Assessment (DA), DV-MOSAIC, Domestic Violence Screening Instrument (DVSI), and Kingston Screening Instrument for Domestic Violence (K-SID). These methods were selected for review because of their popularity and lack of empirical data showing to what degree they assessed the likelihood of future violence. The study makes the excellent point that the science of risk assessment is young. Therefore, whether or not an employer chooses to use one of the aforementioned methods, an employer should always attempt to gather as much background information as possible to assist in predicting the likelihood of an escalation in violence.

45. Id. at Tab F, Ch. 1.

46. Id.

47. *The Prosecutors Deskbook,* "Domestic Violence Policies and Practices," 3d ed., American Prosecutors Research Institute.

48. National Institute of Justice, Assessing Risk Factors for Intimate Partner Homicide, Journal No. 250 (2003).

49. "Domestic Violence: Prosecutors Take the Lead," monograph by the American Prosecutors Research Institute.

50. See supra note 44.

CHAPTER 11

Proactive Planning: Conducting a Site Security Assessment for the Public Sector

Michael Crane and Jack F. Dowling

▊ Introduction

When it comes to workplace violence, it is often easier to convince managers to focus on the problem *after* a violent act has taken place, rather than before an incident occurs. But identifying potential victims, as well as weak points in security procedures, can go a long way toward preventing violence in the workplace.

In its 2002 report *Workplace Violence: Issues in Response,*[1] the Federal Bureau of Investigation (FBI) stresses that no "profile" or litmus test exists to indicate whether an employee might become violent. Instead, it is important for employers and employees to remain alert to problematic behavior, such as major changes in personality or habits, obsession with weapons, dependence on alcohol or drugs, depression, or delusional romantic interests, that could point to possible violence. No one behavior in and of itself suggests a greater potential for violence, but all must be looked at in totality.

Risk factors that can be associated with potential violence include personality conflicts between coworkers or between a worker and a supervisor, disciplinary action for bringing weapons onto a work site, drug or alcohol use on the job, or a grudge over a real or imagined grievance. A former employee who may have been terminated could bring violence back to the workplace. A disgruntled customer also can pose a threat. Risks also can stem from an employee's personal circumstances—the breakup of a marriage or romantic relationship, other family conflicts, financial or legal problems, or emotional disturbance. In rare cases, the perpetrator could be a random outsider.

In the public sector, the potential for workplace violence may depend on the nature, location, and function of the government agency or municipality. A small library, for instance, with a few employees located next to police headquarters may have a lesser chance of workplace violence than an urban-based unemployment claims office with many employees and few security resources in and around its facility. Public schools pose a challenge due to the youthful population and, more recently, due to well-publicized incidents of violence in both urban and rural locations. Some public sector agencies provide day care centers on or near their property. This added service creates the potential of workplace violence related to abductions, molestation, and domestic relations situations, and is a real concern that necessitates consideration in a site security assessment.

Once these risks are identified, a site security assessment is the next logical step in creating a safe environment for employees, customers, and bystanders. A thorough assessment encompasses electronic and design security features, security personnel, policies and procedures, and security and crime prevention education and training. It also requires an executive-led team to drive the program throughout the organization.

▎ Identifying Perpetrators of Workplace Violence

Perpetrators of workplace violence can be divided into five categories:

- Employee-on-employee (current or former)

- Employee-on-supervisor (current or former)

- Domestic related

- Customer-on-employee

- Third-party perpetrator

The perpetrator type will greatly influence the site security assessment and, ultimately, the selection of countermeasures. Looking at these types of offenders in more detail will reveal some of the scenarios to take into consideration during the site security assessment.

An "employee-on-employee" incident is based on a present or past employment relationship and may or may not involve a work-related issue. An "employee-on-supervisor" incident also involves a present or past employment relationship but there is a greater likelihood that such an event is associated with a work-related situation. Disciplinary actions or termination are frequent triggers in this type of workplace violence. A domestic-related incident is connected to a personal or intimate relationship outside the workplace that brings harassment, threats, or actual harm to the employee by the abuser at the job site. "Customer-on-employee" events are based on the service aspect of a public employer and could stem from perceived or actual poor performance, or an amorous advance or romantic obsession that causes harassment, threats, or harm to an individual employee or the agency. The violent act by a third-party criminal, not connected to any employment aspect, is the last category and many times involves a homicide, serious assault, or robbery.

▋ A Security Assessment Approach

The security site assessment of the facility should include four areas of consideration:

1. *Physical, electronic, and design security features.* In this evaluation, barriers, lights, locks, alarms, and video monitoring systems should be examined.
2. *Security personnel.* In this area, type, authority, training, staffing, deployment, etc., should be evaluated.
3. *Security policies, procedures, and practices.* Regulations concerning access control, visitor management, codes of conduct, etc., should be examined in light of workplace violence issues.
4. *Security and crime prevention awareness, education, and training programs.* All current workplace violence programs should be reviewed for relevancy.

Each of these crucial areas needs to be viewed in light of the identified risk. The security site assessment should center on the violence analysis conducted on the specific workplace violence threat or general threat condition. Once all vulnerabilities are disclosed, priorities and hierarchies can be established, and the necessary resources and funds can be distributed.

Since the security site assessment will vary based upon the type of the workplace violence threat or incident, each component of the assessment will be discussed.

Physical, Electronic, and Design Security

When an employee threatens or commits violence against a coworker or supervisor, the existing relationship between the victim and the offender is such that enhanced physical and design security measures should be minimal. Other than separating the offender and the employee/supervisor, increased physical and design controls are not appropriate. Relocating the victim or offender would be a temporary solution. However, electronic security could be utilized by issuing a wireless panic or duress alarm (silent mode) that could be activated by the victim if the situation warranted. Additionally, with the technological advances and reduced costs, installation of an internet protocol (IP) or network camera in or around the target area is another consideration to allow for visual observation and recording.

When a former employee poses a threat, a barrier or entry-control safeguard is appropriate. First, determine whether the former employee still has access to the workplace, either through an ID badge, keys, or equipment associated with the business, or if the employee still has computer access connections to the network.

With the threat level of the offender determined, additional or upgraded security countermeasures can be installed around the exterior of the facility if needed. Physical barriers should be closely examined for any breaches. This is particularly important in the case where the offender is a former employee. Such an offender may be aware of any deficiencies in exterior security (e.g., fencing), or create some. Lighting on the exterior and interior of the property will be an essential element to furnish both psychological and physical deterrence and increase the likelihood of identifying the intruder. Video monitoring systems and intrusion alarms also can be used for additional surveillance and protection, especially on the perimeter of the building. These can be combined with delay mechanisms on perimeter doors, which would prohibit anyone from immediately exiting a facility. It may be necessary to provide visual observation on the potential victim's vehicle or those vehicles utilized by public officials or managers.

Access roads to the employer's facility should be inspected and designed to limit the speed of vehicles as they approach the building to reduce the potential of ramming entry points. Bends in the road or speed bumps can be utilized to slow arriving vehicles.

Keeping Workers Safe Inside

The victim of workplace violence also can take preventive measures. He or she can be issued a personal security alarm that will alert staff security upon activation. This protective action can be combined with video monitoring of the possible affected locations in and around the facility. A hidden duress/panic button can be installed at the reception area to the offices of agency heads and senior staff. Additionally, code words could be developed that would be spoken over the telephone to indicate an existing or unfolding problem. In extreme cases, a personalized security plan could be developed for victim(s) and a "safe room" created where the individual could relocate during an imminent threat situation.

Customer-on-Employee Violence

Access control precautions are the greatest prevention strategy for the employee. Depending on the nature of the public entity's facility and its use, restricting admittance at the entrance may be the best approach. As with a former employee, perimeter barriers, lighting, locks, alarms, and video security are helpful.

Domestic Relations

Since perpetrators in this group generally are not connected to the employer's business operation, the access control system is the first line of defense where the victim does not work in an area open to the public. Strict visitor/guest registration situated away from the general work area limits both visual and physical contact. The visitor/guest area should be protected by both overt and concealed communications, such as panic/duress alarms. Additionally, the registration area should be designed to minimize direct contact between the visitor/guest with the use of glass partitions and wide registration desktops. Constant video monitoring of this area during normal business hours is recommended.

Outsider Threats

This category of workplace violence is the most difficult to control or prevent. However, providing the appropriate security presence at the facility may be a significant deterrent. Security would include well-defined approaches to the facility, signage, speed restrictors, barriers, and security lighting. The security plan can also include visible surveillance cameras and "blue light" emergency phones, which have rapid communications capabilities and, in some cases, links to security cameras that are triggered to record activity at the phone.

Any cash kept at the facility should be stored in safes or vaults, and valuable property secured and alarmed.

Security Personnel

The staffing and deployment of security personnel can prevent or mitigate employee-on-employee or employee-on-supervisor incidents. Security personnel could increase the patrol of the workplace area where the victim and offender are located. In an extreme case, a security officer could be assigned to a fixed post in the area where the alleged victim works. Local law enforcement assistance may be needed. Even if not required initially, they should be advised of the situation so they can be prepared to respond quickly if a situation should arise that requires intervention. Although an internal incident report already may have been filed, a formal police report may be appropriate if the facts warrant.

If a threat involves a former employee, all security personnel should be aware of the status of the former employee, have a current photograph of him or her if available, and be provided basic information about the vehicles that the person owns or has access to, or other identifying data, which may include any past trespassing notices issued. This critical information should be maintained at all vehicle and pedestrian entry points under the strictest confidence and remain there indefinitely or until the threat becomes obsolete. Experience has shown that it is not uncommon for acts of violence by former employees to take place months or years after the person was terminated. Security personnel should review this material on a regular basis and update it if new information is gathered with respect to a former employee's vehicle or his or her appearance.

Deployment and staffing requirements of security personnel may be affected by a potential workplace violence incident. It may be appropriate to post a security officer near the victim's work station or work area. The offices of officials or high-level administrative staff may warrant additional protection, such as a stationary uniformed or plainclothes officer located outside their offices. The vehicles of potential victims may need to be observed and placed under surveillance, either by a security officer or via closed circuit television.

Consistent with the rules, regulations, or past practices of the public employer, a security officer could be assigned to the victim or public official and be provided door-to-door service. Depending on the threat level, a security officer could be assigned to the victim's and/or public official's residences.

Whether to utilize armed security is an issue that will need to be considered by the threat assessment/crisis management team. If the security force is already armed, their ability to carry firearms off the property could be limited. Options such as using local or off-duty police can be discussed, along with relevant legal issues.

Customer-on-Employee Violence

If a customer has threatened an employee with violence, collecting all available personal information on the offender will give the security staff the best chance to prevent an incident. But photographs of and vehicular information for the offender are rarely available to identify the offender prior to entry into the facility. In some cases, security personnel may already be familiar with the customer or may have been involved in previous confrontations.

Domestic Relations

In any domestic situation, violence can escalate quickly, and police or security personnel become the target of both the victim and offender. Since offenders can be current or former spouses, boyfriends, girlfriends, or a relative, the list of possible offenders in this category is potentially extensive but always linked to some current or past personal relationship with the employee. Responding to this class of workplace violence may require two security officers with backup readily available, as domestic situations tend to be the most likely workplace violence scenarios encountered.

Outside Threats

Perimeter patrols and varied routines by the workplace targets will also act as a visible deterrent and reduce the opportunity for an outsider to commit workplace violence. By analyzing the crime patterns and trends on the property and in the immediate area, patrol deployment and staffing can be adjusted to meet the anticipated threats.

Security Policies, Procedures, and Practices

Employers should establish a strong workplace violence prevention policy. Such a policy provides a definition of workplace violence, gives specific examples of acts of workplace violence, contains a weapons prohibition, strongly condemns acts of violence, and outlines procedures for reporting and responding to these acts. An employer's code or standard of conduct, or its work rules and regulations, should be utilized and enforced in such situations. Most public entities have behavior expectations and workplace violence policies (prohibition against threats, harassment) that would cover this kind of conduct and impose sanctions for violations of the same. Making the offender aware of the potential ramifications of his or her actions is the first step in this process.

Termination policies, if based on a workplace violence incident or threat, should include a security provision that prohibits, to the extent legally possible, a former employee from entering onto the property in the future. This prohibition should be issued in writing and kept on file. Basically, the former employee would be persona non grata and subject to arrest for trespassing if he or she is found on the property. Depending on who the public entity is, and the applicable state and local laws regarding trespass, legally barring the former employee from the premises may or may not be feasible. Such a policy may be more feasible to implement in the private sector where employers exercise greater control over who may enter their premises.

Customer Access

Even in the absence of a threat, customers should be limited in their access to the property. Clear policies should restrict customers from going beyond areas open to the public and require an employee escort to enter areas limited to employees. Further, customers should be issued a temporary ID and be required to wear it in plain view whenever on the property. An overall policy also should address any amorous advances by a customer toward an employee and even prohibit socializing between customer and employee during work hours.

Access by Friends or Relatives

To prevent domestic disputes from spilling over into an office environment, companies should institute strict access control policies that prevent employees from allowing friends or relatives into employee-only work areas. Friends and relatives should be restricted to the public areas of the facility, such as the visitor/guest registration area(s) and special parking areas separated from employee parking.

Companies also should implement a process whereby employees who have obtained a court order of protection against an individual can have that person listed. This list should be provided to security and maintained along with information on other persons who should not be given access to the facility.

Outside Threats

Trespassing enforcement policies and procedures assist in safeguarding against outsider incidents. If cash or valuable property is a target, a policy limiting the amount of cash on the premises and periodic bank deposits can reduce the hazards of theft. A policy mandating that valuable property be inventoried, engraved, and properly secured or alarmed can limit the chance of workplace violence related to this target.

Security and Crime Prevention Awareness, Education, and Training Programs

As recommended by the FBI in its report on workplace violence, new and current employees, along with supervisors, managers, and elected officials, should receive regular training in the employer's workplace violence prevention policy, including reporting requirements. This training should include awareness of risk factors that can cause or contribute to threats and violence, early recognition of warning signs, and a standard response action plan for violent situations, including how to get assistance, respond to alarm systems, and communicate threat to leaders.

Former Employee Perpetrators

It is important to warn employees, staff, and administration when a former employee has made a threat. However, caution should be taken to convey this information without violating state or federal privacy laws. This can be a good time to conduct additional training in workplace violence, while focusing on the threat posed by the former employee. Prompt notification of security personnel should be encouraged if the former employee has been seen in or around the property.

Crime prevention training and education for the victim, supervisors, and/or management can be conducted on an individual basis and may include strategies for minimizing the threat of violence both on and off the property.

Customer Threats

Part of any workplace violence training should focus on customer conduct that is considered inappropriate. Employees whose job duties put them in contact with the public on a daily basis should receive additional training on how to handle irate customers, including de-escalation techniques that can help defuse the situation.

Domestic Relations

In this situation, a personal education and training program can be conducted for those employees threatened. Education should stress the importance of promptly reporting any changes in the relationship, either good or bad, or new information on the offender. Training can include certain precautions to be taken both on and off the property.

Outsider Threats

Personal security programs can be conducted on a periodic basis that incorporate awareness, education, and training components, including the distribution of crime prevention material. These programs can include a discussion of crimes against both persons and property. The tenets of these programs can be applied both on and off the job. Topics could include robbery prevention, prevention of rape and sexual assault, theft, and burglary. Instructors should stress the importance of reducing the opportunity for a crime to occur and provide employees with relevant safety skills to avoid becoming a crime victim.

▌ Site Security Assessment Checklist

In order to be comprehensive, many site assessment factors need to be reviewed. A detailed checklist follows.

Perimeter

- *Maintain well-lit approaches.* All areas around the perimeter of the facility, including roadways and walkways, should be lit to the levels suggested by the Illuminating Engineering Society of North America (IESNA).[2] Ensuring sufficient illumination can serve as a physical and psychological deterrent and aid in observation.

- *Provide ample barriers/fences.* Depending on the type of facility, a wrought iron or chain-link fence should be erected around the property to serve as a barrier to a potential intruder or adversary. Also effective are thick, thorny bushes, standing alone or in front of the fencing.

- *Post clear signage.* Post clear signs directing individuals to authorized pathways/driveways and warning against trespassing. These measures inform a potential intruder or adversary that security is a serious issue, which acts as a deterrent.

- *Control access.* Entry points should be limited, if possible, to one entrance for vehicles and one for pedestrians to restrict and better control access to buildings by nonemployees. These entrances and exits should be staffed as an added safeguard.

Parking Facilities (Surface Lots and Structures)

- *Consider prior criminal activity.* Based on the past criminal offenses committed in the parking areas and immediate vicinity, protective measures can be established that are meaningful and cost effective, depending on the identified crime level—low, medium, or high.

- *Adequate lighting.* Parking facilities should establish cones of illumination, using the guidelines established by the IESNA.

- *Concealment points.* Any trees, shrubbery, or plants that detract from security and offer a place to hide, or block lighting, should be trimmed so that there is an unobstructed field of view from about three to eight feet in all directions.

- *Video monitoring system.* With the recent advances in technology, smart/intelligent cameras, video analytics, and use of IP/network transmission, the cost of furnishing security surveillance has decreased substantially, along with more efficient recording, archiving, and retrieval of video images. There is a deterrent effect for visible cameras in addition to the investigative leads furnished by the recordings that can be utilized in disciplinary and/or court hearings. With the IP/network cameras, flexibility of placement allows installation wherever there is a network connection.

- *Emergency phones.* "Blue light" emergency phones are used frequently and can be placed strategically throughout parking facilities. The visible deterrent effect, along with the rapid communications capability, enhance security. Additionally, many phones are equipped with a security camera or linked to a nearby surveillance camera that is triggered to record activity at the phone when activated by an individual.

- *Entry control.* Limiting the number of entrances and exits for both persons and vehicles reduces the opportunity for unauthorized entry. Many facilities use a key card access control or other comparable identification system along with a barrier arm to control traffic. A double gate or swing-arm entry control system can eliminate tailgating into the parking area as the second barrier does not activate until the first barrier is closed.

- *Security patrol routines.* Regular but varied patrol of the parking facility by uniformed security officers either on foot, on bicycle, or in marked vehicles increases protection and enhances deterrence.

■ *Escort system.* Used after regular hours and on weekends or by request of a workplace violence victim, a personal escort from the building to the individual's vehicle serves as an added security feature.

External and Internal Area Lighting

■ *Level measurements.* Regular measurements of the lighting output should be conducted and upgrades made where deficiencies are noted. An illuminance or photo meter should be utilized.

■ *Repair/replacement policy.* A facility's maintenance program should include prompt reporting and repair or replacement of lighting outages.

Internal Access Controls

■ *Strict policy.* A policy that limits who can enter the facility can aid in the prevention of any type of workplace violence that does not involve a current employee as the offender. Only authorized personnel should be allowed beyond the reception area or in non-public areas of the facility.

■ *Reception area barrier.* Depending on the location and security risks, barriers could include bulletproof glass enclosures or a wide and raised platform registration area. This entry point can have video security, a panic/duress button, and remote door controls.

■ *Visitor management system.* Technology today allows companies to preregister visitors, scan and record personal information, and print temporary badges. This can be accomplished in a short amount of time and furnishes a higher level of security, in addition to capturing pictures, business card, or driver's license data.

■ *ID credential verification of employees.* This procedure can be managed by staff who individually recognize each employee or by optical turnstiles that allow both entry and exit. Some optical turnstiles are equipped with anti-tailgate technology.

- *Metal detectors.* Public facilities that house courtrooms or other potentially charged activities should consider metal detectors. In extreme cases, there may be a need to screen for explosives and other weapons.

- *Personal property inspection.* This measure is usually combined with metal detectors by providing either x-ray of contents or personal inspection.

- *Employee termination policy.* Such a policy should contain provisions for obtaining all keys, access devices, and equipment at the time of termination. Access codes to the computer network or doors should be changed, and the former employee removed from any access control databases.

Alarms

- *Intrusion.* These protection measures can be used at the perimeter or, more commonly, for the interior of the facility or building. These alarms can prevent someone from staying on the property after hours or entering unlawfully prior to opening the facility or building.

- *Duress/panic.* These personal alarms are either carried by the individual and operate in a wireless fashion or hidden at the individual's workplace. Most are silent alarms, but some personal protection alerts are battery operated and create a loud sound when activated without security notification.

Cash Handling Procedures

- *Minimize the amount of cash on hand.* To reduce opportunity or motivation, limited amounts of cash should be kept on hand. This fact should be advertised by signage. Regular, periodic bank deposits can be used to accomplish this.

■ *Drop safe*. Where routine bank deposits are not possible, a safe that cannot be opened by the employees should be utilized. This fact also should be advertised by signage. This procedure should be used when the amount of cash on hand reaches a predetermined amount.

■ *Transportation*. Periodic or daily bank deposits should be carried out with great caution and, depending on the crime risk in the area, performed by more than one individual using a varied time and route. In extreme cases, the use of an armored car transportation service should be considered.

Crime Prevention through Environmental Design

■ *Natural surveillance*. The perceived risk of being identified will deter most intruders. Keep an unobstructed view of the entire property from both inside and outside the facility.

■ *Target hardening (locks, doors, windows, etc.)*. Making the facility as physically secure as possible will limit intruder opportunities. The use of sturdy locks, solid doors, strong door frames, and windows that cannot be readily opened and/or protected with security screens/grills will deter most rational criminals.

■ *Signage*. Informational and warning signs signify an orderly facility and warn of possible penalties for criminal activity (trespassing, loitering), serving as a deterrent.

■ *Pedestrian and vehicular movement control*. Directing individuals in and out of areas of the facility via specific pathways and directions can limit the ability of a potential adversary to enter, remain, or escape easily from the property.

Notes

1. This document can be found at http://www.fbi.gov/publications/violence.pdf.

2. Information pertaining to the IESNA can be accessed from their Web site at http://www.iesna.org.

CHAPTER 12

The Role of Law Enforcement in Assisting Employers with Workplace Violence

Richard A. Devine
and Bridget Healy Ryan

▍ Introduction

The traditional role of law enforcement is to react to violence and its aftermath. However, in recent years, law enforcement has engaged in efforts to prevent violence. Today, that greater role includes assisting employers in the prevention of violence in the workplace. The focus of this chapter is to suggest ways in which law enforcement can partner with management, security, and human resources personnel to more effectively respond to and prevent workplace violence. This chapter reinforces recommendations made in other chapters concerning workplace violence prevention and intervention techniques. It also presents ways in which law enforcement can assist employers, either proactively or in the aftermath of a serious threat or act of violence in the workplace.

▌ Who Is the Law Enforcement in Your Neighborhood?

Law enforcement is divided into three levels of service: local, state, and federal. Employers should have a general understanding of various law enforcement organizations in order to know whom to approach about workplace violence concerns.

In all likelihood, employers will interact with local or county law enforcement personnel. The district attorney (DA)—also known as the prosecuting attorney, county attorney, or the state's attorney, depending on the jurisdiction—is the designated official who represents a specific county or other judicial district in criminal and certain types of civil matters. The sole responsibility of the civil division is to act as the attorney for the county; therefore, the division cannot defend or bring an action on behalf of a private citizen or business. However, the office of the DA can assist employers with criminal behavior such as: stalking, harassment, nonfatal and fatal assaults and batteries, criminal damage to property, criminal trespass to real property, theft, robbery, and sexual assault. Typically, local police, detectives, sheriffs, and investigators from the DA's office investigate the criminal behavior and apprehend any suspect.

On the state level, each state, territory, and commonwealth has an attorney general who is responsible for advising the governor and state agencies about legal issues, as well as assisting state prosecuting attorneys. Each attorney general is the chief legal officer of the state and is responsible for protecting the public interest of the state and its citizenry. Typically, an attorney general's office addresses such issues as consumer fraud, environmental protection, sex offender laws, child support enforcement, and utility rate laws. Employers should be aware that an attorney general's office usually offers programs that, upon application, may financially reimburse crime victims for out-of-pocket expenses they incur as a result of a criminal incident.

Generally, an attorney general's office does not prosecute workplace violence unless there has been a request for assistance by the local or county prosecutor. However, many of these state offices have conferences, task forces, and publications that specifically deal with workplace violence. For instance, Mississippi, Hawaii, California, and Maine all have helpful materials (e.g., sample workplace violence policies, dangerous assessment checklists) on the prevention of workplace violence that are available to the general public on their respective Web sites.

On the federal level, law enforcement includes the U.S. Department of Justice and its prosecutors from the U.S. Attorney's Office, as well as investigators at the Federal Bureau of Investigation (FBI). U.S. attorneys are the individuals who prosecute federal crimes. According to the FBI's Web site, its mission, along with the U.S. Attorney's Office, is to "protect and defend the United States against terrorist and foreign intelligence threats and to enforce the criminal laws of the United States."[1] The FBI has jurisdiction over hundreds of categories of federal law, including bank robberies, immigration violations, narcotics, terrorism, some crimes against children, major theft, securities fraud, computer crimes, asset forfeiture and money laundering, and offenses committed on federal government property. Additionally, the Department of Homeland Security's Federal Protective Service (FPS) is the main law enforcement service for responding to incidents in federal facilities, which are under the control of the General Services Administration (GSA), such as federal penitentiaries and safe houses.[2]

Much like state law enforcement, federal law enforcement does not typically respond to workplace violence unless there is a request from local law enforcement. However, federal law enforcement will respond when there is a violation of federal law. This would occur if the workplace incident involved an allegation that a substance such as anthrax or a high-caliber weapon or weapon of detonation was present. Notwithstanding the possible involvement of state or federal law enforcement, it is important to remember that most workplace violence incidents begin with the involvement of local law enforcement. As such, local law enforcement is best equipped to assist businesses in the prevention of and response to workplace violence incidents.

▌ The Role of Local Law Enforcement in Helping to Prevent Workplace Violence

There are many ways that local law enforcement and employers can partner to prevent violence at the workplace. This chapter addresses violence between coworkers, as well as violence perpetrated on an employee by a former coworker or a nonemployee (e.g., customer, client). The focus of the employer should be to ensure that management, human resources, security, and law enforcement are all apprised of the circumstances and are working together. As to these types of incidents, the employer must document and keep track of all reports of workplace violence in an internalized, centralized record-keeping area to assist law enforcement investigations.

Many jurisdictions are departing from traditional methods of police intervention and prosecution and moving toward a more integrated, solution-based approach to eradicate crime, which includes workplace violence. This solution-based approach is referred to as *community prosecution*. These programs generally are based out of the prosecutor's office and work to develop partnerships among prosecutors, law enforcement, the community, and various other private and public agencies in an effort to prevent criminal activity from occurring in the first place. The latest publication from the American Prosecutor's Research Institute's Community Prosecutions Section, entitled "Lessons from the Field," highlights ten jurisdictions which are leaders in the field of community prosecution. These jurisdictions include Dallas, Denver, Atlanta, Minneapolis,

Kalamazoo, Brooklyn, Indianapolis, Portland (Oregon), Austin, and Washington, D.C. According to the monograph, "These jurisdictions are models based upon their efforts in crime prevention, intervention and targeted law enforcement, and each represents a unique response to the ever-changing social and law enforcement challenges of the twenty-first century."

Community prosecution units can be extremely beneficial to private businesses and corporations because they enable members of the community to interact with law enforcement prior to the filing of actual criminal charges. The community prosecution approach brings the community, police, and prosecutors together prior to, during, and after a criminal incident. Many community prosecution programs involve weekly/monthly meetings with citizens, area businesses, the police, and prosecutors. These meetings provide a forum to discuss issues that may not involve actual crimes but are of great concern to an individual or a business.

For instance, if an employee is being harassed at the workplace but no actual crime has been committed (no law violated), the employee and/or the employer could meet with the police and prosecutor to find a solution before the situation escalates further and a workplace incident occurs. The police may reach out to the alleged offender to discuss his or her behavior, or even send extra patrols to the workplace. The prosecutor can double-check to see if any laws have been broken or, at the very least, give the victim information about the availability of a civil protective order.

The first step that employers must take to help prevent workplace violence is to develop, disseminate, and enforce (via both an employee handbook and employee training) a clearly defined code of conduct for employees that mandates a zero tolerance policy for workplace violence. This policy should require that employees report suspicious behavior, such as anything that could be interpreted as communicating an intent to cause harm to another employee or to oneself. Employers should make it known that even emotionally abusive behavior can escalate and require attention and intervention. Employers may wish to utilize a comment box, ombudsperson, telephone hotline, or employee assistance referral system to facilitate the anonymous reporting of such behavior. The employer should ensure that people outside the organization also have a means to submit anonymous reports. The workplace violence policy also should include:

- Disciplinary actions for employee violations

- A process for investigating and resolving reports of policy violations

- A policy of no retaliation against an employee-victim or anyone who reports a good-faith suspicion of potential workplace violence

- An antidiscrimination policy

- An anti-drug use and alcohol abuse policy

- A computer technology policy that expressly provides that employees do not have a right of privacy in their computer, e-mail, or Internet usage

- Privacy expectations vis-à-vis an employee's desk, file cabinets, and lockers

Employers should establish contact and exchange information with the local police or sheriff's office before a violent incident occurs in the workplace. Law enforcement should have accurate and timely information about the workplace, including:

- A list of contact persons (management and security personnel) at the job site

- A list of fire and evacuation, crisis, or threat management plans to be given to emergency responders

- A specific location where these documents will be immediately accessible to emergency responders

- Information regarding potential problems, including specific information that will assist emergency responders

- A list of the location of highly valued goods

- A database of employees' addresses and telephone numbers

- A copy of the employer's floor plan, including power and water locations

Management and security personnel can invite law enforcement to tour the workplace so that they may become familiar with the layout and can recommend security measures. An employer should develop and implement a clear and effective policy for visitor access to the workplace. Reception areas can be locked to prevent intruders and former disgruntled employees from gaining access to offices when there is no reception area. Other actions that law enforcement may recommend include:

- Enforcing a no weapons policy

- Utilizing additional police patrols or security guards when the need arises

- Installing (after consultation with legal counsel):

  - Electronic access control systems

  - Silent or panic alarms

  - Metal detectors

  - Video cameras

  - Closed circuit television or other surveillance systems

- Providing identification badges to all employees

- Screening all mail or packages following a threat of violence

- Providing security escorts to employer-controlled parking lots for employees who have been subjected to threats

- Distributing photographs of potential offenders to security personnel and frontline employees

- Ensuring proper lighting in and around the workplace

- Physically relocating an employee who has been threatened with violence and/or providing that employee with a rapid response distress alarm or cell phone

Local law enforcement also can clarify with management and security personnel which workplace violence scenarios would call for a law enforcement response and when and how they should be notified of an incident. Additionally, law enforcement agencies can state what their standard response (as well as their limitations) would be for a variety of workplace violence incidents, including reports of:

- Unauthorized person(s) on the property

- Person with a firearm on the premises

- Noncriminal but threatening behavior

- Crime in progress at the worksite

- Armed attacker

- Bomb threat

- Hostage situation

- Suspicious packages

- Angry customers or clients

Once a workplace violence policy is in place, employers must be prepared to apply it. Often, employees who act out in a violent manner at the workplace exhibit behaviors that foretell their violence (see Chapter 2, "Basic Principles and Concepts in Threat Assessment Evaluations"). Employers should be aware of general warning signs that may be precursors to an act of violence. If an employee's past or present behavior exhibits any of the following, an employer may need to take action:

- Communication of threats

- Displays of temper or explosive behavior

- Comments that blame others, show feelings of persecution, and/or inability to accept criticism

- Demonstrated interest in violent acts/events, extremist groups, or obtaining weapons

- Problems with job performance due to tardiness/absenteeism, low productivity

- Verbal harassment or menacing behavior

- Recent loss of a significant relationship or loss of job status (e.g., demotion, transfer to an undesirable position)

- History of depression, mental illness, and/or substance abuse

Once a clearly delineated policy is in place and employees understand the warning signs of violence at the workplace, the employer should implement disciplinary procedures, which respond to violations of the policy. Be aware that once disciplinary action has been taken, as in reprimand, suspension, transfers or administrative leaves, demotion, or termination, there is a greater risk of escalation of violence. In consultation with human resources and/or legal counsel, employers should develop and utilize safe termination practices, including an exit interview to identify potential violent behaviors. Employers should involve law enforcement and their own security personnel prior to any announcement of layoffs or an adversarial termination.

Another step that employers can take to help prevent workplace violence perpetrated by an employee is to conduct a thorough background check on prospective employees in compliance with the requirements of the federal Fair Credit Reporting Act. Moreover, employers who rely on temporary agency or contract workers to staff their operations must verify that the temporary employment service they use also conducts background checks on their workers. Businesses should utilize private firms that specialize in civilian background checks, as local law enforcement cannot do background checks for the purposes of employment. Law enforcement, by law, generally can only do criminal background checks as part of a criminal investigation.[3] As a result, law enforcement may have information that it cannot divulge, even when an employer has made a request. This may include information pertaining to whether or not a person has a registered firearm. Regardless of whether the police can divulge this information, it is still important to be in communication with law enforcement. Law enforcement may take its own action as long as it is aware that there may be a problem with an individual. The job application should include a waiver and release to enable the employer to verify information. A thorough background check should include:

- An extensive work history of the prospective employee that extends back at least ten years

- An extensive in-person interview before the applicant is offered a position

- A review of court records and databases that provide access to conviction records in all states to identify applicants who have been convicted of a violent crime

- Making inquiries about prior incidents of violence and/or unexplained periods of unemployment

When the potential perpetrator is a former employee, information that was gathered from the prior background check can later prove helpful to both law enforcement and the employer. The background check may include information on the former employee's history of substance abuse, mental disorders, or suicidal tendencies. It is important to point out here that some of this information (e.g., medical history) cannot be solicited from a job applicant until after the employer has made an offer of employment to the individual. After consultation with legal counsel, this information should be disseminated to law enforcement when the employer has credible information that a former employee poses a potential threat to the workplace. The employer also should provide law enforcement with information as to whether the potential offender has engaged in planning or preparing for violence, such as returning to the workplace, trying to breach security, and/or harassing or stalking a current employee.

Finally, employers can integrate community partners into the workplace violence prevention plan. For example, mental health and domestic violence service organizations are often willing partners. Businesses may contact their local advocacy agency or shelter and request a speaker for special training sessions. In Cook County, Illinois, the local prosecutor's office routinely teams up with several different advocacy agencies to conduct training for companies that request it. Topics have included the dynamics of domestic violence, stalking, threat assessment, and general workplace violence. These trainings can be extremely effective in raising awareness in the workplace and training employees on how to assist other employees who are at risk. It also encourages employees who may be aware of a potential situation to communicate with management so that a workplace violence incident can be avoided. Law enforcement also can recommend alternative law enforcement or security companies and/or threat assessment professionals who can assist the employer. Often these additional resources can prove invaluable in prompting the employer to assemble a threat incident response team at the workplace. Local law enforcement also can present information on criminal statutes, such as stalking, domestic violence, assault, and trespassing.

▮ The Role of Local Law Enforcement During a Workplace Violence Incident

With respect to most incidents of violence in the workplace, the employer should contact law enforcement and other emergency responders immediately. If the employer and local law enforcement already have an *existing* relationship, law enforcement will be able to respond in a more effective manner. Prior to law enforcement's arrival, frontline personnel (such as security and receptionists) should be prepared to act if the offender is attempting to gain entry or contact at the workplace. This includes an emergency plan to keep the possible perpetrator isolated in a safe area away from employees while security and/or law enforcement is contacted. As discussed above, when the offender is a current or former employee, the employer should provide law enforcement with whatever information it has about the offender (including a photo ID, if one is available). Employers also should be prepared to provide law enforcement and other emergency responders with a copy of its building and evacuation plans, and a list of important phone numbers and contact persons. Additionally, in the event of a workplace violence incident, law enforcement also may need to obtain the following information:

- Whether the possible perpetrator is a current or former employee, has a relationship with a current employee, or is unknown

- Names of potential witnesses to the workplace violence incident

- Background on what events led up to the workplace violence incident (if known)

- Any specific language used by the offender and how the communication was made

- Description of the offender's conduct and physical appearance

- Description of any response of others who were involved in the incident

■ Description of how the incident ended and what happened to the offender

■ History of the offender

The employer may be instructed by law enforcement to implement lockdown procedures to secure the area where the workplace incident is occurring. The goal is to minimize the number of people at risk of harm. The employer should be prepared to evacuate a floor or a building to a predetermined location or have a system for reporting the whereabouts of all employees located in the area where the offender is believed to have gained access. These approaches allow the employer to account for all of those who are either safe or missing. Lastly, there should be an established procedure for the employer to provide timely, accurate updates to law enforcement of the events as they are unfolding.

■ The Role of Local Law Enforcement Following a Workplace Violence Incident

Despite everyone's best efforts, workplace violence incidents still may occur. Hopefully, the employer has taken steps to minimize the damage inflicted by the offender. Law enforcement and employers can work together to effectively handle the aftermath of a workplace violence incident. Where there is an ongoing criminal investigation, an employer may request that law enforcement provide a central contact person who will be able to answer questions and provide information to the employer.

During the investigation, law enforcement may require the collection of evidence. An employer should cooperate by consenting to a search of the workplace. Also, the employer can greatly assist in the investigative process by making the following items available without the need for a court-ordered subpoena:

- Video security cameras and equipment

- Voicemail recordings

- E-mail records

- Employee's personnel file if the offender is a current or former employee (employer may be required by law to redact certain personal information)

Additionally, where the victim of the workplace incident is a current employee, the employer should take steps to ensure the safety of the employee/victim. The employer and the victim should stay in contact with the prosecutor's office. The local prosecutor's office can refer the victim to advocacy groups and counseling services. The prosecutor's office can also advise the victim as to the pros and cons of seeking an order of protection, as well as the viability of seeking a restraining order (see Chapter 10, "What Employers Can Do to Minimize the Impact of Domestic Violence and Stalking in the Workplace," for more information about orders of protection). The employer should be prepared to help the victim enforce the order of protection. Where there are criminal proceedings, employers also can support a workplace violence victim by providing the following:

- A flexible schedule

- A transfer or administrative leave

- Work accommodations (e.g., permission to work from home)

- Health insurance

- Sick leave usage to attend court hearings and seek counseling (some state laws mandate such leave)

- Enhanced security measures (e.g., panic alarm)

- Accompaniment to court hearings

- Use of a prepaid cell phone

- A change of the employee's work number

- Information on workers' compensation claims

- Information on financial compensation for crime-related expenses through the state attorney general's office

The actual court process can be arduous. Depending on the jurisdiction, the victim may be required to attend all court hearings, which can be as often as once a month. Some cases are disposed of quickly if the parties can reach an agreement. However, in many instances, the defendant will contest the charges or the issuance of a protective order which then may necessitate several court dates in order to gather the information needed to proceed to trial or hearing (e.g., police reports, pictures, witness statements, and criminal histories). Generally speaking, misdemeanors (i.e., assault, battery, criminal trespass, criminal damage to property) take a shorter period of time to litigate than felonies (i.e., aggravated battery, unlawful restraint, weapons charges). If a victim is going to court for a misdemeanor charge, the perpetrator is either charged immediately by the police or a future date is set for his or her arraignment. Either way, there is a court date set where the victim must appear in order for the charges to go forward. In felony cases, the perpetrator is usually arrested, and then a court date for arraignment is set for three weeks to a month later. These cases may take up to a year or longer depending on whether the defendant is planning to plead guilty or ask for a trial. Either way, it is important for employers to support their employees throughout each phase of the legal process.

Where the offender is also an employee of the organization, legal counsel should be available to respond to any privacy or due process concerns. Independent of the criminal process, the employer should determine what disciplinary action to take as a result of the offender's violent actions.

Conclusion

This chapter is designed to offer some steps that employers can take to actively involve law enforcement in a partnership to more effectively respond to workplace violence concerns. While the true rewards from these efforts can never be known, employers can count on a safer and more productive workplace. Together, law enforcement and employers can make a difference.[4]

Notes

1. See Federal Bureau of Investigation's Web site, available at http://www.fbi.gov/hq.htm.

2. See U.S. General Services Administration's Web site, available at http://www.gsa.gov. See also "Dealing with Workplace Violence: A Guide for Agency Planners," Section 5: Workplace Security, Office of Personnel Management (OPM), available at http://www.opm.gov.

3. Public law enforcement agencies in many states have some flexibility with respect to performing background checks on police job applicants and other law enforcement–related job applicants. Public employers should be careful they do not exceed their authority, however.

4. The following sources greatly aided in the writing of this chapter: "Workplace Violence: Issues in Response," Critical Incident Response Report, National Center for the Analysis of Violent Crime, FBI, U.S. Dept. of Justice, Eugene A. Rugala and Arnold R. Isaacs, eds. (2004); "Workplace Violence Prevention and Response Guideline," ASIS International (2005); "Dealing with Workplace Violence: A Guide for Agency Planners," Section 2: Threat Assessment, Office of Personnel Management (OPM); "Dealing with Workplace Violence: A Guide for Agency Planners," Section 3: Prevention, Office of Personnel Management (OPM); "Dealing with Workplace Violence: A Guide for Agency Planners," Section 5: Workplace Security, Office of Personnel Management (OPM); Steve Kaufer and Jurg Mattman, "Workplace Violence: An Employer's Guide," Workplace Violence Institute, available at http://www.workplaceviolence.com.

CHAPTER 13

Workplace Violence: Managing the Crisis After a Crisis

Larry Barton, Ph.D.

W<small>HILE MUCH OF THIS BOOK</small> has been appropriately devoted to preventing workplace violence in the public sector, the reality is that incidents and threats do occur and their effects must be addressed. The statistical exposure of any public sector employer to critical incidents forces us to think about the crisis *after* the crisis—how managers respond to the myriad challenges that arise after someone has been threatened or injured at work.

Having managed more than eight hundred crime-based incidents over the years, I have identified three principal themes in virtually all cases:

1. *Managers were not ready to respond to the numerous stakeholders who emerge, seemingly immediately and concurrently, after an incident.*

For instance, it is not uncommon for a school or court administrator to forward all press and public inquiries to a public information officer on a routine basis. However, when violence occurs, both vested stakeholders (families of the victim) and public stakeholders (the news media, local officials) have a low tolerance for the public information officer who is often seen as a mouthpiece rather than a decision maker with tangible influence to make decisions and allocate resources. Thus, the role of the senior official becomes paramount. For instance, I have observed that whether discussing a tragic school shooting or a massacre in a local courthouse, the media tend to ignore all statements and news releases issued by the public information officer; instead, they relentlessly pursue the senior official to speak on the record: What did the official know about the incident? When did he or she know it? What is being done about it? The system becomes overwhelmed with dozens—potentially hundreds—of inquiries from these stakeholders. This begs several questions:

- Who has the training to answer questions after a critical incident?

- Can the organization create a series of frequently asked questions (FAQs) *before an incident* so that public officials can "fill in the blanks" depending upon the nature of the actual threat or incident?

- In advance of an incident, can the organization create a shadow Web site with key phone numbers where prerecorded updates (such as the date and time of a community debriefing) can be posted? Shadow Web sites are "hidden" pages that many school districts and government offices prepare in advance of a catastrophe. They list emergency numbers, provide evacuation routes, and "safe haven" areas where employees may be found, but they are only launched after a crisis. This reduces unnecessary repetition of key facts by phone operators to hundreds of neighbors, taxpayers, parents, or others trying to get information about the actual crisis.

2. Managers were in patent denial that they actually were in a crisis.

Somehow, public officials who find themselves managing a case of stalking, or an actual knifing or shooting of an employee, often assume or believe that the initial facts of the incident are correct. As a result, they act on information that is inaccurate and that may minimize the scope of incident. As the minutes tick away, these individuals begin to realize that they are actually dealing with the loss of more than one life; that more than one teacher was arrested in an assault on a cheerleader; that the stalker who attempted to kill a highway employee last night had been known to coworkers for months (not a few days) and that now these coworkers are readily sharing their documented concerns with the news media.

Underestimating a crisis is a dangerous business. It can destroy the credibility of capable public officials. The lack of an appropriate response by these officials can create a threshold of opportunity for litigators who later seek to prove that the administration was at best lax, and at worst incompetent, in recognizing and responding to the clear signals of a real threat.

Thus, it is precautionary to suggest that at the first signs of a crisis caused by violence, or the threat of harm, a public official or manager should assume that initial reports of the incident underestimate the number of victims or scope of the danger or harm. He or she should strive to "overachieve" by deciding to respond to victims with abundant care and concern (reminding employees of employee assistance programs) and by holding town hall meetings with employees to advise them on what actions have been taken and are being planned to address the crisis.

Denial or refusal to take definitive steps to address the problem are common in these cases because officials often claim that they were prohibited from taking action on advice of legal counsel or because of employee confidentiality constraints. In actuality, most lawyers recommend that a crisis manager acknowledge that a crisis exists, make a public statement about steps being taken to reduce the impact of the crisis on employees and the surrounding community, and openly express concern for those who have been victimized— "Our thoughts and prayers are with the victims and their families"— so that the organization under assault is represented by a human face.

3. *Competent administrators admit they have a crisis, acknowledge error, and encourage the support of their stakeholders in returning the organization to a place of normalcy.*

The three principal standards of workplace violence prevention that need to be integrated into a crisis response can be described as follows:

Duty to Warn

A public official should be prepared to discuss what steps were taken to protect the organization from harm. These may include workplace safety training, the presence of video monitoring systems and trained guards, and enhanced employee recruitment and retention. If the organization became aware of the potential threat before the fact, the public official should specify what action was taken to warn coworkers (especially the victim) in a manner consistent with the privacy standards of that jurisdiction—such as obtaining (and circulating) photographs of the possible perpetrator or encouraging those employees who felt anxious to contact human resources or security.

Duty of Care

A public official should be prepared to explain to stakeholders that appropriate care was expended in response to the threat; that once aware of the threat, the organization contacted local law enforcement personnel, notified potential victims of credible evidence, or offered a detailed advisory via e-mail encouraging everyone with concerns or observations to cooperate with human resources or local law enforcement.

Duty to Act

Organizational leaders must be prepared to explain, whether in a news conference or during a meeting with victims' families, that they recognized and were responsive to the threat of potential harm. Lawsuits can be avoided, and public criticism of an administration or management team reduced, if public officials demonstrate that they worked diligently and with a sense of urgency after becoming aware of a tangible threat and cooperated closely with local law enforcement. Organizational response should be documented. For instance, the dates, times, and names of anyone who participated in an advisory meeting with law enforcement should be kept by legal counsel as evidence that the employer embraced a due diligence dialogue with police. In addition, the process may include a fitness-for-duty evaluation for any employee whose mental health status raises questions about his or her ability to perform required job duties safely, or other documented decisions that support the administration's position that it had genuinely integrated the principles of "if you see something, say something" throughout the entire organization.

Other standards of care are also essential to help manage the aftermath of an incident of workplace violence. These include:

■ *Informing victims' families, coworkers, and business associates.* After an incidence of violence, competent officials visit the homes of victims and offer to assist them with making funeral arrangements, arranging memorial services, establishing a memorial scholarship or legacy fund, or other activities. Families later decide whether a lawsuit should be pursued not just by the "facts" but by their emotional response to how well the employer managed the immediate aftermath. The more an administrative team can do to reduce the sense of "us versus them" through proactive communication, the greater the likelihood that a lawsuit can be avoided.

■ *Memorials are important.* When a judge and court reporter were slain in an Atlanta courtroom in 2005, one of the first questions that the courthouse administrative team faced was how to create a public memorial to their former associates. It is more than ironic that one of the great icons of family "togetherness," McDonald's, lost valuable goodwill following a horrific incident of violence in 1984 at a restaurant located in San Ysidro, California. Just days after twenty-one people (both children and adults) were murdered, and another nineteen were injured, the company sought to reopen the restaurant. This produced a perception in the news media that McDonald's management appeared more preoccupied with getting back to business as usual than dealing with a community that was still reeling from the sheer magnitude of the number of lives lost. Only after editorials, talk radio, and community activists accused the leadership of McDonald's of being insensitive and inappropriate in their response, did the company decide to tear down the restaurant and give the property to the city so it could determine what to build on the former site. Thus, it is important to consider how the deceased will be remembered and to do so promptly, making sure to publicize this decision in a timely manner in order to demonstrate the organization's concern for those who have lost their lives and for their mourning families.

■ *Engage subject matter experts.* In both the public and private sectors, it is important to recognize that while most leaders can make positive announcements effectively, such as announcing receipt of a federal grant, managing hostile news media, family members, taxpayers, or community residents angered by a violent incident is a radically different task.

Subject matter experts who are adept at crafting key messages for town hall meetings, departmental briefings, news conferences, and Web sites, are of crucial importance. Often, a public information officer can lack the skills needed to manage criticism or biting sarcasm, or to answer questions like "how could your team have prevented these people from dying?" Subject matter experts in crisis communication are a sound investment because of the range of serious issues and incidents that could compromise your organization. One example is homicide. Government statistics for the period 2002–2005 indicate that, on average, 1.6 individuals are murdered each day at the workplace in the United States. However, individual cases of retribution or robbery that turn lethal are pushed from the media headlines by mass homicides like the Virginia Tech shooting.

It is important to create a comprehensive to-do list that clarifies roles for each team leader. Human resources and legal departments must create a synergistic plan that addresses core and lingering questions: what did we know, when did we know it, what did we do about it?

A victim's coworkers and immediate staff associates are most directly impacted by violent incidents. These are the people most likely to require counseling, as well as access to community resources. Many providers are available at all times, and mandated group sessions are an excellent first step toward holistic recovery.

Public officials also should remind employees that only authorized spokespersons may speak to the press and that they should respect the confidentiality and needs of families and loved ones in the aftermath of an incident. Employees also may need to be reminded to exercise restraint in talking about the situation while an investigation remains ongoing.

The organization should consider launching a Web site and taking out an advertisement in the local newspaper to acknowledge the life and contribution of colleagues lost or injured. Blogs could become an immediate magnet for commentary and criticism about a violent workplace incident. Employers may want to monitor local chat rooms and blogs, particularly if employer sponsored, in order to be prepared to respond promptly to breaches in confidentiality or to unfounded accusations of negligence.

The public sector shares a special burden during a violent incident because, unlike a small business or a nonprofit charity, the public has a vested interest in public sector entities: citizens' tax dollars subsidize operations. As a result, after a tragedy in the public sector many taxpayers may feel not only a sense of loss, but a sense of betrayal because their leaders, often elected officials, are paid by taxpayers to protect the body politic—including the internal body public—from harm, both intentional and random. From responses to the tragedies of Columbine, courthouse shootings, airline terminal bombings, and sexual assaults in public libraries, it has become clear that the public can be demanding—even unrelenting—when a violent incident occurs on public premises. Managing an incident as it unfolds in real time is challenging enough, but managing the crisis after the crisis can be both daunting and overwhelming.

The good news is that numerous lessons can be learned from public officials who have experienced these inquiries from the news media, employees, unions, and their constituents in the past. The challenge is to catalogue these lessons beforehand and to apply best practices to any crisis management response plan.

The following are four composite case studies and their resolution that I recently handled as a consultant. The names of the individuals and organizations have been changed, but the events and sequencing are precisely as events unfolded.

Case One: A State of Denial

Janet Keebough is director of the Burlington Housing Authority, a public agency that provides some four hundred units of elderly housing and over 850 units of family-based subsidized housing to her community. The housing authority engages over twenty full-time administrative and maintenance employees.

An anonymous letter crossed Janet's desk indicating that her chief of engineering, Frank Figueira, was convicted of murder more than twenty years ago and that he spent time in jail for his crime. In fact, the housing authority was his first employer post-jail, and Frank began as a maintenance assistant, working his way up through the ranks.

Janet advised the housing authority board of the letter, and they requested a background search. What emerged was startling, disturbing, and all too real. Frank was indeed convicted of killing another student at a community college at the age of nineteen and spent eleven years in prison. Upon his release, he applied for and was employed by the housing authority. Because his first position was as a part-time maintenance aide, he was employed without any formal application (where questions about his criminal background could have been asked and documented) or background check.

On advice of counsel, Janet decided that she would meet with Frank. Although he had served time for his crime, she was concerned that the anonymous letter would raise questions about negligent retention once she had become aware of his background. This was particularly true since, in a senior post of chief of engineering, Frank was often inside the homes of housing authority tenants. She was concerned that if his temper were to flare up he could become violent even though his employment record with the housing authority was virtually unblemished. "I'm not sure what options we have," she told the housing board. "If we put him on leave for not informing us of his crime, I'm sure he could have a case against us. If we terminate him for failure to disclose, that probably could not be defended. We could offer him a buyout, but that seems to put us at high risk for a media expose. We just need direction."

The board spent three weeks in formal and informal meetings determining the best course of crisis management. But during this period, a second anonymous letter appeared on Janet's desk, this one informing the housing authority that Frank had a gambling problem and frequented Atlantic City casinos at least every other weekend. Because his salary was in the vicinity of $70,000, the note questioned whether he was taking material from the storage garage at the housing authority and selling equipment at flea markets on weekends to generate the cash to fund his gaming habits. The letter continued, "You have poor controls and no security on what happens with your staff. We know it as employees. Why are you so ignorant and why do you fail to act?"

Case Resolution

Labor counsel was engaged by the housing authority board. Counsel suggested that the housing authority was culpable of negligent hiring because best practices, even decades ago, suggested that a formal application for employment was standard practice for any employer, including the smallest enterprise.

Significant debate ensued regarding the premise that would be used to engage discussion on the matter. Since the employee had served time for his sentence, a decision was made to ignore the issue of that crime since it was not pertinent to his current role. Although he may have had an assumed obligation to inform his employer, the fact that he was not specifically asked about past criminal acts meant that he had not lied. The lack of documentation at the time of employment made this issue not worthy of further review. Complicating matters was Frank's performance in his job, which varied, depending on the year, from good to excellent.

The housing board determined that the most prudent route to pursue was to follow the lead of the anonymous letter and determine whether Frank could be selling housing authority property on eBay or at flea markets to generate extra income. However, board members were deeply concerned that, because he had a volatile and violent history, he might become enraged if accused of an ethical breach. The board struggled for six hours in executive session to determine whether it had a duty of care and, if so, how to exercise that duty. It also debated whether it could now be found culpable of negligent retention because an individual with a clearly documented record of a violent act had open access to virtually hundreds of homes.

"We can decide to retain him, but if we do, I want it on the record that I was against this course of action and that we are placing the community at risk," objected one board member. Another was adamant: "We are acting on a phantom complaint and potentially ruining someone's life when he paid his debt to society. We should focus on his work performance and not on accusations." Yet the executive director of the housing authority, the full-time administrator hired by the board to manage the authority, agreed with the crisis consultant on two key issues: (1) Frank's violent history was not only a matter of record but it was now a matter of record at this employer. A duty of care was triggered once the housing authority was made aware of his violent past; and (2) a negligent retention claim, with massive negative publicity, was likely to ensue if Frank ever again committed an act of violence, and possibly even if he never acted again. The board's judgment would be called into question.

In the end, a compromise was reached. The director approached Frank and proposed an early retirement, offering him a six-month severance package if he resigned within one week. Frank was told that information had surfaced regarding his past history and that the board was not comfortable having him in a leadership role that was visible in the community. Frank was also told that the housing authority had received additional information linking him to possible theft of equipment, but that rather than hire a private investigator and subject a good employee to intensive scrutiny, it was in his best interest to retire. Frank accepted and signed a comprehensive release two days later.

▌ Case Two: Behavior Escalation

Saul Heese was the president of the Portland Humanist League, a §501(c)(3) charitable organization that raises money for families who have recently lost a child to suicide. Saul began the charity in 2001 after his son committed suicide. The organization raises in excess of $370,000 per year, mostly from banquets, silent auctions, and the sale of a book that Saul Heese authored, *The Power of One*, that explains how his own failure to get for help for his son led to the terrible outcome his family later faced.

Saul was a community hero in greater Portland. He frequently appeared on local talk shows speaking about young people at risk, and he authored a column in the local alternative weekly newspaper. His health in recent years had been declining; at the age of 71, Saul had suggested that he was likely to retire from his post as president (he received a stipend of $28,000 per year to manage the organization, reporting to an independent board).

The board had grown concerned about Saul because of his appearance and demeanor. At a board meeting, Saul demanded that the board establish a retirement plan for him because, he said, "I don't have a retirement plan and have given my life to this place. I'm realizing that I need to do better and you need to help me." When the board indicated that the Humanist League was created to serve the public need for suicide information and not for personal gain, and that it is not a traditional employer (he received no medical or other benefits and never asked for them), Saul exploded.

"Are you crazy? I started this organization! This is my baby. If my son hadn't taken his life, we'd have no League, no board. I cultivated all of you. I want and expect this, and I expect it funded and in place in the next two months. I plan to retire in five years and that will at least give me something to show for all of this." He wept at the meeting; his outburst created genuine concern among the board members that other issues—psychological, financial—were contributing to Saul's erratic behavior.

One of the board members suggested that the League pursue a fitness-for-duty evaluation for Saul. Other members of the board believed that the fitness evaluation would suggest that he be retained, and that he was of sound mind, just economically unprepared. One board member, in particular, was deeply anxious about what was happening. "Saul told me on the phone that if we don't start his retirement plan, he'll quit the League, start another competing nonprofit, and bad-mouth us to the United Way and other charities and donors that sponsor us. He is full of spite and anger. I'm truly at wits end trying to figure out what to do."

Case Resolution

Board members have a difficult role, especially when they are personally cultivated to serve in this capacity by an administrator. Although large organizations and the challenges they face tend to receive the most media attention, the majority of government and nonprofit agencies lack the formal workplace violence awareness training programs and understanding of obligations to manage these cases.

In this instance, the board had a strong chairperson who, although she had tremendous admiration for Saul, felt that the board needed to evaluate the key issues. Saul was undergoing significant emotional stress. Although there were no clinicians on the board, it was clear that he seemed to be on the verge of a mental breakdown, if not a financial one. The board felt it imperative to intervene in a timely manner. The chair was especially adamant that the organization not "cave in" to any extortion attempts by Saul. "If we approve this package now, he will ask for more. This will be viral. Our duty is to our donors, not to an employee, regardless of what he has done that has been noteworthy." Other board members weren't so sure. Although he had displayed bullying behavior toward others in the past, Saul was a public figure. "If he is sick, we should seek a fitness examination and then decide," stated one long-term board member whose daughter had committed suicide the same year as Saul's son. Although they were friends, this board member felt that an evaluation was necessary to ensure that the organization acted in a comprehensive, and not compulsive, manner.

The chairperson of the board phoned Saul at home to inform him that he was being placed on suspension pending the outcome of a required fitness-for-duty evaluation. He was encouraged to participate in the evaluation. During the conversation, Saul directed racial slurs at the chairperson and indicated that he would not participate in any evaluation by an external counselor. "He basically said that he would end the League on his own volition and that he would sue each of the board members for failing to honor a series of verbal promises regarding his retirement that had been made over the years," she indicated.

There were no files or evidence that Saul had been promised retirement benefits in the past. To be sure that this was true, the board engaged an independent auditor to contact all past living board members to determine if any of them were aware of such promises. They verified that no such promises had been made to Saul, and each person indicated that this behavior was unusual for a man they admired. The day after the chairperson's conversation with Saul, the editor of the local newspaper called to inform her that Saul reported that he had been fired by the board. The chairperson said this was not the case but that she could not discuss the circumstance further because it was a personnel matter. She went "off the record" with the editor (a process not recommended by press experts, but the decision was made nevertheless), who promised to hold the story based on the potentiality that Saul was undergoing mental strain.

The chairperson decided to make a bold move, albeit one that could have legal consequences. She contacted Saul's daughter, Sarah, and informed her that the board was concerned about her father and that she felt he should be evaluated by the family physician. "He has a problem, although I'm not a physician. You need to get him seen immediately. He is saying and doing things that are irrational." The daughter was grateful and indicated that her dad had been taking lithium for years but had unilaterally gone off the medication about six weeks earlier. She indicated that this was the third time he had experienced bouts of depression, anxiety, and potentially violent outbursts, and that all of this stemmed, she believed, from the loss of her brother.

Saul refused treatment and intervention by anyone. Over the three weeks I was engaged by the board, we tried repeatedly, with social service agencies, mental health agencies, the local police, and family members, to get intervention for an individual who previously had been celebrated as a champion for families. Saul began a bizarre letter-writing campaign to the governor, the commissioner of banks in his state, each member of the board, the local newspaper and, for reasons that were not clear to anyone, the Federal Deposit Insurance Commission, in Washington.

Saul took his own life about a month into this tragic saga. To this day, the case remains baffling and emotionally traumatic for virtually everyone who knew and worked with him.

▌Case Three: Escalating Tensions

Matthew Thomas was a rising star in the city clerk's office in Sparklin, Nevada. Ten years earlier, he had served as an intern while attending the University of Nevada, and he was offered a position as an assistant city clerk upon graduation. In his current position as city clerk, he oversaw many of the key administrative functions of the community. With an annual salary of $68,800 per year, and a position that is relatively low profile (he is appointed by the city manager with the consent of the Sparklin City Council), he earned high praise from various constituents for his skill in managing an office of five administrators.

Matthew's behavior began to change after he confided to the city manager that he would be seeking a divorce from his wife, Amy. Matthew had said, "I think this could get ugly, and if the media starts to cover some of her allegations, it will be very bad for all of us." When the manager pressed him to explain what he meant by his remarks, Matthew confided that he was having an affair with one of his office workers and that his wife had learned of it. He and his wife were the parents of four children under the age of ten. His wife was very active in their church, serving as the lead cantor during Sunday services.

While extramarital affairs are neither new nor necessarily provocative, this one had an element of workplace safety that was unique. The woman whom Matthew was dating, Tammy White, became vocal when Matthew told her that the affair had to end as his wife had become aware of their situation. Tammy not only sobbed in his office while other city workers could hear the conversation, but she threw a paperweight at Matthew, hitting him in the head. Matthew required eleven stitches to close the head wound, and as he left the office for the hospital, he said to Tammy in front of other workers: "I should have fired you years ago. You're low-end, you don't have any work ethic, and you're pretty lousy in everything you do—and I mean everything."

Tammy did not report to work following the encounter, which took place on a Tuesday. On Thursday, Matthew was back at work and indicated to the city manager that he and his wife were attending marital counseling in hopes that they might reconcile. Matthew also told the city manager that he admitted having the affair to his immediate staff in hopes that this candor would limit any speculation in city hall.

That same week, one of the other assistants close to Tammy told her that Matthew was putting together the paperwork to have her fired and that a package containing COBRA benefits information and her last paycheck would be mailed to her on Friday. During the conversation, Tammy told the assistant/girlfriend: "I'd urge you to stop coming to work yourself. You have no idea what I'm capable of. But I'm telling you—and I mean it—I have a gun, and no stitches will fix him after I take care of him for good."

The coworker notified the city manager of the threat. The city manager called for an emergency meeting of the city council to determine what steps should be taken and engaged outside counsel for additional guidance.

Case Resolution

Outside counsel conducted a fact-finding investigation that included a criminal background check on both Tammy and Matthew. She also interviewed both parties in the city clerk's office (Tammy brought her own counsel) to ascertain facts. Tammy fully cooperated in the fact finding but denied making any threats against Matthew. Matthew also cooperated with the investigation. Matthew indicated that Tammy had a history of violence and anger that had been shielded from some (but not all) workers at city hall, a fact that was later validated by several city workers.

Outside counsel reported to the city council that the city could be found liable for negligent retention of both employees—Matthew, for not disclosing his relationship with a coworker in accordance with the city's code of conduct, and Tammy because her overt conduct resulted in serious injury to Matthew (head wound) that could have been fatal. Two weeks later, the city reached a settlement with both employees that provided each one a modest payout in return for a release of all claims. Within six weeks, the city instituted whistle-blower and workplace violence policies. The city held a series of training programs that specifically focused on anger management and notification by coworkers of any threats made toward their coworkers or anyone else.

▌ Case Four: Weekend Ventures

Roberta Cornelius served as a police officer for the City of Addison for nearly a dozen years. Her record of community service was impeccable until an anonymous note appeared on the desk of the police chief claiming that, on her weekends, Officer Cornelius participated in boxing matches and was a minor contender for the American Female Guard Federation's middleweight boxing title. "If you don't believe me," the note stated, "go to xx.com and look at her—and anyone who knows Officer Cornelius will know that this is her."

Sure enough, the police chief confirmed that Officer Cornelius (who went by the stage name "The Complete Roberta"), traveled up to two hours on weekends, typically without any conflict with her work schedule, to participate in a highly aggressive and visually disturbing new trend in boxing in which chairs, metal objects, and other items are hurled at other boxers until one of the competitors falls unconscious. Officer Cornelius wore a tight cap and makeup that altered her appearance from how she looked at work.

In the past, when she had been confronted about her various bruises, Officer Cornelius told other officers that she was learning kick boxing and was taking courses in martial arts to supplement her police training. Because Addison is located in a northern climate, many of her bruises were covered by long clothing most of the year. Her boxing activities did not appear to violate the City of Addison

Police Code of Conduct. Nevertheless, the chief was embarrassed for himself, for his department, and for Officer Cornelius.

When he asked for a meeting with Officer Cornelius and her commanding officer, she burst into a tirade that was anything but cordial. "Listen, I put my life on the line for you every day. I need an outlet. Please don't make me stop. I'll go crazy if I had to stop when I'm so close to my dream." When asked what that dream was, Officer Cornelius said it was to host her own television reality show, to launch a line of Complete Roberta clothing and makeup, to begin a series of after-school boxing programs for young women around the country, and to retire at the age of forty-five "after I show all of you losers what I can do with my life."

The commanding officer and the police chief informed Officer Cornelius that she was going to be placed on a paid forty-eight-hour leave of absence while they considered the options.

Case Resolution

Legal counsel for the city indicated that the existing code of conduct did not specifically exclude such activities under "outside interests." Counsel felt that since Officer Cornelius had not used her real name or exploited her police position in her "hobby" there was no immediate danger or threat, per se, from her activities. However, counsel noted that the way she handled herself during the meeting was inappropriate, particularly when she referred to her superiors as "losers." Moreover, counsel thought that the officer's desires for fame and fortune might suggest a latent mental health concern that merited review by a licensed clinician. Counsel recommended that the city extend the officer's leave of absence until a fitness-for-duty (FFD) evaluation could be completed. Officer Cornelius was upset with the FFD referral but agreed to the evaluation all the same.

The psychologist's report was alarming. Findings from the officer's MMPI-2 examination suggested that she had significant mental health issues and a significant distortion of reality. During her interview, Officer Cornelius told the psychologist that she had contemplated committing suicide and murdering her half brother and an aunt in retaliation for being beaten as a child, as well as other alleged abuses.

The psychologist indicated that boxing, while providing temporary relief to Officer Cornelius, may help her master her capacity to harm others. The psychologist recommended that the city immediately release her from employment and offer her a three-month severance payment and one-year intense employee assistance program counseling to be paid for by the city, in order to help her "bridge" to her next employment. He also recommended that Officer Cornelius enter an intensive program of evaluation by a clinician at least twice a week. As of this writing, Office Cornelius has kept her appointments with the clinician and is seeking employment as a private security guard.

The Healthy
Workplace Bill

SECTION I—FINDINGS AND PURPOSES

A. LEGISLATIVE FINDINGS

The legislature finds that:

1. the social and economic well-being of the State is dependent upon healthy and productive employees;

2. surveys and studies have documented between 16 and 21 percent of employees directly experience health-endangering workplace bullying, abuse, and harassment, and that this behavior is four times more prevalent than sexual harassment alone;

3. surveys and studies have documented that abusive work environments can have serious and even devastating effects on targeted employees, including feelings of shame and humiliation, stress, loss of tendencies, reduced immunity to infection, stress-related gastrointestinal disorders, hypertension, and pathophysiologic changes that increases the risk of cardiovascular disease;

4. surveys and studies have documented that abusive work environments can have serious consequences for employers, including reduced employee productivity and morale, higher turnover and absenteeism rates, and significant increases in medical and workers' compensation claims;

5. unless mistreated employees have been subjected to abusive treatment at work on basis of race, color, sex, national origin, or age, they are unlikely to have legal recourse to redress such treatment;

6. legal protection from abusive work environments should not be limited to behavior grounded in protected class status as that provided for under employment discrimination statutes; and,

7. existing workers' compensation plans and common-law tort actions are inadequate to discourage this behavior or to provide adequate redress to employees who have been harmed by abusive work environments.

B. LEGISLATIVE PURPOSE

It is the purpose of this Chapter:

1. to provide legal redress for employees who have been harmed, psychologically, physically, or economically, by being deliberately subjected to abusive work environments;

2. to provide legal incentive for employers to prevent and respond to mistreatment of employees at work.

SECTION 2—DEFINITIONS

1. Employee. An employee is an individual employed by an employer, whereby the individual's labor is either controlled by the employer and/or the individual is economically dependent upon the employer in return for labor rendered.

2. Employer. An employer includes individuals, governments, governmental agencies, corporations, partnerships, associations, and unincorporated organizations that compensate individuals in return for performing labor.

3. Abusive work environment. An abusive work environment exists when the defendant, acting with malice, subjects the complainant to abusive conduct so severe that it causes tangible harm to the complainant.

    a. Conduct. Conduct is defined as all forms of behavior, including acts and omissions of acts.

    b. Malice. For purposes of this Chapter, malice is defined as the desire to see another person suffer psychological, physical, or economic harm, without legitimate cause or justification. Malice can be inferred from the presence of factors such as: outward expressions of hostility; harmful conduct inconsistent with an employer's legitimate business interests; a continuation of harmful, illegitimate conduct after the complainant requests that it cease or demonstrates outward signs of emotional or physical distress in the face of the conduct; or attempts to exploit the complainant's known psychological or physical vulnerability.

    c. Abusive conduct. Abusive conduct is conduct that a reasonable person would find hostile, offensive, and unrelated to an employer's legitimate business interests. In considering whether abusive conduct is present, a trier of fact should weigh the severity, nature, and frequency of the defendant's conduct. Abusive conduct may include, but is not limited to: repeated infliction of verbal abuse such as the use of derogatory remarks, insults, and epithets; verbal or physical conduct that a reasonable person would find threatening, intimidating, or humiliating; or the gratuitous sabotage or undermining of a person's work performance. A single act normally will not constitute abusive conduct, but an especially severe and egregious act may meet this standard.

    d. Tangible harm. Tangible harm is defined as psychological harm or physical harm.

        i. Psychological harm. Psychological harm is the material impairment of a person's mental health, as documented by a competent psychologist, psychiatrist, or psychotherapist, or supported by competent expert evidence at trial.

        ii. Physical harm. Physical harm is the material impairment of a person's physical health or bodily integrity, as documented by a competent physician or supported by competent expert evidence at trial.

4. Negative employment decision. A negative employment decision is a termination, demotion, unfavorable reassignment, refusal to promote, or disciplinary action.

5. Constructive discharge. A constructive discharge shall be considered a termination, and therefore, a negative employment decision within the meaning of this Chapter. For purposes of this Chapter, a showing of constructive discharge requires that the complainant establish the following three elements: (a) abusive conduct existed; (b)

the employee resigned because of that abusive conduct; and, (c) prior to resigning the employee brought to the employer's attention the existence of the abusive conduct and the employer failed to take reasonable steps to correct the situation.

SECTION 3—UNLAWFUL EMPLOYMENT PRACTICE

It shall be an unlawful employment practice under this Chapter to subject an employee to an abusive work environment as defined by this Chapter.

SECTION 4—EMPLOYER LIABILITY

An employer shall be vicariously liable for an unlawful employment practice, as defined by this Chapter, committed by its employee.

SECTION 5—DEFENSES

A. It shall be an affirmative defense for an *employer only* that:
  1. the employer exercised reasonable care to prevent and correct promptly any actionable behavior; and,
  2. the complainant employee unreasonably failed to take advantage of appropriate preventive or corrective opportunities provided by the employer;
  [This defense is not available when the actionable behavior culminates in a negative employment decision.]

B. It shall be an affirmative defense that:
  1. the complaint is grounded primarily upon a negative employment decision made consistent with an employer's legitimate business interests, such as a termination or demotion based on an employee's poor performance; or,
  2. the complaint is grounded primarily upon a defendant's reasonable investigation about potentially illegal or unethical activity.

SECTION 6—RETALIATION

It shall be an unlawful employment practice under this Chapter to retaliate in any manner against an employee because she has opposed any unlawful employment practice under this Chapter, or because she has made a charge, testified, assisted, or participated in any manner in an investigation or proceeding under this Chapter, including, but not limited to, internal complaints and proceedings, arbitration and mediation proceedings, and legal actions.

APPENDIX PAGE 4

SECTION 7—RELIEF

1. Relief generally. Where a defendant has been found to have committed an unlawful employment practice under this Chapter, the court may enjoin the defendant from engaging in the unlawful employment practice and may order any other relief that is deemed appropriate, including, but not limited to, reinstatement, removal of the offending party from the complainant's work environment, back pay, front pay, medical expenses, compensation for emotional distress, punitive damages, and attorney's fees.

2. Employer liability. Where an employer has been found to have committed an unlawful employment practice under this Chapter that did not culminate in a negative employment decision, its liability for damages for emotional distress shall not exceed $25,000, and it shall not be subject to punitive damages. This provision does not apply to individually named co-employee defendants.

SECTION 8—PROCEDURES

1. Private right of action. This Chapter shall be enforced solely by a private right of action.

2. Time limitations. An action commenced under this Chapter must be commenced not later than one year after the last act that comprises the alleged unlawful employment practice.

SECTION 9—EFFECT ON OTHER STATE LAWS

1. Other state laws. Nothing in this Chapter shall be deemed to exempt or relieve any person from any liability, duty, penalty, or punishment provided by any law of the State.

2. Workers' compensation and election of remedies. This Chapter supersedes any previous statutory provision or judicial ruling that limits a person's legal remedies for the underlying behavior addressed here to workers' compensation. However, a person who believes that s/he has been subjected to an unlawful employment practice under this Chapter may elect to accept workers' compensation benefits in connection with the underlying behavior in lieu of bringing an action under this Chapter. A person who elects to accept workers' compensation may not bring an action under this Chapter for the same underlying behavior.

2006 New York State Workplace Violence Prevention Law

* § 27-b. Duty of public employers to develop and implement programs to prevent workplace violence.

1. Purpose. The purpose of this section is to ensure that the risk of workplace assaults and homicides is evaluated by affected public employers and their employees and that such employers design and implement workplace violence protection programs to prevent and minimize the hazard of workplace violence to public employees.

2. Definitions. For the purposes of this section:

a. "Employer" means: (1) the state; (2) a political subdivision of the state, provided, however that this subdivision shall not mean any employer as defined in section twenty-eight hundred one-a of the education law; and (3) a public authority, a public benefit corporation, or any other governmental agency or instrumentality thereof.

b. "Employee" means a public employee working for an employer.

c. "Workplace" means any location away from an employee's domicile, permanent or temporary, where an employee performs any work-related duty in the course of his or her employment by an employer.

d. "Supervisor" means any person within an employer's organization who has the authority to direct and control the work performance of an employee, or who has the authority to take corrective action regarding the violation of a law, rule or regulation to which an employee submits written notice.

e. "Retaliatory action" means the discharge, suspension, demotion, penalization, or discrimination against any employee, or other adverse employment action taken against an employee in the terms and conditions of employment.

3. Risk evaluation and determination. Every employer shall evaluate its workplace or workplaces to determine the presence of factors or situations in such workplace or workplaces that might place employees at risk of occupational assaults and homicides. Examples of such factors shall include, but not [be] limited to:

a. working in public settings (e.g., social services or other governmental workers, police officers, firefighters, teachers, public transportation drivers, health care workers, and service workers);

b. working late night or early morning hours;

c. exchanging money with the public;

d. working alone or in small numbers;

e. uncontrolled access to the workplace; and

f. areas of previous security problems.

4. Written workplace violence prevention program. Every employer with at least twenty full time permanent employees shall develop and implement a written workplace violence prevention program for its workplace or workplaces that includes the following:

a. a list of the risk factors identified in subdivision three of this section that are present in such workplace or workplaces;

b. the methods the employer will use to prevent incidents of occupational assaults and homicides at such workplace or workplaces, including but not limited to the following:

(1) making high-risk areas more visible to more people;

(2) installing good external lighting;

(3) using drop safes or other methods to minimize cash on hand;

(4) posting signs stating that limited cash is on hand;

(5) providing training in conflict resolution and nonviolent self-defense responses; and

(6) establishing and implementing reporting systems for incidents of aggressive behavior.

5. Employee information and training.

a. Every employer with at least twenty permanent full time employees shall make the written workplace violence prevention program available, upon request, to its employees, their designated representatives and the department.

b. Every employer shall provide its employees with the following information and training on the risks of occupational assaults and homicides in their workplace or workplaces at the time of their initial assignment and annually thereafter:

(1) employees shall be informed of the requirements of this section, the risk factors in their workplace or workplaces, and the location and availability of the written workplace violence prevention program required by this section; and

(2) employee training shall include at least: (a) the measures employees can take to protect themselves from such risks, including specific procedures the employer has implemented to protect employees, such as appropriate work practices, emergency procedures, use of security alarms and other devices, and (b) the details of the written workplace violence prevention program developed by the employer.

6. Application.

a. Any employee or representative of employees who believes that a serious violation of a workplace violence protection program exists or that an imminent danger exists shall bring such matter to the attention of a supervisor in the form of a written notice and shall afford the employer a reasonable opportunity to correct such activity, policy or practice. This referral shall not apply where imminent danger or threat exists to the safety of a specific employee or to the general health of a specific patient and the employee reasonably believes in good faith that reporting to a supervisor would not result in corrective action.

b. If following a referral of such matter to the employee's supervisor's attention and after a reasonable opportunity to correct such activity, policy or practice the matter has not been resolved and the employee or representative of employees still believes that a violation of a workplace violence prevention program remains, or that an imminent danger exists, such employee or representative of employees may request an inspection by giving notice to the commissioner of such violation or danger. Such notice and request shall be in writing, shall set forth with reasonable particularity the grounds for the notice, shall be signed by such employee or representative of employees, and a copy shall be provided by the commissioner to the employer or the person in charge no later than the time of inspection, except that

2006 NEW YORK STATE WORKPLACE VIOLENCE ... PAGE 3

on the request of the person giving such notice, such person's name and the names of individual employees or representatives of employees shall be withheld. Such inspection shall be made forthwith.

c. A representative of the employer and an authorized employee representative shall be given the opportunity to accompany the commissioner during an inspection for the purpose of aiding such inspection. Where there is no authorized employee representative, the commissioner shall consult with a reasonable number of employees concerning matters of safety in the workplace.

d. The authority of the commissioner to inspect a premises pursuant to such an employee complaint shall not be limited to the alleged violation contained in such complaint. The commissioner may inspect any other area of the premises in which he or she has reason to believe that a serious violation of this section exists.

e. No employer shall take retaliatory action against any employee because the employee does any of the following:

(1) makes an application pursuant to paragraph a of this subdivision;

(2) requests an inspection as authorized in paragraph b of this subdivision;

(3) accompanies the commissioner as authorized in paragraph c of this subdivision;

f. The commissioner may, upon his or her own initiative, conduct an inspection of any premises occupied by an employer if he or she has reason to believe that a violation of this section has occurred or if he or she has a general administrative plan for the enforcement of this section, including a general schedule of inspections, which provide a rational administrative basis for such inspecting. Within one hundred twenty days of the effective date of this paragraph the commissioner shall adopt rules and regulations implementing the provisions of this section.

g. Any information obtained by the commissioner pursuant to this subdivision shall be obtained with a minimum burden upon the employers.

h. When a request for an inspection has been made in a situation where there is an allegation of an imminent danger such that an employee would be subjecting himself or herself to serious injury or death because of the hazardous condition in the workplace, the inspection shall be given the highest priority by the department and shall be carried out immediately.

* NB: Effective March 4, 2007

12 NYCRR Part 800.6 Public Employer Workplace Violence Prevention Programs

800.6(a)

(a) Title and Citation: Within and for the purposes of the Department of Labor, this part may be known as Code Rule 800.6 Public Employer Workplace Violence Prevention Program, relating to requirements of public employers to develop and implement programs to prevent and minimize workplace violence; allows any employee or representative of employees who believes that a serious violation of this safety or health standard exists, or an imminent danger exists, to request an inspection by the Department of Labor; and provides for the enforcement of such requirement by the Commissioner of Labor. It may be cited as Code Rule 800.6 "Public Employer Workplace Violence Prevention Programs" as an alternative and without prejudice to its designation and citation established by the Secretary of State.

(b) Purpose and Intent: It is the purpose of this Part to ensure that the risk of workplace violence is evaluated by affected public employers and their employees and that such public employers design and implement protection programs to minimize the hazard of workplace violence to employees.

(c) Application: This Part shall apply throughout the State of New York to the State, any political subdivision of the State, public authorities, public benefit corporations or any other governmental agency or instrumentality thereof.

This part shall not apply to any employer as defined in Section twenty-eight hundred one-a of the Education Law.

800.6(a)

DEFINITIONS

(a) Terms: As used in or in connection with this Part, the following terms mean:

(1) Authorized Employee Representative. An employee selected by the employees or the designated representative of an employee organization recognized or certified to represent the employees pursuant to Article 14 of the Civil Service Law.

(2) Commissioner. The Commissioner of Labor of the State of New York or his or her duly authorized representative for the purposes of implementing this Part.

(3) Employee. A public employee working for an employer.

(4) Employer. The State, any political subdivision of the State, public authorities, public benefit corporations and any other governmental agency or instrumentality thereof. But, shall not apply to any employer as defined in Section twenty-eight hundred one-a (2801a) of the Education Law.

12 NYCRR PART 800.6 PUBLIC EMPLOYER ... PAGE 2

(5) Imminent Danger: Any conditions or practices in any place of employment which are such that a danger exists which could reasonably be expected to cause death or serious physical harm immediately or before the imminence of such danger can be eliminated through the enforcement procedures otherwise provided for by this Part.

(6) Participation of the Authorized Employee Representative. The Authorized Employee Representative is given an opportunity to contribute information, assist with analyzing statistics and conducting the workplace risk evaluation and determination and participate in incident reviews. The responsibility for preparing, determining the content of, and implementing the requirements of this part remain with the employer.

(7) Retaliatory Action. The discharge, suspension, demotion, penalization or discrimination against any employee, or other adverse employment action taken against an employee in the terms and conditions of employment.

(8) Risk Evaluation and Determination. An employer's inspection or examination of their workplace to determine if existing or potential hazards exist that might place employees at risk of workplace violence. A risk evaluation shall include, but is not limited to, a review of previous workplace incidents, review of the Log of Work-Related Injuries and Illnesses, a survey of employees asking what conditions could be contributing to potential incidents, site security and inspection surveys.

(9) Serious Physical Harm. Impairment of the body so as to render the body part affected functionally useless or substantially reduced in efficiency.

(10) Serious Violation: A serious violation shall be deemed to exist in a place of employment if there is substantial probability that death or serious physical harm could result from a condition which exists, or from one or more practices, means, methods, operations, or process which have been adopted or are in use, in such place of employment.

(11) Supervisor. Any person within the employer's organization who has the authority to direct and control the work performance of an employee, or who has the authority to take corrective action regarding the violation of a law, rule or regulation to which an employee submits written notice.

(12) Workplace. Any location away from an employee's domicile, permanent or temporary, where an employee performs any work-related duty in the course of his or her employment by an employer.

(13) Workplace Violence. Any physical assault, threatening behavior, or verbal abuse occurring where a public employee performs any work related duty in the course of his or her employment.

(14) Workplace Violence Incident. A workplace violence incident is defined as one or more of the following:

(i) An attempt or threat whether verbal or physical to inflict injury upon another employee;

(ii) Any intentional display of force which would give an employee reason to fear or expect bodily harm;

(iii) Intentional and wrongful physical contact with a person without his or her consent that entails some injury or offensive touching;

12 NYCRR PART 800.6 PUBLIC EMPLOYER ... PAGE 3

(iv) Harassment of a nature that would give an employee reason to fear escalation or make it difficult to pursue a normal life when the harassment arises out of or in the course of employment;

(v) Stalking an employee with the intent of causing fear when such stalking has arisen through or in the course of employment.

(15) Workplace Violence Prevention Program. An employer program designed to prevent, minimize and respond to any physical assault, threatening behavior or verbal abuse occurring in the workplace. Article 2 Section 27b of the New York State Labor Law requires that employers must develop and implement a Workplace Violence Prevention Program. The Workplace Violence Prevention Program shall be in writing if the public employer has 20 or more full time permanent employees.

800.6(b)

MANAGEMENT COMMITMENT AND EMPLOYEE INVOLVEMENT

(1) Workplace Violence Policy Statement:

The employer shall develop and implement a written policy statement on the employers' "Workplace Violence Prevention Program" goals and objectives and provide for full employee and employee representative participation.

(i) The Workplace Violence Policy Statement shall be posted where notices to employees are normally posted.

(ii) The policy statement shall briefly indicate the employer's workplace violence prevention policy and alert and notification policies for employees to follow in the event of a workplace violence incident.

(2) The responsibility for preparing and implementing the requirements of this Part remains with the employer. Local governments and all other public employers may elect to share resources in the development and implementation of their workplace violence prevention programs.

800.6(c)

WORKPLACE EXAMINATION

(1) Record Examination:

The employer shall examine any injury, illness, accident, incident or statistical record in their possession to identify trends and the type and cause of injuries. The examination shall look to identify patterns of injuries in particular areas of the work place or incidents which involve specific operations or specific individuals.

(2) Workplace Evaluation and Determination:

The employer, with the participation of the Authorized Employee Representative, shall evaluate the workplace to determine the presence of factors or situations

12 NYCRR PART 800.6 PUBLIC EMPLOYER PAGE 4

which may place employees at risk of workplace violence. The Department of Labor has tools to aid employers in performing this evaluation which will be posted on the Department's internet site.

Factors which might place an employee at risk include but are not limited to:

(i) Working in public settings (e.g. Social Service Workers, Police Officers, Firefighters, Teachers, Public Transportation Drivers, Health Care Workers, other Governmental Workers or Service Workers).

(ii) Working late night or early morning hours;

(iii) Exchanging money with the public;

(iv) Working alone or in small numbers;

(v) Uncontrolled access to the workplace; or

(vi) Areas of previous security problems.

800.6(d)

THE WORKPLACE VIOLENCE PREVENTION PROGRAM

(1) Employers with 20 or more full time permanent employees, with the participation of the Authorized Employee Representative, shall develop a written workplace violence prevention program.

(2) The Workplace Violence Prevention Program shall include the following:

(i) A list of the risk factors identified in the workplace examination;

(ii) The methods the employer will use to prevent the incidence of workplace violence incidents at such workplace or workplaces, including but not limited to:

(A) Making high risk areas more visible to more people;

(B) Installing good external lighting;

(C) Use of drop safes or other methods to limit cash on hand;

(D) Post signs stating that limited cash is on hand;

(E) Providing training on conflict resolution and non violent self defense responses; and

(F) Establishing and implementing reporting systems for incidents of aggressive behavior.

(iii) The program shall adhere to a hierarchy of controls as follows: engineering controls, work practice controls, and finally personal protective equipment;

(iv) The employer shall address the methods and means to address each specific hazard identified in the workplace evaluation and determination;

(v) The employer shall address when crisis counseling will be provided, following generally accepted practices, after a workplace violence incident for employees;

(vi) The employer shall design and implement a workplace violence reporting system for any workplace violence incidents that occur in the workplace. The reports must be in writing and maintained for the annual program review;

(vii) An outline or lesson plan of employee training shall be made part of the written program;

(viii) The program shall be reviewed and updated as necessary at least annually.

12 NYCRR PART 800.6 PUBLIC EMPLOYER ... PAGE 5

800.6(e)

EMPLOYEE INFORMATION AND TRAINING

(1) Upon completion of the Workplace Violence Prevention Program every employer shall provide each employee with information and training on the risks of workplace violence in their workplace or workplaces at the time of the employees' initial assignment and at least annually thereafter. Retraining shall be provided whenever significant changes are made to the workplace violence program. At a minimum training shall address the following:

(i) Employers shall inform employees of the requirements of this Part and the risk factors in their workplace that were identified in the risk evaluation and determination;

(ii) The measures that employees can take to protect themselves from the identified risks including specific procedures that the employer has implemented to protect employees such as incident alert and notification procedures, appropriate work practices, emergency procedures, use of security alarms and other devices;

(iii) Employers with 20 or more full time permanent employees shall inform employees of the location of the written workplace violence program and how to obtain a copy.

(iv) A review of procedures for providing crisis counseling to affected employees after an incident and the protocol developed to determine when such counseling should be made available.

800.6(f)

RECORDKEEPING AND RECORDING OF WORKPLACE VIOLENCE INCIDENTS

(1) Employers shall develop and implement protocols for the reporting of workplace violence incidents which includes procedures for reporting incidents that may be of a criminal nature to the appropriate police agency. An employee's right to pursue a criminal complaint shall not be infringed upon.

(2) Employers at sites where there is a developing pattern of workplace violence incidents which may involve criminal conduct or a serious injury shall attempt to develop a protocol with the District Attorney or Police to insure that violent crimes committed against employees in the workplace are promptly investigated and appropriately prosecuted. The employer shall provide information on such protocols and contact information to employees who wish to file a criminal complaint after a workplace violence incident.

(3) Workplace violence reports and recordkeeping:

The employer shall develop and maintain a workplace violence incident report that can be in any format but at a minimum contains the following information:

(i) Workplace location;

12 NYCRR PART 800.6 PUBLIC EMPLOYER ... PAGE 6

(ii) Time of day/shift;
(iii) Incident description including what happened immediately prior to the incident and how the incident ended;
(iv) Names and job titles of involved employees;
(v) Name or other identifier of individuals involved;
(vi) Extent of injuries;
(vii) Names of witnesses; and
(viii) An explanation of the actions the employer has or is in the process of taking to mitigate future incidents with a time table for correction where appropriate. Interim protective measures shall also be listed. The employer shall address global (all similar worksites) enhancements which become apparent are necessary to protect all employees.
(4) The Workplace Violence Incident reports must be maintained for use in annual program review and updates.
(5) This Requirement does not relieve an employer of the recordkeeping requirements of 12 NYCRR Part 801.
(6) The employer with the participation of the authorized employee representative shall conduct a review of the workplace violence incident reports at least annually to identify trends in the types of incidents in the workplace and review of the effectiveness of the mitigating actions taken.

800.6(g)

EMPLOYEE ACCESS TO INFORMATION

(1) Every employer with at least 20 permanent full time employees shall make the written workplace violence prevention program available to Employees, Authorized Employee Representatives, and the Commissioner, for reference in the work area during the regularly scheduled shift.

800.6(h)

EMPLOYEE REPORTING OF WORKPLACE VIOLENCE PREVENTION CONCERNS OR INCIDENTS

(1) Any employee or their representative who believes that a violation of the employer's workplace violence protection prevention program exists, or that an workplace violence imminent danger exists, shall bring such matter to the attention of a supervisor in the form of a written notice and shall afford the employer a reasonable opportunity to correct such activity, policy or practice.
(2) Written notice to an employer shall not be required where workplace violence imminent danger exists to the safety of a specific employee or to the

general health of a specific patient and the employee reasonably believes in good faith that reporting to a supervisor would not result in corrective action.

(3) If following a referral of such matter to the employee's supervisor's attention and after a reasonable opportunity to correct such activity, policy or practice the matter has not been resolved and the employee or the employee representative still believes that a violation of a workplace violence prevention program remains, or that an imminent danger exists, such employee may request an inspection by giving notice to the Commissioner of Labor of an alleged violation of this Part. Such notice and request shall be in writing, shall set forth with reasonable particularity the grounds for the notice and shall be signed by such employee or their representative. A copy of the written notice shall be provided by the Commissioner to the employer or the person in charge no later than the time of inspection, except that at the request of the person giving such notice, such person's name and the names of individual employees or representatives of employees shall be withheld. Such inspection shall be made forthwith by the Commissioner.

(4) No employer shall take retaliatory action against any employee because the employee exercises any right accorded him or her by this Part.

800.6(i)

EFFECTIVE DATES

(1) The Employers Policy Statement required by section 3-1 shall be complete 30 days after the effective date of this Part.

(2) The workplace examination required by section 4 of this Part shall be completed within 60 days of the effective date of this Part.

(3) The workplace violence prevention program required by section 5 shall be complete within 75 days of the effective date of this Part.

(4) Employers shall be in compliance with the entire Part within 120 days of the effective date of this Part.

Table of Cases

Index